Explorations with Young Children

Explorations

with
Young Children

A Curriculum Guide from
The Bank Street College of Education

● ● ● ●

Edited by Anne Mitchell and Judy David

Sara, Age 5

gryphon house
Beltsville, Maryland

© 1992 The Bank Street College of Education
Published by Gryphon House, Inc., 10726 Tucker Street, Beltsville, MD 20705
ISBN: 0-87659-160-8
Library of Congress Catalog Number: 92-74062

Illustrations: Debby Dixler, Nina Woldin, Catherine Minor, Joan Auclair
Cover Design: Beverly Hightshoe

Publisher's Cataloging in Publication
(Prepared by Quality Books Inc.)

Explorations with young children: a curriculum guide from Bank Street
  College of Education / editors-in-chief, Judy David, Anne Mitchell.
    p.cm.
    Includes bibiographical references and index.
    ISBN 0-87659-160-8

  1. Education, Preschool—United States—Curricula. 2. Education, Primary—United States—Curricula. I. David, Judith A., 1945- II. Mitchell,
Anne W., 1950- III. Bank Street College of Education

Contents

Acknowledgments

We are grateful to those people whose vision has made possible *Explorations with Young Children: A Curriculum Guide from Bank Street College* and the companion videotape *Social Studies: A Way to Integrate Curriculum for Four-and Five-Year Olds.* Donna T. McCurdy of the W. Alton Jones Foundation encouraged us to begin. Shelby Miller, formerly of the Ford Foundation, believed in the importance of Bank Street communicating its approach to the early childhood community and was responsible for funding the planning phase of our work. Cynthia Massarsky, marketing consultant, worked with us to create a marketing plan to determine the feasibility of our producing written and audiovisual materials. Patricia Gallatin of the NYNEX Corporation and Tom Skrobala of the NYNEX Foundation supported us at the critical juncture between development and final product. Thanks are also due Margie Barclay, at Bank Street, who put us in touch with NYNEX.

Clennie Murphy and Dollie Wolverton from the Head Start Bureau, Washington, DC, encouraged us at every stage and strongly believed in the value of this project for the Head Start community. Whenever the going got tough, Joan Lombardi, early childhood policy consultant, reminded us how valuable the work would be to the early childhood community and encouraged us to persist. The last phase of our work, including the field testing of the Guide, was made possible through funding from the East Coast Migrant Head Start Project (ECMHSP). We are grateful to Sister Geraldine O'Brien, Executive Director (ECMHSP), and Sherrie Rudick, Program Development Manager (ECMHSP). Sherrie's insights about staff development helped shape the Guide in many ways.

The videotape was jointly developed by Ann-Marie Mott and Eileen Wasow. Production was supported by the W. Alton Jones Foundation. Jeff Hall, Media Specialist at the Bank Street Library, produced the tape with professional skill and much good humor. The feasibility of producing videotapes on other topics using existing video footage was fully explored by Josie Oppenheim and Kathleen Hayes with Jeff's help.

Field testing the Guide was a tremendous learning experience for us. We enjoyed working with Ramona Merlino and her staff at Bright Horizons Child Enrichment Center (ECMHSP) in Bridgeton, New Jersey and with Raynita Smith and her staff at Kiddie Kastle Migrant Head Start (ECMHSP) in Mt. Vernon-Glennville, Georgia. We appreciate the creativity and expertise of Maritza Macdonald and Susan Soler who field tested the Guide with the ECMHSP in these sites, and of Amy Dombro and Judy Jablon who field tested the Guide with Program Development Specialists from ECMHSP. Nancy Klein field tested excerpts from the Guide at the Region II Head Start Conference; Toni Porter field tested selections from the Guide with parent education groups. Judy Catell and Nancie West from Front Range Community College used the videotape and chapters of the Guide with their students and gave us invaluable—and enthusiastic— feedback, as did Sheila Hanna from Westchester Community College and Sherry Johnson from Glendale Community College. Earlier drafts of the Guide were reviewed by members of the National Advisory Panel and the Bank Street Advisory Group. They made many helpful suggestions, as did other Bank Street faculty who offered to read sections of the Guide or incorporated chapters into their course work with Bank Street students. We thank them all.

There are many people whose commitment and talents are reflected in the Guide. The authors have worked hard and successfully to communicate the Bank Street approach. Collaborating with them (and learning from them) has been a pleasure: Roberta Altman, Nancy Balaban, Joan Cenedella, Amy Dombro, Susan Ginsberg, Judy Jablon, Nina Jaffe, Leah Levinger, Maritza Macdonald, Janice Molnar, Ann-Marie Mott, Edna Shapiro, and Liz Westfall. Amy and Judy have read and commented on many of the chapters and have been instrumental in defining the purposes and scope of the Guide. Angel Centeno worked on an earlier version of "Valuing Diversity," as did Beth Norford on "Integrated Curriculum for Four- through-Eight-Year-Olds" and Ann Schafer on "Literacy in Early Childhood." Many individuals interviewed by the authors contributed their ideas to chapters in the Guide: Don Cook, Harriet Cuffaro, Barbara Dubitsky, Dick Feldman, Kathleen Hayes, Lois Lord, Hal Melnick, Kathy Modigliani, Sal Vascellero, Eileen Wasow, and David Wolkenberg. Maritza Macdonald helped to conceptualize the curriculum chapters; her vivid examples of the Bank Street approach in action appear throughout the Guide.

The illustrators have helped the text come alive with their wonderful drawings of children, families, teachers, and classrooms: Debby Dixler, Nina Woldin, Catherine Minor, and Joan Auclair. Debby's willingness to do any task, no matter how big or small, is greatly appreciated. Joan and Debby also assisted with the layout and design, as did Reneé Creange, Ruth M. Kolbe, and Maria Licitra. In addition, we are very grateful for Ruth's meticulous proofreading of the final manuscript. The editors, Paddy Yost and Jeffrey Fisher, worked tirelessly and carefully; their comments and questions clarified our thinking. Paddy's common sense (and sense of humor) made many tasks so much easier. Attention to all the details of the bibliographic references was the responsibility of Nina Liu and Sharon Cohen.

In the final stages of production, the skills (and patience) of the word processors were essential: Maureen Cunningham, Naomi Hupert, Irene Mordkowitz, and Theresa Thornton. Lois Robarge also typed, scheduled meetings, and solved problems with efficiency. Laura Bryant was always available to assist with budget matters. The computer experts at Bank Street College helped at many critical moments: Deondra Drumgold and Rafael Busto.

Liz Westfall, Project Manager in the first years with Anne Mitchell, orchestrated the work of dozens of advisors, authors, and reviewers, skillfully managed the technological aspects of production, and launched herself as a writer as well. From July 1991 to the last word of the camera-ready copy, Maria Licitra, Project Manager with Judy David, gave generously of her time, expertise, and good humor. She coordinated the work of many people, made useful suggestions about the text and illustrations, and made sure that the Guide met her own high standards.

Joan Cenedella, Vice President for Academic Affairs at Bank Street, has been supportive of our work in so many ways; she has read and commented on every chapter, written one of them, made resources at the College available to us, and throughout has helped us articulate the Bank Street approach. She has believed in the importance of this undertaking from beginning to end. Her wisdom and her wit are greatly appreciated.

Anne Mitchell, Editor-in-Chief
and Project Director
(July 1989–July 1991)

Judy David, Editor-in-Chief
and Project Director
(August 1991–June 1992)

Foreword

From its founding in 1916 as the Bureau of Educational Experiments to this last decade of the twentieth century, Bank Street College has held a distinctive position in the field of education, influencing educational practices in the city, across the nation, and around the world. Founded by Lucy Sprague Mitchell and Harriet Johnson, the Bureau was initially characterized by a diversity of interests that grew out of the context of early progressivism—educational testing, rural schools, vocational education, day nurseries, public school nutrition. By 1919, the Bureau staff had established a focus for its work that continues to this day: to understand through study, experimentation, and research the complex development of children, and to create environments that support and promote their development.

Combining research, practice, publishing, and outreach, Bank Street is now composed of a Graduate School of Education, a model School for Children and Family Center, a Division of Continuing Education, a Publications Group, and a Research Division. Through the efforts of all these divisions, Bank Street works to improve the education of young children by preparing teachers and educational leaders; demonstrating our approach in programs for children at Bank Street and in many other educational settings; conducting research; and creating materials in various media for teachers, children, and parents.

Explorationns with Young Children: A Curriculum Guide from Bank Street College of Education is a logical extension of these efforts—our way of reaching out to all those who work with young children and their families. The plan for putting together this Guide and making the companion videotape, *Social Studies: A Way to Integrate Curriculum for Four- and Five-Year-Olds,* originally emerged from a College-wide strategic planning process begun in 1988 with support from the W. Alton Jones Foundation. We asked ourselves: What would really help people who are trying to create quality programs for young children? Making the Bank Street approach to early childhood education accessible to many more people than we can reach directly through our programs in New York City seemed to be the answer.

Thus, we decided that our priority would be the production of a set of materials (written and audiovisual) that could be disseminated widely. The Ford Foundation supported this phase of our work. Planning involved many of our current and former colleagues at

Bank Street—the Bank Street Advisory Group—as well as colleagues from the larger early childhood community—the National Advisory Panel. They reviewed the early drafts of materials and commented on them. Their contributions were invaluable, and we thank them again.

National Advisory Panel

Don Bolce
National Head Start Association

Sue Bredekamp
National Association for the Education of Young Children

Peggy Crichton
American Association of Community College Early Childhood Educators

Harriet Egertson
National Association of Early Childhood Specialists in State Departments of Education

Kay Hollestelle
The Children's Foundation;
National Association for Family Day Care

Deborah Jordan
Council for Early Childhood Professional Recognition

Pauline Koch
National Association of Regulatory Administration

Peggy Pizzo
National Center for Clinical Infant Programs

Tutti Sherlock
National Association of Child Care Resource and Referral Agencies

Margaret Spencer
Division of Educational Studies, Emory University

Bank Street College Advisory Panel

Nancy Balaban	Bill Hooks
Harriet Cuffaro	Maritza Macdonald
Dick Feldman	Ann-Marie Mott
Sam Gibbon	Edna Shapiro
Susan Ginsberg	Sal Vascellaro
Judith Gold	Eileen Wasow
Laura Guarino	

Writing the Guide and making the companion videotape were collaborative processes that brought together the skills and talents of colleagues from every part of the College. The writers, reviewers, editors, illustrators, photographers, typists, and administrators among us all contributed their best to bring these materials into being. As the materials were nearing completion, they were also being field tested in a variety of early childhood settings and reviewed by staff developers, trainers, and other teachers of adults. Our work during this period was generously supported by the NYNEX Foundation and the East Coast Migrant Head Start Project.

We hope these materials will enrich the important and valuable work you do every day with young children and their families. The process of creating them has been a deeply rewarding learning experience for us at Bank Street. We hope that using them will be the same kind of experience for you.

Anne Mitchell, Editor-in-Chief and Project Director (July 1989-July 1991)

Joan Cenedella, Vice President for Academic Affairs Bank Street College

Introduction

Explorations with Young Children: A Curriculum Guide from Bank Street College of Education is written for early childhood professionals who are serving infants, toddlers, preschoolers, and young school-age children (6 to 8 years old) in a variety of educational settings—family day care homes, center-based care, Head Start, and public schools. By early childhood professionals, we mean teachers, caregivers, staff developers, teacher trainers. (We use the words "teacher" and "caregiver" interchangeably throughout the Guide, eschewing the common distinction that one teaches and the other cares for. We believe that *all* early childhood professionals both care for children and educate them.) Teachers and caregivers will find the Guide and its companion videotape, *Social Studies: A Way to Integrate Curriculum for Four- and Five-Year-Olds,* helpful in planning and putting into practice every aspect of their program; staff developers and education directors will find the materials useful supplements to their inservice work with staff; and college instructors and Child Development Associate (CDA) trainers will be able to incorporate chapters from the Guide into their courses (see Appendix A). Finally, for those readers, whether educators or not, who have an interest in the theoretical roots of the Bank Street approach (also referred to as the developmental-interaction approach), the Guide presents an overview and examples of how theory is translated into practice.

Whatever your setting, as an early childhood professional you are a vital part of your children's early, critical years of learning and growth. Our goal in writing this curriculum guide is to offer a framework for planning and carrying out work with young children. At Bank Street, we believe that a sound framework based on an understanding of how children grow and learn—rather than a series of lesson plans and specific curricula—is the best guide for those working with children. The curricula, the lessons, the pacing—these will grow out of the particulars of the school or setting, the needs and interests of the children, and the professional's own strengths and interests.

This Guide offers a way of thinking about, or helping others to think about, program issues and make decisions on what to teach and how to teach it. It is meant to encourage early childhood professionals to develop their own curricula based on a few important principle, which, together, we think of as a framework for educators, no matter who they are or in what setting they work with

Who is this Guide for?

children. These principles, extensively developed in the Guide, include the following:

- Your work with children is based on knowledge of child development, and especially of the interdependence of social, emotional, physical, and intellectual growth.

- You learn about your particular children through observation and recording, through children's works or products, through children's families, and through others who have worked with them.

- You create a physical environment for children that encourages their active participation in their own learning.

- You create a social/emotional environment that encourages a sense of community and of the value of each individual in the community.

These principles are discussed in the first seven chapters of the Guide; the remaining chapters give examples of how these principles can be applied in your program and in specific areas of curriculum. The examples throughout the book come from many different schools and settings. Some, but by no means all, come from Bank Street's Family Center and School for Children; some come from schools and child care settings that Bank Street works with; others come from settings where Bank Street places graduate students for field placements; still others come from settings our faculty have worked in. The settings are private, public, suburban, urban, and rural. We have deliberately included a wide diversity of settings to make the point that the framework can work in many different situations. (The principles of the Bank Street approach are applicable to children with special needs. However, the Guide does not address issues specific to their disabilities.)

How can the Guide be used?

We urge you to make this Guide yours, to use it in the way that best suits your needs and interests. For many readers, this will mean reading the Guide from beginning to end, chapter by chapter. This strategy would immerse you initially in the theoretical bases and general framework of the Bank Street approach, as described in the chapters "Principles of the Bank Street Approach," "Child Development," and "Observing and Recording Children's Behavior." With a grounding in the underlying theory and ideas of the Guide, you would then see how they can be put into action as you read about planning the learning environment, valuing diversity, developing curriculum, working with families, fulfilling your role as teacher, and conducting assessment.

For some readers, it may make sense to review the Table of Contents and then begin by reading the chapter that addresses a particular concern or interest. For staff whose priority is to involve families in the program, the chapter on "Working with Families" would be relevant. If you are thinking about general curriculum issues—for example, what developmentally appropriate practice means for your setting—then a good starting point would be one of these curriculum chapters: "Creating Curriculum," "Planning for Infants, Toddlers, and Threes," or "Integrated Curriculum for Four-through Eight-Year-Olds." Ideas about how to enrich a curriculum area, such as math or music, and how to integrate it with other curriculum areas are presented in the respective chapters. Although you can begin by reading any one chapter in the Guide, we do recommend that, at some time, you look at the initial chapters, which provide the framework for the Bank Street approach.

In general, the chapters in the Guide have a similar format. The topic or subject is first defined; for example, what is child development, discipline and management, or science in early childhood? Then a rationale is presented—why incorporate movement into the curriculum or why value diversity? The third section is "how to"; for example, how to observe and record, support emerging literacy, develop an integrated curriculum, or assess through the curriculum. This section provides guidelines and recommendations, not fail-safe recipes. (At the heart of the Bank Street approach is the recognition that the specifics of any early childhood program will reflect unique characteristics of the children, families, and staff.) The next section provides vivid examples of what caregivers and teachers do to implement a curriculum area (e.g., art or movement) with different age groups—infants and toddlers, preschoolers, young school-age children—and with families. Each chapter concludes with a series of exercises for you to try and a list of resources for further reading. Throughout the Guide, Bank Street's respect for diversity is reflected in references to males and females from many ethnic and cultural backgrounds.

One of the reasons we at Bank Street wanted to create the Guide was to support current national efforts to improve the quality of programs for young children and to reform schools. The ideas in the Guide support these efforts in numerous ways.

Our materials are consistent with the efforts of the National Association for the Education of Young Children (NAEYC) to define "developmentally appropriate practice" and with NAEYC's standards for accrediting programs (1987). The Bank Street approach is characterized by its emphasis on age-appropriateness and individual appropriateness in early childhood programs. *The Guidelines for Appropriate Curriculum Content and Assessment in Programs Serving Children Ages 3 through 8*, published by NAEYC in 1991, focuses on

How does the Guide support current efforts to improve programs?

the "what" and "when" issues of teaching and learning, and on assessment. Here are two important examples of how the Guide is consistent with NAEYC's guidelines:

The first curriculum guideline is:

> The curriculum has an articulated description of its theoretical base that is consistent with prevailing professional opinion and research on how children learn (p. 29).

The first chapter in the Guide, "Principles of the Bank Street Approach," describes our theoretical base and its relevance to research on children's growth and learning.

The sixth guideline is:

> Curriculum content reflects and is generated by the needs and interests of individual children within the group. Curriculum incorporates a wide variety of learning experiences, materials and equipment, and instructional strategies to accommodate a broad range of children's individual differences in prior experience, maturation rates, styles of learning, needs, and interests (p. 30).

The Bank Street approach is an integrated curriculum rooted in social studies. As you will see in the chapters, "Creating Curriculum" and "An Integrated Curriculum for Four- through Eight-Year-Olds," these studies are designed to arise from children's interests and are developed to meet individual children's needs. Other chapters, including "Observing and Recording Children's Behavior" and "Valuing Diversity," also reflect this guideline. Throughout the Guide and highlighted in the chapter "Assessment through the Curriculum," the curriculum approach we present is consistent with this important guideline.

In 1988, the National Association of State Boards of Education (NASBE) convened a Task Force on Early Childhood Education, Their report, *Right from the Start*, called on schools to recognize the early childhood years (ages 4-8) as a distinct period, and to restructure teaching in those years on the basis of child development and the child in context of family and community (1988). The themes of child development, diversity, and families which run through every chapter in the Guide will make it a useful tool for schools working to implement the recommendations of the report.

The Guide is also consistent with the standards put forth by the National Association of Elementary School Principals (NAESP) for programs serving 3- through 8-year-olds (1990). The chapters focusing on curriculum, assessment, and working with families are particularly relevant.

In an effort to improve programs for very young children and their families, the National Center for Clinical Infant Programs has identified core concepts for professional practice (1990). The core concepts of developmental processes and the interrelationship and transaction between the infant and the environment are addressed in the chapters "Child Development," "The Learning Environment," and "Planning for Infants, Toddlers, and Threes." Nearly every chapter of the Guide includes sections on infants and toddlers and on families.

Thus, the approach to early childhood education articulated in the Guide supports all the current major national efforts to improve the education of young children. This is true, despite the fact that the essential principles of the Bank Street approach were developed in the late teens and early twenties of this century. Indeed, much of what is perceived today as "new" in early childhood education was part of Bank Street's theory and practice some seventy years ago. We are delighted to have so many influential allies in our ongoing efforts to provide the best possible education for young children in all the settings in which they grow and learn. And we hope this Guide will add valuable momentum to the movement toward child-centered, developmentally appropriate programs for our nation's children.

Anne Mitchell, Editor-in-Chief   Judy David, Editor-in-Chief
and Project Director   and Project Director
(July 1989-July 1991)   (August 1991-June 1992)

Joan Cenedella, Vice President
for Academic Affairs, Bank Street College

Bredekamp, S. (Ed.). (1987). *Developmentally appropriate practice in early childhood programs serving children from birth through age 8.* Washington, DC: National Association for the Education of Young Children.

National Association for the Education of Young Children and the National Association of Early Childhood Specialists in State Departments of Education. (1991). Position Statement: Guidelines for appropriate curriculum content and assessment in programs serving children ages 3 through 8. *Young Children,* 46(3), 21-38.

National Association of Elementary School Principals. (1990). *Early childhood programs and the elementary school principal: Standards for quality programs for young children.* Alexandria, VA: Author.

National Association of State Boards of Education Task Force on Early Childhood Education. (1988). *Right from the start.* Alexandria, VA: Author.

National Center for Clinical Infant Programs. (1990). *Preparing practitioners to work with infants, toddlers and their families.* Washington, DC: Author.

Resources

1 | Principles of the Bank Street Approach

The way we teach reflects the way we think people learn. Over the years, many philosophers, psychologists, and educators have devised ideal educational systems that follow from their images of what human beings are like and theories about how we become the people we are. Theories about development are not a luxury or an add-on to practice; theory governs action, even when we are not fully aware of why we do what we do. The principles of Bank Street's approach to education are based on a coherent set of values and goals for optimum development and anchored in knowledge of processes of growth.

Bank Street was founded in 1916 and was originally called the Bureau of Educational Experiments, a name that reflected the idea that educational practice should be based on studying children to better understand their development. Lucy Sprague Mitchell, the founder of Bank Street, like others of her time, believed strongly in the power of education to affect and improve society. Education takes place in a social context and has profound consequences for the larger society.

Bank Street's approach to education is not limited to any one educational institution. But while the general outlines and theoretical bases are shared by a number of other educators and psychologists, Bank Street has a uniquely long-term experience in putting the theory into practice.

Theoretical roots

The approach flows from three main sources: (1) the dynamic psychology of Freud and his followers, especially those who were concerned with development in a social context, for example, Anna Freud and Erik Erikson; (2) developmental psychologists like Jean Piaget and Heinz Werner, whose theories focused primarily on cognitive development but who were not especially concerned with education; and (3) educational theorists and practitioners like John Dewey, Harriet Johnson (the founding director of Bank Street's early education program), Susan Isaacs, and Lucy Sprague Mitchell. These have been the main theoretical sources. However, there are many other psychologists and educators whose ideas are compatible with Bank Street's approach to education, and who have influenced its continuing development and refinement, for example, Kurt Lewin, Lois Murphy, Lev Vygotsky. Barbara Biber, a psychologist who had a long and distinguished career at Bank Street in research and teaching, helped to define the connections between psychology and educational philosophy and practice.

As we already have said, Bank Street's approach is not unique to Bank Street, and therefore we wanted to give it a name that indicated its generality, and also its distinctiveness from other educational models. We have called it the developmental-interaction approach. Developmental refers to the patterns of growth and ways of understanding and responding that characterize children and adults as they mature. Interaction points, first, to an emphasis on interaction with the environment, an environment of children, adults, and the material world. And, second, it points to the interaction of cognitive and affective development; that is, thinking and emotion are not seen as separate but as interconnected spheres of development.

These concepts apply to the education of children and adults of all ages. However, a basic principle is that one has to understand the stage of development of those one is teaching. Therefore, concepts need to be adapted or translated for children and adults of different ages, capabilities, and cultures. Perhaps most important, children are different from adults. They are not just a smaller version, or even a smaller, less-knowing version; their ways of taking in and relating to the world, their ways of thinking and expressing themselves are different from those of adults. In these chapters, we are focusing on the way the developmental-interaction approach relates to the education of young children, from birth through the primary years, through age eight.

Governing principles

Six general principles of development are basic to understanding the Bank Street approach.

1. Development is not a simple path from less to more; and it is not an unfolding, like the unfolding of a flower. Development involves changes or shifts in the way a person organizes experience and copes with the world, generally moving from simpler to more complex, from single to multiple and integrated ways of responding. The concept of stages of development is crucial, and is also a convenient way of talking and thinking about developmental change and growth. Stages are approximate and are only loosely related to age.

   This leads to a second principle:

2. Individuals are never at a fixed point on a straight line of development, but operate within a range of possibilities. Earlier ways of organizing experience are not erased, but become integrated into more advanced systems. While people will want to function at the highest possible level, they are also able to use less mature ways appropriately. (Even after a child knows how to hop and jump, there are times when it is a good idea to crawl; even adults find

moments when it is appropriate to be silly.)

One of the biggest puzzles of development is how one moves from one stage to the next. No one really understands the process, but one aspect is clear:

3. Developmental progress involves a mix of stability and instability. A central task for the educator is to find a balance between helping a child consolidate new understandings and offering challenges that will promote growth.

The fundamental concept that development involves the interaction of the individual with the environment leads to our fourth principle:

4. The motivation to engage actively with the environment—to make contact, to have an impact, and to make sense of experience—is built into human beings. The growing child gradually adds more ways of actively engaging with the world as she develops. Generally, the progression is from more physical, body-centered ways of responding to perceptual and then more conceptual, symbolic ways.

Probably one of the most agreed-upon principles of development is the importance of developing a sense of self as a unique and independent individual:

5. The child's sense of self is built up from his experiences with other people and with objects; knowledge of the self is based on repeated awareness and testing of one's self in interaction.

Finally, an equally important principle:

6. Growth and maturing involve conflict—conflict within the self, and conflict with others. Conflict is necessary for development. The way conflicts are resolved depends on the nature of the interaction with significant figures in the child's life and the demands of the culture.

Educational goals

The educational system is seen as responsible for fostering the child's development in a broad sense; the aim is not simply to promote specific learnings but to provide many opportunities for physical, social, and emotional as well as cognitive development. A fundamental principle of the developmental-interaction approach is that cognitive growth cannot be separated from the growth of personal and social processes. Further, the school should be an active community, connected to the social world of which it is a part, rather than an isolated place for "learning lessons." This means that the school shares responsibility with children's families and with other neighborhood institutions.

Educational goals are conceived in terms of developmental processes, not as specific achievements. The school is responsible for fostering the individual's ability to deal effectively with her environment. The development of competence is central. Competence means being as able as possible in all areas of development, and being motivated to use one's abilities. A second goal is the development of a sense of autonomy and individuality. This involves a strong sense of identity, the ability to act on your own, to make choices, take risks, and be able to accept help.

Coupled with this is the development of social relatedness and connectedness. This means caring about others, learning to feel part of larger social groups, being able to form friendships, cherishing diversity, developing awareness of human interconnectedness, and seeing human beings in an ecological context.

The encouragement of creativity is a fourth goal. Creativity does not focus only on the product but honors the processes of making. It involves having a range of means for expressing feelings and ideas-logical, intuitive, subjective. Children's (and adults') creative work can take many forms—physical movement; drawing, painting, sculpting; spoken and written words; melody or rhythm; dramatic enactment; mathematical and scientific ideas. Finally, the school promotes integration rather than compartmentalization. Integration means pulling together different ways of experiencing the world—joining thinking and feeling, making connections between how one feels and how others might feel, communicating in both original and conventional ways, connecting the self to the world.

It is critical to understand that these broadly stated goals need to be thought of and made concrete in terms that are appropriate to the child's developmental stage, and also to the cultural context.

Educational concepts

How does this translate into educational practice? How do we put the theory into action?

The Teacher's Role

The teacher creates the climate of the young child's learning environment. Within the constraints of what is possible, she structures the physical and psychological atmosphere. Teachers vary in personal style, temperament, cultural background, and the kinds of experience they bring to teaching. In enacting the developmental-interaction approach, the teacher's personal qualities do matter; in this way of teaching, the teacher does not leave her personal self at the classroom door. This framework is compatible with a wide range of personal and teaching styles. The essential and overriding principle, however, is that the teacher should respond and relate to each child with respect. The task is to enable the child to have trust in himself, and in the adult caregiver and teacher. This means that the teacher herself must be trustworthy.

It is the teacher's responsibility to know the children in her charge as individuals. Knowing means understanding patterns of child development, and knowing each child—her talents and weaknesses, her tolerance for frustration, her pace of learning, her sources of pride and concerns about inadequacy, and her family. A good deal of this knowledge is based on close, careful, and frequent observation of the children in a range of different situations, an essential part of the educator's task.

Work and Play

Adults make a major distinction between work and play; young children learn these concepts from us. There are activities children like and those they don't like, or "hate," but the difference has nothing to do with what we consider work or play. Learning and play can and should be joyful and fun, a source of pleasure. Play offers ways of trying out new ideas, new combinations, of expressing emotions, of taking different roles, and of repeating known ways of enjoyment.

Learning, especially in the early years, is active, physical exploration—touching, tasting, hearing, seeing, moving. An infant drops something to see what happens. The sequence of learning moves from open exploration to more structured engagement with materials and ideas. Children learn through active doing, through experimenting with materials, with language; they learn from each other and from adults. Even very young children are capable of sustained concentration when their interest is captured. Unless they are taught otherwise, they enjoy learning, discovering, and mastering.

The Educational Environment as a Community

Every child, every person, is part of a number of communities—family (or families), neighborhood(s), cultural and ethnic group(s). Programs for children are another kind of community that children become part of. They learn how to relate to others in the group, they learn the "rules of the game" of the center, the preschool, the elementary school; they learn from and teach each other. Positive experiences of belonging, of cooperating with others, of being a group member, of dealing with differences of opinion and styles of interaction are necessary for functioning well in a democratic society.

Connections with the Larger World

A good part of children's learning takes place at home, and in the neighborhood—that is, outside of the "formal" educational environment. Sometimes there is continuity between home and school in the kinds of learning that are valued, the expectations of appropriate behavior, and the customs. More often, in this country of diverse national and ethnic groups, there are sharp breaks between the cultures of school and home. Educators must connect with the child's world, both in the sense of knowing the child's experience and also as interpreters of educational programs and goals. Educators should be a resource to parents and others who also are responsible for the child's welfare and development.

There is no simple recipe for fostering children's development. If you believe that all you have to do is "lay out the facts" and the child will learn, then you can say, "too bad," and blame the child or the family when she doesn't. But if you believe that the educator needs to meet the children where they are, then you have to find out where they are. If you want genuine and mutual trust and respect, you have to give as well as receive. You have to be willing to join with the children in an exploration of possibilities, to accept that what worked yesterday may not work tomorrow. Like the children, you have to learn from experience. But first, you have to give such learning a chance. The chapters that follow give practical information about how to put the Bank Street approach to work in your program. It is not always easy, but when it works, you will find much pleasure and satisfaction in enhancing the development of the children you care for.

Resources

Antler, J. (1987). *Lucy Sprague Mitchell: The making of a modern woman.* New Haven, CT: Yale University Press.

Biber, B. (1977). A developmental-interaction approach: Bank Street College of Education. In M. C. Day & R. K. Parker (Eds.), *Preschool in action: Exploring early childhood programs* (2nd ed.). Boston: Allyn & Bacon.

Biber, B. (1984). *Early education and psychological development.* New Haven, CT: Yale University Press.

Biber, B., Shapiro, E., & Wickens, D. (1977). *Promoting cognitive growth: A developmental-interaction point of view* (2nd ed.). Washington, DC: National Association for the Education of Young Children.

Cuffaro, H. K. (1977). *The developmental-interaction approach.* In B. D. Boeghehold, H. K. Cuffaro, W. H. Hooks, & G. J. Klopf (Eds.), *Education before five.* New York: Bank Street College.

Gilkeson, E., & Bowman, G. W. (1976). *The focus is on children: The Bank Street approach to early childhood education as enacted in Follow Through.* New York: Bank Street College.

Shapiro, E., & Biber, B. (1972). The education of young children: A developmental-interaction point of view. *Teachers College Record, 74,* 55-79.

Zimiles, H. (1987). The Bank Street approach. In J. L. Roopnarine & J. E. Johnson (Eds.), *Approaches to early childhood education.* Columbus, OH: Charles E. Merrill.

About the Authors:

Edna Shapiro, Ph.D., a senior researcher in the Research Division at Bank Street College, is a developmental psychologist interested in the application of psychological principles to educational thoery and practice. Dr. Shapiro is the author of a number of articles in psychological and educational journals, and is co-author of The Psychological Impact of School Experience, *with Patricia Minuchin, Barbara Biber, and Herbert Zimiles (Basic Books, 1969), and co-editor with Evelyn Weber of* Cognitive and Affective Growth: Developmental Interaction *(Erlbaum, 1981).*

Anne Mitchell, M.S., is an early childhood policy researcher at Bank Street College where she did a national study of public schools as providers of programs for children under six and then developed the Early Childhood Curriculum Project. She has taught Education Policy and is the founder of Bank Street's master's program in Early Childhood Leadership. She has been a trainer and consultant with early childhood teachers and family day care providers, and was the director of two child care centers where she worked with toddlers, preschoolers, and children with special needs.

2 | Child Development

Here are children in action:

- A 1-year-old rolls a ball behind a chair and does not seem to notice it has disappeared.

- A 3-year-old kicks a ball back and forth to an adult.

- A 7-year-old makes up a game with a friend—one throws the ball in the air, shouts out "ten," and the other catches it on the tenth bounce.

How does the 1-year-old who does not go after the ball become the 3-year-old who can focus her energy on kicking it, and eventually mature into the older child who creates her own game? The study of child development helps us understand the changes we see as children grow and develop. It describes patterns that occur in the way children mature. To make it easier to talk about, a child's development is usually divided into four areas: *physical, emotional, cognitive,* and *social.* Although we will discuss each area separately, keep in mind that they are intertwined. Together, they make up the whole person.

Physical development refers to increases in bodily size and strength. It includes motor development, which is the ability to control large and small muscles. Changes in the nervous system and brain structure affect physical and motor development.

Emotional development describes how a child feels about himself, other people, and the world he lives in. During the first years of life, children are working on answering, "Who are the important people in my world?" and establishing a sense of self separate from others. As children get older, their sense of who they are becomes more complex and abstract. Emotional development also involves children's learning to distinguish different feelings and express them in culturally acceptable ways.

Cognitive development refers to how children think and learn. People used to believe that children were like empty bottles, waiting for adults to fill them up with what they had to know. Now we know that, from birth on, children are active learners. They learn by interacting with their environment—objects, adults, and other children. They learn by doing and by using their bodies and their senses. Cognitive development includes growth in memory, attention, reasoning, problem-solving strategies, and language abilities.

What is child development?

Social development is concerned with how children, at different ages, relate to other people. At first, the social world of children is limited to family members and other caregivers. Over the course of development, their world expands to include playmates and other adults in their community. Social development includes learning how to make friends and get along with other people.

Throughout childhood, these areas of development interact with and affect each other. Imagine a 5-year-old walking on a balance beam, a task that requires physical coordination. He takes great satisfaction and pleasure in this feat; his physical ability fosters a positive self-concept. He has to wait his turn, so he is learning to cooperate. As he gets close to the end, he poses a problem for himself: how to take three big steps before he finishes. Figuring out how to do this involves thinking hard. In the life of this 5-year-old—and for children of all ages—physical, emotional, cognitive, and social development are brought together in the context of everyday play.

In this chapter, we are going to look at why knowing about child development is important and how to use this information in your setting. Then there will be exercises you and your colleagues can do together.

Why is it important to understand child development?

What your program is like is based largely on who the children in your group are—their stages of growth as well as who they are as individuals. As caregiver or teacher, you need to know about both to plan a strong program. Child development gives you some guidelines to consider as you plan how to meet the needs of children of a certain age. There are reasons for what children do that stem from their level of development, even though those reasons may not at first be apparent. Knowing how children's experience of the world differs depending on their age can help you make sense of what they are doing and plan appropriate curriculum. (In another chapter, "Observing and Recording Children's Behavior," you can read about how to use observing to help you get to know each child as a special person.)

Here are examples of children's behavior at different ages and how insights from child development can be applied.

- Imagine Rachel, 18 months old, who is playing in a pail of soapy water. In the course of a few minutes, she splashes the water, sucks her wet fingers, and puts a little bit in her hair. Then she pours some water on the table top, spreads it around with both hands, and chants, "Wa, wa, wa."

Knowing that young children learn through their senses—taste, touch, sound, smell, and sight—can help you understand that Rachel is not doing this to make cleaning up harder. Rather, she is learning about water—that it feels warm on her head and makes a loud sound when she splashes it. She is using language to describe her experience.

- Several 4-year-olds are talking. Kyle asks Timmy, "Are you my friend?" Timmy replies, "No, I'm Ali's friend. He has a new truck."

Young children think differently from adults about many aspects of their world. Children focus on what is immediate and concrete. Timmy likes Ali's new truck, and to 4-year-olds friendship means that someone lets you play with his toy. This is not a selfish or materialistic viewpoint; rather, it reflects a particular developmental level. Not until children are older do they understand that friendships are based on personal qualities, like trusting and helping one another.

- In preschool, Yolette loved to paint and draw, especially pictures of her family and her kitten. When she entered elementary school, she still liked art activities. But sometimes she would begin a picture of her kitten, scratch it out or erase it, and say, "I can't draw it." Even when adults encouraged her, she would get frustrated and often give up. Her parents and teachers wondered what had caused this change in her behavior and attitude.

During the school years, children's creative efforts reflect their increasing awareness of standards and their desire to be competent. Like Yolette, they want to draw a kitten that really looks like one; as preschoolers, they were more interested in the process and perfectly satisfied with their very own version of a kitten. Knowing that children's creativity is affected by their developmental level helps adults find ways to encourage school children.

Learning about child development is an ongoing process. You can learn about it by reading books, articles, and other materials and by talking with colleagues and parents. You can also learn a great deal by observing the patterns of growth and behavior in the age group you are teaching.

In this section, we use information about child development to begin creating a picture of infants and toddlers, preschoolers, and young school-age children. We will present a developmental profile of each age group, describing general patterns in their physical, emotional, cognitive, and social functioning. To help complete the picture, we suggest that you add your own knowledge about children's development to the descriptions.

As we describe the different ages, we also refer to theories of child development. The theories offer explanations of how a child changes; they help us see how all aspects of development are interrelated.

How can you learn about child development?

There is no one accepted theory for understanding development; rather, there are a number of theories that emphasize different aspects of development and different processes at work.

As discussed in the chapter "Principles of the Bank Street Approach," several theoretical perspectives have informed the developmental-interaction approach. The dynamic psychology of Sigmund Freud and his followers has contributed to our understanding of children's emotional development. Erik Erikson delineates stages in social-emotional development (referred to as psychosocial crises) that are shaped by the child's culture and pose both challenges and risks to development. The Swiss psychologist, Jean Piaget, describes stages in cognitive development that occur as children's biological development matures and as they build up experiences with objects and people. Lev Vygotsky, a Soviet psychologist, emphasizes the role of the social environment in children's learning. Each of these theories of development, and many others, have shaped the Bank Street approach. Findings from biology, sociology, and anthropology have also provided insight into children's growth and development.

As you read the developmental profiles, keep these points in mind:

- Patterns of development are just guidelines. No one fits exactly on a developmental chart. Usually, but not always, the sequence of development is the same for children, even though their rate of development varies. For example, most children speak in single words before they put together two or three words, but some children will say their first word before, and some after, their first birthday.

- Heredity and environment interact to affect the course of development for any one child. Although heredity (genetic make-up) largely determines how tall a person will become, in the absence of proper nutrition and stimulating, nurturing experiences, a young child's physical growth may be stunted.

- Not all areas of development progress at the same pace for an individual child. One area may develop more rapidly than another; for example, a toddler may make tremendous gains in physical development while his language lags behind. It may be a while before his energy for learning is directed into verbal skills.

- Development does not occur along a straight line. Growing consists of steps forward and backward. A child who has been toilet trained may insist on going back to diapers for a while. An older child who is showing many signs of growing up, such as tying her own shoes, may begin to act "helpless," especially if there is a major change in her life, like starting a new school or the birth of a sibling.

- Children are born with their own unique temperaments. Some children are rather easygoing; others are intense. Some are slow to warm up and need lots of time to adjust to changes in their environment; others will plunge in right away. Children's temperaments will determine in part how they experience different stages of development.

Developmental Profile of Infants and Toddlers: One- and Two-Year-Olds

Physical Development

Children grow more rapidly when they are infants and toddlers than at any other period of life. Physical development proceeds in two related directions: "head-to-tail," that is, the baby's head becomes functional before his hands or feet; and "near-to-far," that is, development proceeds from the center out to the periphery. For example, the child uses his whole hand as a unit before he can control individual fingers. Many of the physical advances in the early years are stimulated by growth and specialization of areas of the brain.

At birth, physical actions are guided by reflexes, such as sucking, swallowing, and grasping. A few months after birth, infants begin to coordinate the acts of looking and reaching—the first signs of goal-directed behavior. Now their reflexes are coming under voluntary control and are coordinated and transformed into very complex actions. As their fine-motor control improves, infants learn to use a spoon and a cup—evidence of their growing independence.

During the first year, infants learn to roll over, sit, and crawl. Around their first birthday, most children begin to walk. Because of their wobbly movements, they are now called toddlers. By the time they are 3 years old, they are skilled at running, climbing, and jumping with two feet.

Emotional Development

During the first year, infants form a deep bond—a primary *attachment*—with adults who nurture and care for them. We can see how strong this connection is when, toward the end of the first year, children everywhere begin to protest when they are separated from their primary caretakers. This suggests that attachment is a universal feature of development.

It is in the context of their attachments that children begin to learn the language, the behaviors, and the values of the adults they love. When children feel emotionally secure, they are willing to explore and play. According to Erik Erikson, the goal of emotional development in infancy is to establish a sense of *trust* in the world and

themselves which individuals will carry with them the rest of their lives. If infants do not have the opportunity to form attachments, then they will form a sense of *mistrust* and their development will be at risk.

What is commonly called the "terrible twos" is the result of toddlers' struggle to be their own person—in Erikson's words, to forge a healthy sense of *autonomy* (or, on the other hand, to develop a lasting sense of *shame* and *doubt*). Children's "no" or "me do" is their way of saying, "I am my own person, apart from you." At the same time, toddlers are developing a sense of adult standards, and evaluate themselves and their behavior in simple terms: "I am a good boy," or "I wear big socks—I'm a big girl."

Understandably, young children may feel both eager to try out their new abilities and overwhelmed by the big world. Toddlers often swing between extremes of independence and dependence; for example, wanting to walk down the street by themselves and then wanting an adult to carry them. They may develop an attachment to a transitional object, like a blanket or stuffed animal, which will comfort them and ease their sense of separateness. As much as they may assert their independence, they also depend on the sense of security that familiar people and places provide. Changes in their routines at home or in the early childhood setting may upset them.

Many toddlers express their feelings intensely and in physical ways, although this may depend somewhat on the child's temperament. Joy can be expressed in exuberant running, anger in hitting, or even biting. When they want something, they want it now and have difficulty waiting. Toddlers tend to be impulsive; they do not yet have the cognitive ability to think ahead, to anticipate that taking all the toys off a shelf means they will then have to be picked up. Their feelings often seem to overwhelm them and push them out of control; it can be difficult to get toddlers back on an even keel. With your support and with development, they will learn to express their feelings in more restrained ways, primarily through verbalizing them.

Cognitive Development

In Piaget's theory, the first period of cognitive development is called the *sensorimotor stage*, referring to how infants experience the world: through their senses and motor activity. They suck on their fingers, shake a rattle, watch an interesting sight. They experiment to see what happens when they bang on a pot or tear up a piece of paper. All of these activities help them develop early concepts about cause and effect and spatial relationships and help them acquire information about the world—that some objects feel soft, others feel hard, some taste good, others do not.

Up until 9 to 12 months, infants do not realize that an object (or person) still exists when it is out of sight—that it has an independent, permanent existence apart from their sensorimotor experience of it. Thus, very young babies will not look for the ball that rolls under the bed. The development of infants' understanding of *object permanence* and their increasing ability to remember people and categorize them as familiar (and unfamiliar) are related to the development of attachment.

During the second year, children enter a new phase of mental development. They develop the capacity to symbolize, to think abstractly. Their symbolic capacities are expressed in make-believe play, such as pretending to feed themselves, turning a block into a car, or making a birthday cake out of sand. They enjoy peek-a-boo, which is a playful enactment of separating and reappearing. They are active explorers and problem solvers, quick to figure out that if they move the chair, they can reach the toy on the shelf.

As infants and toddlers hear language directed to them and used in conversation around them, their language skills progress from vocalizations to babbling to words. In all languages, the names of important people and things and words relating to action, such as "bye bye," are usually spoken first. Their ability to use language—to make a word stand for something—reflects the young child's capacity for symbolic thought.

Although Piaget emphasizes the child's construction of knowledge through her own sensorimotor activity, Vygotsky assigns a greater role to adults (or older children) who guide the child's learning. In the course of daily interactions, parents and teachers stimulate cognitive development by offering support that goes just beyond the child's competence, thereby building on her existing capacities and drawing her toward accomplishing these actions on her own.

Social Development

Children's first relationships are with caregiving adults in their lives. Usually these include their parents and maybe others, such as grandparents or child care providers. When the adults are sensitive to them as individuals and responsive to their needs for food, comfort, and play, infants and toddlers learn to love and trust them. Although most 1-year-olds are fearful around strangers and prefer to be around familiar adults, as they grow older, they actively seek out contact with other people. Toddlers will greet strangers on the street with a big "hi" and want to learn the names of people they see regularly, such as shopkeepers and neighbors.

Infants and toddlers are very curious about other children. If they have older siblings, they may be very attached to them. Even at an early age, some children seem to develop special friendships, especially if they share similar interests, such as playing on large motor equipment. Young children tend to play next to one another in a kind of parallel fashion. But sometimes toddlers show the beginnings of turn taking and cooperation. Much of their play is imitative and based on what they have observed in their families—Daddy shaving in the morning, grandma making tortillas.

Since young children are learning through their bodies, their play is often active and physical. When they argue or get upset with a playmate, they may hit or push, not yet having the words to express themselves. They are egocentric, tending to see the world from their own perspective, so they cannot always understand why somebody else needs a turn. They are too young to share; you can encourage but not expect it at this stage. Toddlers' assertion "it's mine" is actually a positive step in their self-development because it indicates that they have a sense of themselves distinct from others.

Think about the infants and toddlers you work with. What would you add to this description of their development?

Developmental Profile of Preschoolers: Three-, Four-, and Five-Year-Olds

Physical Development

By the age of 3, children are losing their baby fat and their legs are growing longer and thinner. They are steady on their feet and love to run, jump, climb, and throw a ball. Preschoolers become interested and skilled in using their small muscles to draw, fasten buttons, pull up zippers, use scissors, and put puzzles together. To the delight of adults, they have usually achieved bowel and bladder control, an important step toward independence. The exact timing of toilet training will vary, depending on the child's biological readiness and her own family's and culture's expectations. During the preschool period, growth within and between areas of the brain occurs and is related to changes in behavior.

Emotional Development

Preschoolers are continuing to learn about themselves. Their sense of identity includes knowledge that they are a boy or girl (gender), and a member of a particular family, racial, religious, or ethnic group. Yet, their sense of self is unstable; a boy may think that he can grow up to be a Mommy or that if he wears skirts, he will be a girl. They feel proud about all the things they can do, such as feeding and dressing themselves and helping out around home and school.

Preschoolers are aware of how people feel about them. They want to please the adults in their lives and look to them for approval and praise. As they internalize the standards of their culture ("Don't pick the flowers"; "Say please"), they exhibit increasing self-control over their impulses. Yet, a preschooler's conscience is still very fragile and is easily overcome by immediate desire. They need firm but reasonable limits. Erikson describes the psychosocial conflict of the preschool period as children learning to take *initiative* in thinking and acting without getting out of control versus feeling *guilty* over their attempts at independence.

Children between the ages of 3 and 5 have strong emotions. They can feel exuberant one minute when they reach the top of the climbing structure, but panic the next because they are not sure how to climb back down. They may be afraid of animals or being in the dark. Although the basis for some of their fears may be imaginary, the "monsters" or "ghosts" seem real to them. They can swing back and forth between feeling independent and dependent, wanting to make their own sandwich and then demanding that you do it for them.

Cognitive Development

Compared to the infant who relies on sensorimotor activity to learn and understand, preschoolers can think in more complex and abstract ways. Because they can think symbolically, using a mental symbol to stand for something else, they now rely on symbolic forms—as in language, art, and dramatic play—to express themselves. They will make marks on a paper to represent "my mommy" or pretend to be a bus driver going to the zoo. They need many varied, direct experiences to support their new cognitive abilities. For example, they learn best about their community when they visit real places, such as a grocery store or library, and then re-create these experiences back in the classroom through drawing, block building, and story writing.

Piaget calls the period from about 2 1/2 to 6 years the *preoperational stage*, which is characterized by many paradoxes and inconsistencies in thinking. The way things look or appear impresses preschoolers and is the basis for much of their reasoning. A classic example from Piaget's work involves presenting a child with two identical glasses filled with the same amount of water. One glass is poured into a third, narrower, taller glass so that the level of water is higher. From this change in level, preschoolers conclude that the amount of water has somehow increased. They confuse a change in appearance with a change in reality. They focus on one aspect of the situation, the height of the water, and cannot consider simultaneously the height and width of the glass. Not until the next stage of cognitive development will children be able to consider all aspects of the problem and logically think it through.

Preschoolers have vivid imaginations, and the line between reality and fantasy is often blurred. They may think that their dreams are real, that superheroes really fly, that putting on a Halloween mask can turn someone into a witch. Magical thinking flourishes and reflects preschoolers' immature understanding of cause and effect. When a 4-year-old wishes for a sunny day and the sun comes out, he will think *he* caused it! A preschooler may think that her anger at a family member was the reason that person became sick. Young children do not yet understand natural processes; they see little connection between water from the faucet and ice cubes in the freezer.

Language development is rapid between 3 and 5 years of age. Vocabulary blossoms at the rate of nearly 1,000 words a year. Preschoolers have mastered many complex language forms, though they have not learned all the exceptions to the rules. For instance, saying "the mouses ate the cheese" instead of "mice" or "he goed yesterday" instead of "went" are typical errors in learning English and a normal part of development. These errors are evidence that children are constructing knowledge because these incorrect forms of speech are not learned from adults. Young children are intrigued by words, rhymes, and silly songs. Language is understood literally, and so when an adult says, "I have a frog in my throat," preschoolers react with amazement. They are famous for asking all kinds of questions, from "Why is the car red?" to "Where does the sun go at night?"

Many preschoolers are beginning to understand what letters and words stand for. They are eager to make scribbles and say, "It's writing"; often they know some of the letters in their names and try to write them. They may ask adults to write down a story that goes with their drawing, or try to write it down themselves. It is important to encourage these efforts because these are first steps toward reading and writing.

Throughout the preschool period, children's thinking tends to be egocentric. They think their viewpoint is the only one, especially when they are emotionally involved in a situation. They do not understand that another child's ideas for play are just as valid as their own. They believe that their experience is universal—that everyone eats with chopsticks as they do or has a Mommy who goes to work.

Although Piaget's theory emphasizes the development of children's understanding of the physical world and concepts about number, space, time, and causality, children also develop ideas about the social world. This capacity is referred to as social cognition and has to do with thinking about individuals and groups. Preschoolers' concepts about gender, race, culture, and socioeconomic class reflect their preoperational thinking. They focus on visually salient features, "Boys wear pants and have short hair," and reflect their egocentric interpretation of information, "People who speak

Spanish eat chili, like my friend José does."

Throughout development, children's perceptions and experiences of the physical and social world are organized into mental structures. Although this process is far from understood, Piaget and others describe it as an active process in which children both *assimilate* new experiences into their existing structures and, in turn, modify or *accommodate* these structures to fit in the new information. For example, a young child has a notion of "dog," which initially he applies to all four-legged creatures. As he encounters new experiences, his concept of "dog" becomes refined and he distinguishes "dog" from "cow," "horse," and other animals. In this way, he accommodates his idea of "dog" to reality. These dual processes of assimilation and accommodation are occurring all the time and cause change and growth in children's thinking.

Recent research challenges Piaget's conclusions about the limited cognitive capacities of young children. In some situations, preschoolers do adjust their needs to those of others, and they do seem to understand others' viewpoints. There are also individual differences in children's level of awareness of self and others that may reflect differences in their social environments. Nevertheless, Piaget's description of how children construct knowledge and how their thinking changes with age provides a useful framework for understanding some aspects of development.

Social Development

Preschoolers are developing new social skills. They can usually share and take turns (even though they may not always want to and may need adult help). Leaders often emerge in the course of play. Usually, they are children who have good ideas for keeping the play going and who are cooperative and sensitive to others. Preschoolers demonstrate increasing empathy toward their peers. They ask, "What's wrong?" and may offer a blanket to a tired child or reassurance to a child who is missing her mother. These advances in their social behavior also reflect changes in their emotional and cognitive functioning.

Preschoolers' ideas about friendship express their egocentrism and their focus on the here and now: "She's my friend because she gave me a cookie," or "He's my friend because we sit next to each other at snack." Friendships often have a momentary quality, although some friendships may be quite stable, especially if children have known each other a long time. Some children who are temperamentally shy may take longer to make friends or need adult help in joining other children's play.

Often preschoolers' preferences in activities and toys reflect sex stereotypes; many boys exhibit more active, physical play than girls, which may be due to both genetic and environmental factors. As children gain more experience interacting with others, their ideas and concepts about individuals and groups are modified and reorganized to reflect a deeper understanding of people's similarities and differences.

A description of preschoolers would be incomplete without a closer look at how play contributes to their growth and development. Play fosters children's emotional well-being, providing them with a forum to express and resolve the feelings they cannot yet put into words. "Going to the dentist" becomes less scary when a 4-year-old can take on the role of dentist and have another child be the patient. In play, children are in charge (not adults) and they can take risks without fear of failure. Play builds preschoolers' sense of confidence and competence.

Play stimulates cognitive development. When children pretend to be "big sister" or make "hamburgers" with playdough, they are engaged in making something stand for the real thing. This kind of symbolic play is an important precursor to the mastery of written and numeric symbols. Play involves thinking and problem solving as preschoolers experiment with sinking and floating objects in the water table or figure out how many blocks they need to make a garage big enough to hold the buses. By building houses, pizza parlors, and roads and by becoming zookeepers and farmers, children bring the real world closer and make it comprehensible. In the words of Barbara Biber (1984), a well-known Bank Street psychologist and educator, they are "learning about the world by playing about it."

Play and social development go hand-in-hand. Play offers many opportunities to be with other children and to share, take turns, disagree, and compromise. In dramatic play, preschoolers try out social roles and activities. Whereas 3-year-olds enact family roles, 5-year-olds are likely to take on the roles of adults at work or characters from stories and television. Social play challenges children's egocentrism; they see that their way is not the only way to build a castle or play "Daddy."

Finally, play promotes physical development, as preschoolers climb, run, and jump. They develop fine motor control when they handle puzzles, paint brushes, and sand toys.

In short, play offers essential learning experiences for preschool children.

Think about the preschoolers you work with. What would you add to this description of their development?

Developmental Profile of Young School-Age Children: Six-, Seven-, and Eight-Year Olds

Physical Development

During the school years, also called "middle childhood," children's size and strength increase, but not so rapidly as in earlier years. Young school-age children become more coordinated, enabling them to ride bikes and write with a pencil. They can dress and undress themselves and can take care of their own toileting needs. They are curious about the human body—their own and others—and they are often interested in where babies come from. They take great pride in the loss of their baby teeth, a sure sign that they are growing up. By the age of 5 or 7, most children's brains have achieved a level of complexity comparable to adults. Changes in brain size and functioning have been linked to some of the advances in children's behavior and thinking seen during this period of development.

Emotional Development

Young school-age children are still developing a sense of "who am I?" They are moving toward a more objective, detailed view of themselves: "I am a Jewish girl who likes ice cream and scary movies." Doing well in school—learning to read and write and do math—helps them feel competent. For children growing up in some families, a sense of competence may be derived from taking care of younger siblings or working in the fields. In Erikson's terms, this age group is developing a sense of *industry*, "I can do," or a sense of *inferiority*, "I can't do," in relation to the real world.

Increasingly, 6- through 8-year-olds verbalize a range of emotions, from "That infuriates me" to "I feel scared" to "I'm lonely." They are sensitive to social contexts and are learning where and how to express their feelings in culturally acceptable ways. For example, it may be all right to admit fear to a parent but not to a peer. Their increasing ability to see themselves objectively and from another's perspective means that they may feel embarrassed or ashamed when their behavior does not meet expectations.

Children this age are developing a stronger conscience, a sense of right and wrong. They tend to hold themselves and others to very strict standards. Breaking a rule in a game can cause a major upset. It is as if their new conscience is constantly "on the alert." They may "tattle" on each other, motivated more by the desire to show adults they know the rules than to get a peer in trouble. Because older children can formulate goals and resist temptation in meeting them, adults hold them far more responsible for behaving themselves in school and at home than preschoolers. Yet, young school-age children still need help from adults to set limits and to boost their confidence in their ability to exercise self-control.

Cognitive Development

In societies around the world, a major shift begins occurring in children's thinking between 5 and 7 years, and lasts until about age 12. Piaget calls this the period the *concrete operational stage*. Internalized mental actions (operations) now fit into a logical system and are applied to concrete, real-world matters. When children begin to think in logical ways, they become capable of mentally combining, separating, ordering, and transforming information and objects. Preschoolers can physically manipulate objects, but cannot do so mentally, which means that changes in how things look mislead them. But the world becomes more predictable when young school-age children attain concrete operations. They understand that when the same amount of water is poured into a different-sized container, the amount remains constant. Now children are not so tied to their own sensory experience, to what they can see and hear and touch, and can begin to understand what they themselves may never have experienced. Young school-age children have a firmer understanding of concepts of number, time, space, size, and distance than preschoolers. Their thinking becomes more flexible and they can formulate alternative ways of solving problems. The line between reality and fantasy becomes clearer; they can organize experience and understand ideas in new ways. These new forms of reasoning and an increased memory capacity help 6-, 7-, and 8-year-olds understand many of the ideas they are learning in school.

In comparison to preschoolers, more of their thinking takes place inside their own heads instead of being acted out in their behavior. They daydream and begin to turn their fantasies into stories, poems, artwork, or musical expression. Their imaginative life may draw heavily on media characters or real life heroes.

In the realm of social cognition, young school-age children's concepts are becoming more differentiated. They recognize that physical appearance alone does not define gender: "Girls can wear pants and have short hair." They are less likely to generalize from one instance to another: just because José likes chili does not mean that all Spanish-speaking people do. They know that one's identity—gender, racial, cultural—remains stable and constant regardless of superficial changes. This means they can understand some of the subtle and complex issues surrounding diversity and group membership in a way that younger children cannot.

Children of this age range are becoming more comfortable working with symbols, such as numbers and letters, although they still need many opportunities to work with real materials and objects. They begin to sound out words and write them out ("km" for "come"). Adults need to support these efforts, even though they may be incorrect, because they show the child's desire for mastery and for learning new things. Linked to their increasing competence is a sense of pride in their accomplishments. Again, though, it is important to have realistic expectations; young school-age children do not yet think like adults.

There is no one entity called intelligence that can describe the range of individual abilities and competencies in school children. Work by Howard Gardner (1983) suggests that there are multiple intelligences: linguistic, musical, logical; mathematical, spatial, bodily; kinesthetic, interpersonal, and intrapersonal. Each follows a different developmental path.

According to Piaget's theory, the cognitive achievements in middle childhood constitute a separate stage of concrete operations, distinct from the forms of thought associated with the preschool and adolescent periods. Yet, some child development specialists propose that the changes seen around 5 or 6 years represent a gradual build-up of capacities already present in younger children. As we find out more about what children are learning in different social environments, we will gain insight into cognitive development in middle childhood.

Social Development

Peers are very important to young school-age children. They offer companionship and a sense of security as children move into the wider world away from their families. Friendships are often intense and joyous, based on more of a give-and-take than was true for preschoolers. There can also be rocky times because it is inevitable that children's wills sometimes clash. Yet, these are important growing experiences, as children learn to compromise and to assert themselves. Their increased ability to take other people's points of view means that 6- through 8-year-olds are more likely to show considerate, cooperative behavior than younger children. But the values of their family and culture will also affect the likelihood of children displaying these behaviors. Each culture has expectations about how to relate to adults and other children, and learning the "acceptable" ways is an important part of social development in young school-age children. (You can read more about the influence of culture and family on children's development in the chapters "Valuing Diversity" and "Working With Families.")

Children's developing consciences lead them to be critical at times of people who do not conform to their ideas of the way things should be. They can be very hard on one another and may need adult help to learn how to settle disagreements about rules and to make their expectations of each other reasonable.

Play is still important to school-age children. They like to play games with rules, such as card or board games or sports. Because they understand better the logic and consistency of rules, they can keep a game going and deal with conflicts over cheating in a way that preschoolers cannot. If given the opportunity, they still like dramatic play; in fact, they may even act out their own plays. Children's play in the school years is often sex-segregated, which to some extent may reflect boys' and girls' different interests. Also, by sticking with the same sex, boys and girls tend to feel reassured about their own gender identity.

Six- through 8-year-olds often enjoy stumping each other or adults with riddles and jokes. It gives them a sense of control and "being in the know." Given their new mental abilities, school-age children can see the humor when logic is violated or when language has a double meaning. ("What has four wheels and flies? A garbage truck.")

Think about the young school-age children you work with. What would you add to this description of their development?

Putting knowledge of child development into action

Infants and Toddlers

Sandra is a new teacher in an infant/toddler program. She is feeling very frustrated with Paul, 20 months old. In her weekly conference with Eileen, the Director, she reports, "Paul does not obey me. For example, he runs away when I try to put on his jacket to go outside." Eileen replies, "This sounds like a classic battle between adults and toddlers." They agree that Eileen will visit Sandra's classroom to observe, and later they will talk.

During their next conference, Eileen explains to Sandra that toddlers are learning to be very independent. In fact, several times, she heard Paul say, "Me do it." When Sandra did let Paul do things for himself, Eileen observed that he was more cooperative. This was good for Sandra to hear because she had the impression that Paul was always negative. Sandra decides to try letting Paul help with his jacket. She gives him a choice, "Which arm do you want to put in first?" Then, she says, "Great. Now I'll start the zipper. But you pull it up." Paul struggles a bit with the zipper, but persists on his own.

Seeing that Paul can be cooperative if she presents the task appropriately makes Sandra feel more effective as a teacher. She and Eileen agree that it would be helpful to learn more about child development in order to set realistic expectations for the age group she is working with.

Preschoolers

In a classroom of 4-year-olds, Barbara, the teacher observes these play episodes:

- Kira announces, "We're selling oranges." She asks Roland if he wants to buy some. He wants three and Kira counts out three blocks. Roland takes them over to other children and tells them the oranges cost $100. They pretend to pay. When Roland returns with the good news that he has sold the oranges, Kira explains, "We're not *selling* things. Get them back. We're only letting people *borrow* things."

- Joan pretends to wash her doll's hair. When the baby gets soap in her eyes, Joan not so gently wipes it away and scolds, "Now that's not so bad. It's just baby shampoo." Then she consoles, "Don't cry. Just one more rinse." At the end, she rewards the good baby: "Here's some candy, yum, yum."

- A small group of children is mixing dough for sugar cookies. One child says, "It feels delicious," as he squeezes a small piece of dough between his fingers. Another adds, "You know what I wish—a tidal wave of this stuff would come into the room, then we could eat our way out!" Everyone laughs and giggles at the thought.

Later, Barbara reflects on what she observed and thinks about what it tells her about preschoolers' development. The class visited the local grocery store last week; it seems that Kira and Roland are expressing their ideas about buying and selling and how much things cost. She wonders if the children need more opportunities to clarify the difference between selling and borrowing—maybe a trip to the library to borrow books is a good idea.

Like many children her age, Joan does not like to have her hair washed. In her play, she reverses roles and becomes the mother. Joan's activity shows how play is an opportunity for children to cope with their fears. Barbara wants to tell Joan's mother how she is portrayed—as a kind mother who scolds a bit, but who ultimately comforts her unhappy baby, even rewards her.

The sensory experience of making the cookies appeals to these 4-year-olds. Barbara sees how this experience elicits the children's cognitive and language abilities as well as their infectious sense of humor! These scenes from her classroom point out to Barbara that play is the cornerstone of learning and development in the preschool years.

Young School-Age Children

Mrs. Jackson has been teaching pre-kindergartners and now she teaches first graders. She is amazed at how much the children argue over rules and what is fair and unfair. She has brought checkers and other games into the classroom, but is tempted to remove them to cut down on the arguing. Often, she hears the children bickering over the rules for a tag game during recess. And sometimes the loudest arguments occur when a child has momentarily stepped out of line, and others will not let him back in.

Another first grade teacher tells Mrs. Jackson that all of this behavior is very typical of 6-year-olds. Her colleague suggests that before Mrs. Jackson ban all games she take another look at her children and how they think about rules. Later in the day, she observes another incident: Roberta is waiting in the lunch line, but has forgotten her woolen scarf. She takes a few steps to get it out of the closet, but then Greg insists, "You can't get back. Go to the end of the line." Roberta retorts, "I had to get my scarf." Their argument escalates into pushing and shoving.

Mrs. Jackson, remembering her colleague's advice, decides to use this incident as the basis for a group discussion. She describes what she saw happening between Roberta and Greg and asks if this happens to other children and how it makes them feel. She asks the children for suggestions as to what to do. Roberta suggests, "Let's make a list of when it is okay to get back in line and when it is not." Others agree and Mrs. Jackson writes down their ideas: "It's fair if you've forgotten something, need a drink of water, or have to tie your shoelace. It's not fair if you just want to go talk to a friend or are showing off."

Mrs. Jackson is delighted to see how much careful thought the children give to this, and in the end she thinks their decisions are fair ones. Over the next few days, the line is much more manageable and the children are enforcing the rules they made up. She can see that these older children can take more responsibility for themselves and for others than the preschoolers she is used to working with.

Families

Your knowledge of child development can be helpful to children's families by giving them a broader perspective about their children's development. Jerry's parents are concerned when their 5-year-old begins acting clingy. They worry that Jerry seems to be going backwards and acting in a way that they think is "babyish." They share their concern with his teacher and say that there are no changes at home that might be accounting for his behavior. The teacher explains that development is not a straight path from point A to point B, but rather, at every age, it is a process of taking steps forward and backwards. She says that, in a way, Jerry's seeming to go backwards was really a sign of how much growing he was doing—his backward steps allowed him to take a break in his rapid development. She suggests that he is clinging because he is more aware of how big the world is and how much he has to learn. He feels vulnerable and maybe not quite ready to give up being "little" and being cuddled.

Seeing patterns helps Jerry's parents understand that what they are seeing is common in children his age. Rather than pushing him to be a "big boy," they are able to be more understanding and patient, which helps Jerry feel more secure.

Learning about child development can seem like an enormous assignment at first. But by reading about and watching children of different ages, you will begin understanding patterns of development. You, the children in your group, and their families will all benefit.

These activities will help you learn more about child development and how you can apply it in your work with children. The exercises can be done with one or more colleagues.

1. As children develop, they experience the same event differently. Take a walk around your neighborhood. Think about what the experience of taking a walk is like from the point of view of an infant, toddler, preschooler, and young school-age child. Answer the following questions:

   - What would each of these children be interested in during the walk? What kinds of questions might they ask? What might each of them learn about himself? about other people? about things in the world?

   - What would you do to keep each age safe during a walk? What would you do that is similar and different for each age?

   - Imagine a walk with a toddler (in a stroller), a 4-year-old, and a 7-year-old. How might they interact with each other?

   - How would you explain the value of taking a walk to a family member?

2. Growing up involves trying new things, thinking in new ways, and learning new skills. To help yourself get in touch with the feeling of what growing up is like for the children in your group, think of a time in your childhood when you were learning something new, such as how to multiply or play a new game, or when you were facing a new challenge, such as going to a new school or leaving your family to go to camp. Consider the answers to these questions. Discuss them with your colleagues.

   - How did you feel about learning something new or facing the new challenge?

   - How did you feel if you made a mistake or did not understand something right away?

   - What did the people around you do to support you? Did they do things that were not helpful? If yes, what were they?

   - How can you apply your own experiences to your teaching?

   - How do you feel about learning something new or taking on a challenge now?

3. Think about time, space, equipment, and activities that relate to physical development in your age group. Make a list of all the

indoor opportunities you provide for children to develop and practice large- and small-muscle skills. Can you think of other opportunities to provide?

4. Young children are developing a sense of who they are. How do you help the children in your program develop a positive self-image? Consider the answers to these questions:

   • How does your physical environment help children feel competent?

   • What kinds of things do you say that help children feel positive about who they are?

   • How do your daily activities help children feel good about themselves?

   • How does your program validate children's experiences at home or in their community?

5. Choose an activity in your early childhood setting that you think works well. Try to look at it through children's eyes. What are the children learning in this activity? Based on what you know about their level of cognitive development, how does this activity support their learning? How does it support different learning styles?

   Then choose an activity you are not sure about. Based on what you know about children's cognitive development, how could you change this activity? Try out your ideas for changing it and see how they work.

6. If children learn how to treat others by the way they themselves are treated, then your relationship with children in your room is a way to enhance children's social development. Take some time to think about your relationships with children. Answer these questions:

   • What does it mean to respect children? How do you show children respect? What do you do and say?

   • How do you help children know they can trust you?

   • What do children learn about how to get along with other people when they watch you with your co-workers and members of their families?

   • How do you deal with disagreements you have with adults in your program? How do you help children deal with their disagreements?

7. As you think about the children you work with, ask:

   • What kinds of previous experiences contributed to their development?

   • What kinds of experiences do they need now in order to continue to develop?

By addressing these questions, you will get an idea of "where your children have been" and "where they are going" in terms of development. Often it is useful to refer to Erikson's stages in this exercise. For example, if you teach preschoolers, ask:

- What kinds of experiences contributed to a sense of trust in infancy, and autonomy in toddlerhood?

- What kinds of experiences can I provide now to foster a sense of initiative?

8. There is a wide range of individual differences at any one age. Select one age that you work with. For example, if you teach 4-year-olds, ask:

- What are the general characteristics of this age?

- What is the range of individual differences you see in physical, emotional, cognitive, and social functioning? Are there some 4-year-olds who are like 3-year-olds; others who are like 5-year-olds?

9. Think about some aspect of child development that interests you, such as empathy, humor, understanding of right or wrong, pretend play, or language development. Then learn about it from books, by watching children, by talking to co-workers. Consider how the phenomenon you have studied changes to reflect children's growth and development. For example, if you focus on empathy, ask:

- How do infants and toddlers, preschoolers, and young school-age children express empathy?

- How does empathy change with age?

- How do changes in empathy reflect changes in other areas of development (such as cognition)?

- What experiences in the family, peer group, and community help children develop a sense of empathy?

- What can I do, as caregiver or teacher, to foster the development of empathy in the children with whom I work?

Resources

Biber, B. (1984). *Early education and psychological development.* New Haven, CT: Yale University Press.

Biber, B., Murphy, L., Woodcock, L. P., & Black, I. S. (1952). *Life and ways of the seven- to eight-year-old.* New York: Basic Books.

Bredekamp, S. (Ed.). (1991). *Developmentally appropriate practice in early childhood programs serving children from birth through age 8* (rev. ed.). Washington, DC: National Association for the Education of Young Children.

Cohen, D. H. (1988). *The learning child.* New York: Schocken Books.

Cole, M., & Cole, S. (1989). *The development of children*. New York: W. H. Freeman.

Cowan, P. (1978). *Piaget with feeling: Cognitive, social, and emotional dimensions*. New York: Holt, Rinehart & Winston.

de Villiers, P., & de Villiers, J. (1979). *Early language*. Cambridge: Harvard University Press.

Erikson, E. H. (1950). *Childhood and society: The eight stages of man*. New York: W. W. Norton.

Fraiberg, S. (1984).*The magic years: Understanding and handling the problems of early childhood*. New York: Macmillan.

Galinsky, E., & David, J. (1991). *The preschool years: Family strategies that work from experts and parents*. New York: Ballantine Books.

Gardner, H. (1983). *Frames of mind: A theory of multiple intelligences*. New York: Basic Books.

Hartley, R., Frank, L., & Goldenson, R. M. (1952). *Understanding children's play*. New York: Columbia University Press.

McGhee, P. (1979). *Humor: Its origin and development*. San Francisco: W. H. Freeman.

Miller, P. (1989). *Theories of developmental psychology* (2nd rev. & exp. ed.). New York: W. H. Freeman.

Minuchin, P. (1977). *The middle years of childhood*. Monterey, CA: Brooks/Cole.

Paley, V. (1984). *Boys and girls: Superheroes in the doll corner*. Chicago: University of Chicago Press.

Piaget, J. (1986). *The construction of reality in the child* (Margaret Cook, Trans.) New York: Ballantine. (Original work published 1937.)

Rogoff, B., & Lave, J. (Eds.). (1984). *Everyday cognition: Its development in social context*. Cambridge: Harvard University Press.

Rubin, Z. (1980). *Children's friendships*. Cambridge: Harvard University Press.

Singer, D., & Singer, J. (1990). *The house of make-believe: Children's play and the developing imagination*. New York: Teachers College Press.

Vygotsky, L. S. (1978). *Mind in society: The development of higher psychological processes*. Cambridge: Harvard University Press.

Werner, E., & Smith, R. S. (1982). *Vulnerable but invincible: A longitudinal study of resilient children and youth*. New York: McGraw-Hill.

About the Authors:

Judy David, Ed.D., is on the faculty at Bank Street College where she advises student teachers and teaches courses in Child Development and Observing and Recording Children's Behavior. From July 1991 to March 1992, she was Director of the Early Childhood Curriculum Project. She has been a researcher and consultant to early childhood programs and a Head Start teacher. She is co-author of The Preschool Years *(Ballantine, 1991).*

Amy Laura Dombro, M.S., headed the Bank Street Infant and Family Center from 1976 to 1983. She is now a consultant with Head Start Parent Child Center programs. She is the senior author of The Ordinary is Extraordinary: How Children under Three Learn *(1989, Fireside) and* Sharing the Caring: How to Find the Right Child Care and Make it Work for You and Your Child *(1991, Fireside).*

3 | Observing and Recording Children's Behavior

What is observing and recording?

Have you ever watched a child and tried to figure out what that child was feeling or thinking, so you could decide how best to respond to her? *Observing* is watching a child with the purpose of trying to understand what she is experiencing. It is trying to see a child from the inside out. Looking at the world from a child's point of view helps you understand that child. *Recording* is the system(s) you use to note what you have seen and heard. In this chapter, we focus on writing up brief descriptions of a child's behavior although other recording techniques, such as checklists and rating scales, are sometimes used in early childhood settings.

Observing is a powerful technique that caregivers and teachers can use to find answers to their questions. Your questions may range from concerns about a particular child: "How does Louis enter a play group?" to issues having to do more with your role as curriculum planner: "What materials are children using in the science area?" Becoming a careful observer of the children will help you think about the work you are doing with them. (You can learn more about observing your curriculum-in-action in the chapter, "Assessment through the Curriculum.")

In this chapter, we are going to look at why observing and recording children's behavior are important and how to use them in your early childhood setting. Then there are exercises you and colleagues can do together to practice.

Why observe and record?

You are trying to create a program that is right for children of a certain age *and* right for each child in your group. You can use what you have learned about child development to help you recognize the basic patterns typical of children at different ages. However, when it comes to getting to know each child in your group, you will need more specific information. Observing over time is a way of getting that information, of getting to know each child.

Children tell us about themselves by their actions as well as their words. Young children feel and think with their bodies. From the outside, we can observe children's expressions, their actions, and what they say to try to understand what is happening on the inside. We observe children to get an idea of what they know and feel about themselves and their world, and to help us figure out their current interests. To really know each child in your group, you must be able to "hear" all the ways children have of telling us who they are.

47

Observing can help you:

Keep track of a child's emotional, social, cognitive and physical development over time.
By observing a child at the beginning of the school year, you will be able to gather information on how he adjusts to a new setting. As you continue to watch him, you will see how he makes friends and what activities he enjoys. By the end of the year, you will have a well-rounded picture of his progress and will be able to make recommendations to his next year's teacher.

Identify a child's strengths and interests.
You can see, for example, 6-year-old Lorenzo's persistence when he continues trying to solve a math problem instead of getting frustrated and giving up.

Identify concerns you may have about a child.
Observing, for example, that Samantha, a preschooler, always asks "What?" when someone speaks to her may lead you to get her hearing checked.

Decide how best to respond in a certain situation.
Is Grace, a first grader, so frustrated with trying to read a book that she needs you to help or to suggest another book? Or is she managing the challenge on her own?

Figure out how to handle problem situations.
Noticing that 4-year-old Joey falls apart at clean-up time and during other transitions, you conclude that times of change are hard for him to manage. You can think of ways to make transitions easier for him. You might decide to give him more time to get ready for changes or give him a special job near you, such as setting the lunch table. If you had not taken time to observe, you might have focused only on his behavior (kicking over the blocks) and missed the pattern (falling apart at transition times) that helps you understand the reasons behind the behavior.

Improve your physical environment and materials.
Noticing that you never have the supplies you need within reach, for example, may lead you to reorganize the diapering area so you can focus on building relationships with infants rather than on finding a fresh diaper.

Modify your curriculum.
If, for example, you see that every time you have outdoor play scheduled, a few infants are sleeping, you might decide to divide the

group so some children can go outside with one caregiver while those who are sleeping stay inside with another.

Give you specific examples of behavior to share with parents, colleagues, and specialists.
What better way to start off a parent conference than, "Let me tell you how Louisa is learning to read."

Sometimes you might feel that you cannot take time away from what you are doing to observe. Someone might think that you are not doing your job, that you are just taking a break. But stepping back for a few minutes to focus on what a particular child is doing is one of the most valuable kinds of work you can do in your classroom. The children, their parents, you, and your co-workers will all benefit from the time you spend observing.

How can you observe and record?

Observing is not something you learn to do all at once. Rather, it is a skill that takes lots of practice. The more you practice, the better observer you will be. Make observing part of your daily work. As you watch a child, alone or with others, ask yourself: "What is he or she experiencing?" To observe, pay attention to how a child moves, the expression on her face, and what she says. Focus not only on what a child does but on details that reveal *how* that child feels about what she is doing. Notice *how* she does something as well as *what* she does.

As an observer, you are the filter of everything you see. Being a good observer means being aware of yourself and what you bring to an observation. Your temperament, your childhood experiences, even your mood on a particular day can color what you observe. You may find a very enthusiastic 6-year-old's behavior to be disruptive, while a co-teacher finds the same behavior vital and spirited.

Observations are useless if you cannot remember them. A necessary part of observing is recording what you saw. Because it is impossible to remember all the details, take "on-the-spot" notes that describe what the child is doing at a particular moment. Later, you can fill out your rough notes to make a complete written observation.

Written observations should have these three parts:

- A **heading,** which tells the name of the child being observed, his or her age, the date, where the observation is taking place, and the name of the observer. When observing older children who might be able to read names, you can use initials.

- The **observation,** which describes what the child says and does. This may be a few sentences or a paragraph or two.

- A **discussion,** in which the observer tries to make sense out of the observed behavior. Here you should ask yourself, "What does the observation reveal about this child's social, emotional, cognitive, and physical functioning?" This is the place to raise questions, identify patterns, or note inconsistencies in behavior.

Part of observing is paying attention to the words you use. You want to use descriptive words, but not judgmental ones. Here are two versions of an observation of a toddler made at the same time by different adults:

- Jim is breaking the rules and drawing on the table. He shouldn't do that. He is naughty.

- Jim holds the crayon in his left hand. He draws big, sweeping circle-like marks. They fill up the entire paper and sometimes, the crayon goes onto the table. He looks at the paper and smiles as he draws.

What do you learn about the child in each of these observations? Which one creates a "picture" of the child's behavior? The first observation tells you about the *observer*, and what he or she considers unacceptable behavior. All you learn about what the child is actually doing is that he is drawing on the table. In the other version, you "see" what Jim is doing and his attitude toward it. His drawing on the table is an "accident" caused by his large, uncontrolled movements. He is not "naughty"—which is a negative judgment. Rather, he is drawing in a typically toddler way!

What can be said in the discussion about this observation of Jim's behavior? You might comment on his mood, "Jim enjoys drawing"; and his style, "Jim uses his whole arm when he draws"; and the shapes he makes, "A month ago, Jim only made lines; now he can make circles."

Observing the behavior of children 6 and older can be difficult for several reasons. They are self-conscious, and may be aware that you are observing them. Also, much of their social life happens in peer groups—away from adults so it may be difficult to witness some of their behavior. In comparison to younger children, whose thinking and feeling is revealed primarily in their actions, older children tend to express themselves verbally and in their written work. Thus, as an observer you often have to rely more on recording what older children say than on what they do. You may find that in order to learn about a young school-age child, you need to spend time talking with the child and listening to his ideas. You can also collect samples of his work. In some schools, this is called a portfolio. The teacher works with the child to collect representative samples of his reading, writing, math, and art work. The child can use these materials as the basis for self-assessment, for identifying his own areas of strength and weakness. Portfolios can also be used as the basis for family-teacher conferences. It is often useful to work with colleagues if you

Name of child:
Age:
Date:
Setting:
Observer:
Observation:

Discussion:

want to develop a formal portfolio system.

Following these steps can help you make observing and recording part of your day:

Getting ready to observe:

- Develop a recording system that works for you. Some people like to take notes on scrap paper and transfer them later. Other people like to write in a spiral notebook or on large, gummed address labels that can be stuck in a child's folder. You may prefer to use index cards or a notebook with tabs for each child, or to design a simple form you can xerox. You may want to keep a notebook for each child that is divided into sections such as: Interactions with Peers, Interactions with Adults, and Interactions with Materials. No matter which system you choose, be sure to keep a pencil handy at all times.

- Make a plan for who and what you will observe. You may want to make a checklist to keep track of who was observed and when, to be sure you have records for everyone. Sometimes there will be a specific child, activity or part of the day you want to focus on.

- Arrange for a staff person who speaks the child's language to observe that child and write up the observation. The meanings of words (or body language) are best understood by someone from a similar linguistic or cultural background.

- If you have co-workers, figure out a system that allows you to cover for one another while someone steps out of the action to observe for a few minutes. You may develop a signal such as a nod or wave that says, "Something is happening that I want to observe."

- Think about what you will tell children and parents who ask you what you are doing. You may, for example, explain that you are observing to help you be a better teacher or that you are taking notes to help you remember details of what you see. At first, people might be uncomfortable, reacting much as if you were taking pictures with a camera. However, everyone will soon get used to seeing you with your paper and pencil.

Observing and recording:

- Treat your observations professionally. Never leave your notes lying around. Observation records are confidential.

- Observe for 2 or 3 minutes at a time. You will be amazed at how much happens in such a short period.

- Remember that you, as caregiver or teacher, can be a part of an observation you record. Your interactions with a child are important data and may reveal a great deal about many facets of the child. You will want to write down what a child says to you or how he responds to your efforts to comfort, teach or discipline him. It is also important to observe the child at times when he is not interacting with you.

- Observe children in a variety of situations and settings during the day and on different days to get a well-rounded picture of who they are. Observe them in different activities and in different parts of the room as well as outdoors. The behavior observed during the reading of a story may reveal a side of a child that you do not see during a daily routine, such as eating lunch or clean-up.

- Listen to children and talk with them. Posing open-ended questions to children is one way to elicit their thinking. Asking preschoolers "Why do you think the caterpillars live in a cocoon?" or first graders, "What kinds of rules are fair and unfair?" will uncover their ideas, hypotheses, and misconceptions, revealing information about the individual child as well as about developmental levels.

- Whenever possible, note what you see "on the spot," even if it is just a few words. Later, when you have a few minutes, you can go back and fill in the missing details. If you cannot take time to record when you see something happening, do try to get your observations on paper as soon as possible—during a break or at the end of the day. Everybody's memory fades over time!

- Checklists and rating scales can also help you learn about a child. These tools are best used to supplement more detailed observations of children's everyday behavior. Here is a checklist that one kindergarten teacher used every day to keep track of the children's experiences in learning centers:

Name	Library	Blocks	Math/ Science	Art	Dramatic Play
Ruth	xx	xxx	xx	x	
Ari	xxx	x		xx	x
Mei-lin	x	x	xx	x	xx

Learning from your observations:

- Do not worry if your observations do not seem to make sense right away. With work, you will discover they contain important information that can help you better understand who a child is. Keep observing.

- Collect children's work to accompany your written observations. Keeping samples of a child's art or writing over the school year will help you see patterns and identify the progress made. You can take photos of block buildings or group projects. You may want to develop portfolios of children's work.

- Consider your observations in light of what you know about developmental stages and the child you are focusing on. You may discover, for example, that Shelley, 20 months, has more difficulty saying goodbye to her family on Mondays after a weekend at home, that 4-year-old Reggie thinks cartoon characters are real, or that Gretchen, 7 years old, has plenty to say when she is talking with a friend, but never says a word during a class meeting.

- Some people find it useful to write a general description of a child, based on all their observations. You might divide your observations into those about physical, social, emotional, and cognitive development, and then summarize what you have learned about each area of development.

- Remember that observing a child's development is an ongoing process. Answers are not guaranteed. Sometimes your observations may lead to even more questions. You may, for example, find that you need more information about a child's family life or culture to help you understand what you are seeing. You may want to learn more about second-language acquisition after you have observed children newly arrived from another country in your class.

Everyone will benefit when you and your co-teachers make observing part of your everyday lives. You will become a stronger team as you work together to observe and understand what you see. You will gain insight into who individual children are. What you learn will help you decide how to respond to children in ways that encourage their learning and development. While you experience the satisfaction of being even more effective, the children in your room will have the advantage of the individualized support you can offer.

Infants and Toddlers

Putting observing and recording into action

Irene's parents are worried about her physical development. She is almost 7 months old and not sitting up yet, while Katie, another child in the group, who just turned 6 months, is sitting up by herself. Irene's caregiver can use observations to help Irene's parents see that she is developing normally—according to her own schedule, not Katie's.

Here are the observations she recorded and shared with Irene's parents during the month of October.

October 7th at 2:30. In the living room.

Irene is sitting propped up against some pillows, chewing on the leg of a rubber cow. She sits up straight for a moment

53

and then sinks back against the pillow.

October 16th at 10:30. In the living room.

Irene is sitting propped against some pillows, smiling as the rattle she is shaking makes a sound. She sits up straight and looks around the room before toppling forward and ending up on her tummy.

October 25th at 1:30. In the bedroom

I put Irene on her stomach in her crib, pat her back as I always do, and say "goodnight." A few minutes later, when I look in, Irene is sitting up in her crib.

Preschoolers

At the beginning of each year, the teachers in Shelley's preschool program observe children's arrivals to help them figure out how to support each child and family with separation.

Here is a copy of an observation Mrs. Li recorded this morning about Shelley, her mother, and Mrs. Davis, the assistant teacher:

9/22/91

Shelley, 3

preschool room

S & mom arrive. S holds on, looks at floor. Serious—mouth tense. Mrs. D asks S and mom feed fish. Tiny smile. Feed fish. Mom says bye. S cries. Mrs. D talks with S. S listens. S says fish—Mommy. Excited. Look at fish.

When Mrs. Li rewrites her notes at the end of the day and adds some details, they look like this:

Date: 9/22/91

Child: Shelley

Age: 3 years

Setting: preschool room

Observer: Mrs. Li

S & her mom arrive. S holds her mom's skirt, looks at the floor, back and forth several times. Her expression is serious. Mrs. D (assistant teacher) suggests S & her mom can help feed fish. S has a tiny smile. They feed fish. Then S's mom tells S she will be back after lunch and that S can tell her about the fish then. They hug and S cries. Mrs. D sits next to her. "You are sad that your mommy had to say goodbye." S looks up and stops crying. Mrs. D suggests they go look at the fish so S can tell her mother about them later. "I tell mommy about fish," S says excitedly, and walks over to aquarium with Mrs. D.

Mrs. Li then writes the discussion section to take to a staff meeting which will focus on children's adjustment to school.

S is worried about mother leaving. Has she been away from her mother before? She protests quietly. Is this her style of expressing her feelings? When Mrs. D talks with S about what she is feeling, she listens and looks up. Does putting words to her feelings help her feel safe?

S seems interested in the fish, even though she is worried about her mother leaving. Her mother used the fish to make a connection. Why don't we try to strengthen this connection? We can look at the fish with S and read a book about fish with her. Tomorrow I will write a book with her about feeding the fish with her mommy.

Young School-Age Children

When Betty overhears this conversation she records it.

Jake (age 7):   I don't want to play with you today.

Cordelia (age 8):   But we made a plan to play together.

Jake: I know, but Jimmy and Bill want me to play dodge-ball with them.

Cordelia: Wait a minute, let's all play dodge-ball for half of recess and then you and I can play for the other half.

Jake: OK! Let's go!

Betty has been working with children all year on preventing discrimination. They have studied Martin Luther King and Rosa Parks. They have talked about the lives and deeds of famous women like Amelia Earhart. At the beginning of the year, they agreed that teasing or excluding someone because of a person's identity (for example, their gender, race, disability) was never okay. Rereading her notes, Betty thinks about how well these two children were doing at solving their own problems and how much more often the girls and boys were playing together. Betty puts her notes into Jake's and Cornelia's files so she will remember this incident for her next family conferences.

Families

Observing is a skill you can use in your work with parents. Zachary's parents are worried about how much he is really *learning* in his preschool program—a program that focuses on group life and daily activities rather than on "academic skills." His caregiver, Mr. Rollins, and Zach's mother spend some time observing Zach.

They see that he is learning about numbers when he counts cups and plates for snack, and that he is learning to read when he helps make a shopping list for a class trip to the supermarket. Mr. Rollins suggests Zach's parents observe at home to see what kinds of things he is learning in the course of everyday life. Here are two of their observations:

His mother writes:

> This afternoon, Zach walked out to the mailbox with me to get the mail. On the way back to the house, he pointed out some of the letters on an advertisement. Later, he wanted an envelope to write a letter.

His father writes:

> When I helped Zach get dressed this morning, he told me he wanted to wear his maroon shirt. I didn't even know he knew such a color existed.

Do you have questions about a child, your physical environment, or your curriculum? If you do—and who does not have a question about something—you have the perfect starting place to begin observing.

Observing may seem like a lot of work—and it is. But it is a skill that is unquestionably worth all the effort and time you devote to it. Like any new skill, it will take some time to get used to doing. But after a while, it will become second nature and you will wonder how you ever managed before you became a good observer.

Exercises

Here are some exercises you can do and some other resources you can use to learn more. These exercises will help you sharpen your observing skills. They can be done with a colleague or group of colleagues. Remember, observing takes a lot of practice to do well.

1. The goal when observing is to focus on the child and describe what you see and hear without interpreting or judging. To do this, you must be aware of yourself and what you bring to the situation. To help you become a more self-aware observer, do the following exercise with a small group of colleagues.

   • Choose a photo (from a magazine, a poster, or one you have taken) of a child engaged in an activity. Study it by yourself. Then, each of you take five minutes to record what you observe.

   • Share your observations with one another. How were they the same? How were they different? How did your feelings and backgrounds—who you are—influence what you saw?

   • Now observe the same picture again. Make an effort to be as objective as possible. As you observe, try to separate what you see happening from how you feel about it. Record only what you see. Compare your observation to that of your colleagues. If you are each being more objective, your observations should be more similar to each other's than they were the first time.

2. One of the main purposes of observing is to understand the world from a child's point of view. This is a critical skill for teachers because children experience the world differently from adults. And their view is constantly changing, as they mature and gain more information and experience over the months and years.

   In this exercise, you will observe three children—an infant or toddler, a preschooler, and a young school-aged child—engaged in the same daily routine. As you observe each child helping to make snack, getting dressed to go outside, or helping to clean up the room, record what the child is doing as well as what he or she is saying. Then, answer the following questions:

   • What are the ages of the children you observed?

   • What daily routine or activity did you observe?

   • How do the observations differ? For example, a toddler helping to make pancakes for snack may have spent most of his time rubbing his hands in the flour, while a 6-year-old carefully measured the ingredients.

   • Based on your observations, what do you think each child is experiencing?

3. It is important when you observe to note not only what a child is doing but how he or she is doing it—the quality of his or her behavior. How you describe what you see is limited only by your language. The purpose of this exercise is to help you think about your vocabulary and to practice making it more descriptive.

   Take five minutes to list how many different ways you can describe a child moving across the room. Share your lists. How many of these words did you think of?

   > walking, crawling, racing, prancing, hopping, stagger-
   > ing, stumbling, toddling, charging, strolling, saunter-
   > ing, rolling, marching, shuffling, wandering, running,
   > plodding

   What other words did you come up with? Try again. This time think of how many ways you can describe a child approaching a new material such as playdough, or a hammer in the woodworking corner, or a new challenge, such as reading a book on an unfamiliar topic or learning a computer program. You might use these words:

   > timidly, enthusiastically, fearfully, shyly, energetical-
   > ly, excitedly, cautiously, impatiently, eagerly, reluc-
   > tantly, dubiously, doubtfully

   What other words can you think of?

4. In this exercise, you and your co-teachers design a system that will work for you. Part of your system will include figuring out a time

to share your observations. This is critical, because no matter how detailed and accurate they are, observations left sitting in a file box or viewed in isolation are of little use. Use the questions below to guide your planning:

- What form will your observation system take? Will you use index cards, notebooks, file folders?

- Where will you store your observations? Be sure this is a secure, private place.

- How will you decide who observes which children and when?

- How will you keep track of completed observations and those still to be done?

- When will you meet to share and discuss your observations?

When you have established your system, give it a tryout period. After two weeks or a month, review how it is working. Make any necessary changes. Most important of all, continue observing.

5. As a teacher or caregiver, you make countless decisions about activities, the environment, and how to respond to various situations throughout the day. The insights and information you gain from observing will help you make the best decisions possible.

In this exercise, you will apply what you learn from observing to a situation in your program. Throughout this activity, remember that sharing your work with colleagues can often reveal insights you may not see when you are working in isolation. Follow these steps:

- Think about a question you have. For example, say Jason, 22 months, has been falling apart at the end of the day—clinging to you, crying, and refusing to put his coat on and get into his stroller—much to the dismay of you and his grandfather, who regularly picks him up. You might ask yourself: "Why is Jason behaving this way? How does Jason experience the end of the day? What can I do to make this transition easier for him?"

- Make a plan to observe.

- Observe for a few days.

- Review your observations in light of what you already know about toddlers and who Jason is. See if there is any additional information you need. Look for any patterns that may emerge. It may be, for example, that Jason is a child who needs time to change from one activity to another and that lately his grandfather has been arriving later than usual and having to rush Jason out the door. It may be that Jason finds it easier to say goodbye when you help him put on his coat or when he and his grandfather can walk out with another family. It is possible that, rather than finding patterns, you have found new questions. If so, make a note of them and continue observing.

• Apply your new insights to the situation. For instance, see if Jason's grandfather could come a few minutes earlier or develop a routine in which you help Jason put on his jacket and then walk him to the door to say goodbye.

• Plan a staff meeting in which you and co-teachers share how observing has influenced your daily practices.

Resources

Almy, M., & Genishi, C. (1979). *Ways of studying children: An observation manual for early childhood teachers* (rev. ed.). New York: Teachers College Press.

Biber, B., Murphy, L., Woodcock, L. P., & Black, I. S. (1952). *Life and ways of the seven- to eight-year-old.* New York: Basic Books.

Boehm, A. E., & Weinberg, R. A. (1987). *The classroom observer: Developing observation skills in early childhood settings.* New York: Teachers College Press.

Carini, P. F. (1982). *The school lives of seven children: A five-year study.* Grand Forks, ND: University of North Dakota.

Cohen, D., & Stern, V., with Balaban, N. (1985). *Observing and recording the behavior of young children.* New York: Teachers College Press.

Dodge, D. T., Koralek, D. G., & Pizzolongo, P. J. (1989). *Caring for preschool children: A supervised, self-instructional training program.* Washington, DC: Teaching Strategies.

Paley, V. (1981). *Wally's stories: Conversations in the kindergarten.* Cambridge: Harvard University Press.

Ramsey, P. G. (1987). *Teaching and learning in a diverse world: Multicultural education for young children.* New York: Teachers College Press.

Woodcock, L. P. (1941). *Life and ways of the two-year-old: A guide for teachers and parents.* New York: Dutton.

About the Author:

Amy Laura Dombro, M.S., headed the Bank Street Infant and Family Center from 1976 to 1983. She is now a consultant with Head Start Parent Child Center programs. She is the senior author of The Ordinary is Extraordinary: How Children under Three Learn *(1989, Fireside) and* Sharing the Caring: How to Find the Right Child Care and Make it Work for You and Your Child *(1991, Fireside).*

4 | The Learning Environment

All programs for children happen somewhere—inside a home, a school classroom, or a center, and outdoors. Children, caregivers, and teachers spend a great deal of time together in these physical spaces. Wherever the space is located, it has furniture, equipment, and other materials arranged in it and some kind of schedule of how time is spent during the day. The space, the objects in the space, and the organization of time are each parts of the environment. The learning environment is all of these together.

The environment is a powerful force on the behavior and feelings of the people—adults and children—who live and work in it. The shape of the room, how the space is divided up, the equipment, the daily schedule, the temperature, what colors are there, how much light comes in, and how the space is decorated affect how people feel and act.

Children learn through their interactions with the people and things around them. You can promote interaction, and thus learning, by creating an environment that supports and challenges children and, at the same time, is comfortable for both adults and children. For example, by providing comfortable seating, you make it more likely that caregivers, teachers, and children will spend time sitting together reading books, working with puzzles, or talking. This means having small chairs for children and bigger ones for adults. Depending on how much room you have, you might want to put an armchair in your space. Having "messy" materials such as water, sand, paint, or clay is important for children. Having an easy way to clean them up is important for adults (and for children as they grow older and assume more responsibility for taking care of their space). You can make clean-up easier by setting out these materials near a water supply and in areas of the room with linoleum flooring that can be easily swept and wiped clean. This increases the chances that these materials will be put out for children to explore rather than be kept in the closet because they are too much trouble.

The learning environment you create is a reflection of your philosophy and your curriculum. Your environment "speaks" to everyone who enters it. A display of each child's art says you respect individual differences and value children's work. A message board and shelf of resources for parents says they are welcome in your space. A daily schedule posted on the wall that gives children time

What is a learning environment?

Why be concerned with the environment?

61

each day to choose their own activities says you believe children learn by pursuing their interests.

How can you create a learning environment?

Safety and Health

The most basic aspect of a learning environment is that it is safe. For example, equipment is in good repair, windows have guards, radiators are covered, and dangerous substances like cleaning products are locked away. Maintaining a healthy environment where adults and children wash their hands frequently and where nutritious meals and snacks are served is also important. These aspects of health and safety in programs for children are included in regulations in every state. Every program for young children should know about and abide by these regulations. You can find out about them by calling the local office of your state's department of health or social services.

Activities, Interactions, and Schedules

The environment should support children's development by offering many opportunities for interactive experiences that are challenging yet safe for their age group. This means that the space you work in has to accommodate a variety of activities—sitting quietly looking at books, reading and writing stories, moving about with dramatic play props, climbing on things, messing around with clay, eating snack and other meals, painting on large sheets of paper, working puzzles, building large structures with blocks, conducting science experiments, caring for pets.

The space must support different kinds of interactions between people—being all together in a group, working in smaller groups, in pairs, or alone. Cooperation among children is supported by arranging furniture to create small areas or protected places for a few children to work or play together. Creating a sense of the group as a community of learners requires a large enough area for everyone to gather together for meetings during the day. Having a space to be alone—to escape from group life for a time—is essential, too.

The schedule of the day reflects the rhythm of life in a program for children younger than 5—arriving, playing, eating, cleaning up, and going home (and sleeping in some child care programs). It is the routine that shapes each day and makes life predictable and secure for children. The schedule should balance active/quiet, indoor/outdoor, small-group/large-group activities so there is variety. It should allow plenty of time for children to become involved in an activity. A typical schedule for toddlers and preschoolers might include an hour of child-choice activity both in the morning and the afternoon. During this time, toddlers may do many different activities, such as climb on a climber, work on a puzzle, and read a story with a caregiver, while some preschoolers might build with blocks, paint, or engage in dramatic play.

Young school-age children often need even longer periods of time so that they can concentrate on a particularly interesting or complicated activity. A long work period also allows a child enough time to choose more than one activity. The daily schedule might include two periods of one to one-and-a-half hours each (one in the morning and one in the afternoon) with one period devoted to the current topic of study and the other to reading and writing. It should be flexible to allow for things that just happen, like going for an extra long walk when the weather is nice or shortening the time allotted for mural painting when interest wanes.

An Environment to Live—and Learn—In

The space should reflect the fact that children (and adults) spend a large amount of time in it. It should be comfortable—more like what we think of as "homey" than what we usually think of as "school-like." Introducing softness by having soft chairs or a couch, rugs on the floor, pillows in the reading area, and curtains on the windows helps to create a sense of home. A home has a personality and a sense of style that reflects the taste of the people who live in it—so should a learning environment. Having children's artwork decorating the walls at their eye level and displayed on shelves for all to admire, charts and signs hand-lettered by the teacher and children, comfortable places to sprawl, and music that everyone enjoys listening to all contribute to creating a place that children and adults feel comfortable in.

The culture and language of children and adults is also part of the personality of the space, reflected, for example, in the language used on signs, the music listened to, and the kinds of dramatic play props that are available. By adding wooden crates, work gloves, and a basket of oranges to the dramatic play area, caregivers in a program for children of migrant workers bring their out-of-school lives into the environment. This tells the children that their experience is important and that the space is theirs. (You can read more about incorporating diversity into your program in the chapter "Valuing Diversity.")

While some amount of clutter is a necessary part of the personality of a comfortable space, order is also an important aspect of a learning environment. Children need a protected space to keep their personal belongings. This can be in a cubby-type piece of furniture or on shelves, using dishpans as personal storage bins. Children's names should be clearly visible. The storage and display of the equipment and materials that everyone uses should be sensible. The water table should be near the source of water. Art materials are kept

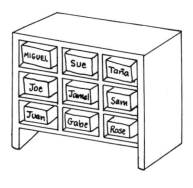

near the art-work area and away from the reading place. Things that are used together are kept near each other. Storage and display of most materials should encourage independent use by children—on open shelves at their height. Storing things in closed cupboards means that adults control the material. (Obviously, some materials need to be under adult control and used with adult supervision; for example, the hot plate used for cooking projects.)

There needs to be space set aside for your things, too, so they are safe and easily accessible. Arrange for a secure place to keep your coat and other personal belongings. Think creatively about where to keep your professional books and records. Many teachers automatically assume they need a desk like their teachers had. The reality is that teachers' desks are bulky and take up a lot of space. An alternative, such as a set of adult-height shelves with doors that can be locked or a small file cabinet pushed against the wall, can meet your storage needs and give both you and the children more room. Make space for things that make the environment pleasing to you. For example, use adult-height space on the wall to hang up a calendar with pictures you enjoy, or clear off a spot on the window sill for a plant. (You can read more about this in the chapter "You as Teacher or Caregiver.")

The environment also needs a space for information and resources for parents. A designated bulletin board for notices and a shelf for pamphlets and books means parents can find and take advantage of the resources you have to offer. (You can read more about this in the chapter "Working with Families.")

Arranging Activity Areas

The learning environment is organized into several distinct areas that correspond to the kinds of activities that you want children to be able to do. The number and kind of activity areas you set up depend on the ages and interests of children in your group. But certain kinds of activities are necessary no matter what age the children are:

- a space to do messy, creative art activities;
- a soft, comfortable space with reading materials;
- a space just big enough for one child to be alone;
- at least two areas large enough for a group of children to play in together;
- space for each child to store personal belongings (coats, extra clothes, lunch boxes, and his or her creations);
- access to an outdoor playing area.

Generally, the nature of these areas will change as children grow older. Other activity areas may be necessary only for one age group, such as a diapering area for infants and toddlers. For preschoolers and young school-age children, an area large enough for everyone to gather for a group meeting is a necessary part of the environment. This area does not have to be used only for meeting, but can double as the reading corner or an indoor movement area. Being able to eat together in small groups is important for infants, toddlers, and pre-schoolers. Work tables used for activity areas can all double as snack and lunch tables. Most older school-age children can handle eating in a cafeteria, although eating in small groups is still important for social development.

Deciding where to place the activity areas in the space should take into account noise, light, heat, traffic patterns, which activities should be encouraged to mix and which should not, and how many children each area can accommodate. Quiet activities, like reading, should be separate from noisy ones, like dramatic play. The block-building area needs to be protected from traffic so that children's structures will not be disturbed and large enough for five or six children to use it at once. The location of light sources helps determine where to put areas that require light, such as reading, writing, and painting, and those that do not require as much, like block building or dramatic play. An area where children will be reading or sitting still should not be in a cold or drafty place.

Pathways through the space should be clear and obvious to children. Pathways lead children from one area to another, but should not run the whole length or width of the space or they will become runways. Areas for activities that can be integrated can be near one another. For example, having large hollow blocks near dramatic play props encourages children to build structures to support their role-playing. Ones that conflict should be separated; the reading area should not be right next to woodworking. Order helps create a sense of familiarity and belonging that makes the space welcoming and enjoyable to children and adults. Flexibility in the arrangement of equipment and materials in the space is important, too. Adding new materials (or rotating familiar ones) or rearranging the furniture to support different activities can add variety and spice to your program. Broken toys should be removed (and repaired or replaced). When they are not, the message they send to children is, "I only deserve broken toys," which undermines children's sense of self-esteem.

Observing how children use the space will help you decide how to arrange and rearrange it until it works for everyone. When Louisa, a teacher of young school-age children, notices that Hannah cannot maneuver her wheelchair from area to area without knocking things over, she widens the pathways. Louisa also put blocks under the legs of a work table so that Hannah's chair can fit underneath and she can be part of the group.

Materials

Active exploration and discovery, messing around with materials, and hands-on activities are all necessary for learning in the early years. The environment for young children must be well-stocked with materials that support "learning by doing" in a space arranged so that active explorers can navigate easily. Nearly all the materials that are usually found in early childhood programs can be classified according to their openness and complexity (Jones & Prescott, 1978; Prescott, 1984). Open materials are those that can be used in a variety of ways and have no correct outcome—like clay or sand or water or playdough. Closed materials are ones that are meant to be used in a particular way with a certain outcome—like a puzzle, a matching game, a shape sorter, or a worksheet. Many materials fall in between open and closed, such as wooden unit blocks or Legos. They can be used creatively but must fit together in a certain way. In terms of complexity, a simple material can be used in only one way, like a rattle or sand without any digging toys. More complex materials are ones that can be used in different ways and together. For example, a wide variety of shapes and sizes of unit blocks combined with people, vehicles, and sign props is complex. Sand with water and a variety of tools is complex. A well-equipped learning environment offers materials ranging from simple to complex and closed to open, with most materials falling nearer to the open and complex end.

Getting the Equipment You Need

There are many excellent equipment lists you can use to help you decide exactly what you need, depending on the ages of children in your group and your budget.

Many companies offer early childhood furniture, equipment, and materials; some sell only one product or one kind of product, such as books for children. Other companies are distributors that handle the products of many companies; both manufacturers and distributors exhibit at early childhood conferences. You are probably already on the mailing list of many of them. Some companies have lists of what is needed to equip a program for children of various ages. When you are ready to buy, it is a good idea to check a couple of catalogs for the items you want so you will get the best price. The magazine *Child Care Information Exchange* includes a regular feature called "Buying Guide" that describes a different kind of equipment, like playground equipment or small-motor manipulatives, and gives an exhaustive list of companies' products.

Outdoor Environments

The outdoors is an extension of the indoor environment you create for children. Nearly all of the activities that you can do indoors can be done outdoors, weather permitting. The curriculum and the goals you have for children, such as cooperation, are the same indoors or out. The additional opportunity that outdoor play offers is a chance to use large muscles in ways that are more exuberant than is often possible inside (although hallways offer good indoor large-muscle play spaces). Climbing equipment, riding toys and, for preschoolers and young school-age children, material to build with, such as hollow blocks and boards, and plenty of space to move make an appropriate outdoor environment. Depending on the age groups, balls of different sizes are fun and challenging equipment.

The starting point in designing an environment for the children you work with is the children. How many are there? How old are they? What kinds of things do they like to do? Your beliefs about learning—what is important and how learning happens—help you shape the environment. What sorts of activities and opportunities for experience do you want for children? How much time should be given to different activities? The specific learning environment you create depends on the answers to all of these questions and, obviously, on the physical space you have to work with. The learning environment is a dynamic part of the total curriculum—the whole program you are creating for children. As you read further in this Guide, you will see that many of the chapters refer to the learning environment.

Putting what you know about the learning environment into action

Infants and Toddlers

As described in the chapter "Planning for Infants, Toddlers, and Threes," activities for very young children flow naturally out of the experiences of everyday living and are designed to create a sense of security and trust. Their environments should be as home-like as possible, to ease the transition between home and program and to support development. The routines of diapering, sleeping, and eating take up much of the day.

Safety and health are especially important aspects of the environment for very young children. Hand washing before eating and after toileting can dramatically reduce the spread of illness. Sanitary diapering practices are extremely important in group care. The diapering area should be at adult waist height (so the caregiver does not strain her back) and near a source of hot water so that hands can be washed before and after each diapering. The diapering table should have a paper cover that is discarded after each diaper change or that can be washed off thoroughly with a disinfecting solution and air dried (Aronson, 1991). Additional details on safety and health should be available in your state's regulatory standards. Diaper-changing time is also a learning opportunity, as you talk to a baby about what you are doing and what she sees near her, while gently and caringly changing the diaper.

Physical development is advancing very rapidly during the first three years of life and a great deal of cognitive, social, and emotional development happens through physical activity. Active learning in this period means using the whole body to explore the world. Infants need safe spaces to roll in and to crawl about. Toys such as soft balls are easy for beginners' grasping hands to hold. Toddlers are on the move and need ample space. Climbing onto and in and out of things are favorite activities; plastic milk crates or cardboard boxes are perfect. Small slides and mats to tumble on are also popular with toddlers. (You can read more about infant and toddler development in the chapter "Child Development.")

The emotional development of very young children requires cuddling and holding. Furniture such as upholstered couches and easy chairs offer comfortable places for adults to sit with children on their laps, as well as safe climbing for toddlers. Rocking chairs are a must if infants are in your group; for many babies, rocking while being fed a bottle and talked to is the ultimate in comfort and security. The reading area can be a rug in the corner with large, soft pillows against the walls and a low shelf with picture and story books (displayed with their covers facing out). A separate area for napping can be helpful for those children who need quiet to sleep and can be used for other activities when children are not sleeping. In a group program, this can ease the strain of everyone being in one space all day long. The nap area can be used for other activities when children are not sleeping.

For very young children, playing with sand and water (separately and together) is an important learning experience. Sand and/or water can be put into a specially made table, or set up in a dishpan for each child. Filling the sink (in the kitchen or bathroom of a family day care home, or the wash-up sink in a classroom) halfway with water makes a perfect two-person water table. Adding soapsuds offers a different sensory opportunity. Playing with tactile materials (things you can feel) is a full-body experience for toddlers—they will be up to their armpits in shaving cream or finger paint and will often want to paint with their hands instead of with brushes. Offering these activities in an area that is right next to the sink makes set up and clean up easy. Smocks, aprons, or other coverings should be kept nearby. Many activities can be done on the floor. One or two large tables can double as art areas and eating places.

Dramatic play is important to the social development of toddlers, who are beginning to have a sense of themselves as separate from others. Toddlers will try on roles that imitate their family members and will play out home and family themes. Home-like props such as phones, shoes, and hats, and housekeeping furniture such as sink, stove, kitchen table, and baby beds will support their dramatic play.

Representational block building will become interesting to children as they reach the age of 3 years or so. Before this time, they will enjoy laying blocks out flat or building small towers to knock down. Cardboard blocks rather than wooden ones are safer and easier to handle.

Infants and toddlers have not yet developed the ability to share. Having enough toys for everyone to be able to choose something they want, and having multiples of the more popular ones, helps to cut down on fights over toys, allowing each child to have "mine."

Very young children often have large quantities of personal belongings—diapers, two or more changes of extra clothes, strollers—that require space to be stored. Labeling cubbies, hooks for hanging up strollers, and bins with children's photographs and names helps adults and children know whose things belong where and also creates a comforting link between home and child care.

Preschoolers

Three-, four-, and five-year-olds are developing greater control over their small muscles and need lots of opportunities to use them. They need to use their large muscles as well. Socially, 3-year-olds are still very much "me-centered," but in the next few years, their social world moves out from self to family and to community. Sharing and cooperating become easier. They are beginning to think symbolically and have more ways to express themselves, but they still need many direct experiences to construct their understanding of the world. Play is essential to their learning and to their self-expression.

The learning environment for preschoolers supports their expanding abilities and interests by including more varied and complex materials than those used by younger children. The areas that offer opportunities for symbolic representation (blocks, dramatic play, art) are increasingly important. The block-building area for preschoolers is large and includes more shapes and props. Building with wooden unit blocks that are made in proportionate sizes helps children discover relationships and provides them with the opportunity to represent their experiences on a small scale. The block area may take up to one third or one half of the space your group uses. Working with wood using real tools, such as hammers and saws, and nails and glue, is an additional activity for the preschool classroom, allowing children to experience a new medium for creativity.

Dramatic play for these children takes on a wide variety of roles and themes beyond family, which require props like hats of different kinds of workers, and more open-ended building materials, such as large hollow wooden blocks instead of housekeeping furniture.

Children's growing interest in print means that opportunities for writing and reading expand. Signs, charts, and graphs are used to record children's expressions and experiences. The reading corner will have a wide variety of books, including picture books, simple stories, and age-appropriate children's literature. Paper and a type-writer can be added to the dramatic play area. The art area can offer a variety of writing tools, such as pencils and markers, along with notecards and different kinds of paper.

The variety of media that children use to express themselves expands. Modeling with different kinds of clay, creating collage, painting, and drawing are done both as a sensory experience and to communicate one's thoughts and represent experiences in different ways. The art area will have many materials available for independent use. (See the chapter "Art in Early Childhood" for more information.) A large rectangular table in the art area can double as a snack and lunch table. In a family day care home, the kitchen table makes a good art table when covered with oilcloth.

Small manipulative toys, such as matching games, Legos, and pattern blocks, need to be organized into an area with storage and a work table with enough chairs. The group meeting area is usually a carpeted space where children and adults gather and sit on the floor. It is often also the reading area. With preschool children, it is helpful to have a second area with storage and seating that can be changed to suit the curriculum. This area may display apples and drawings of the trip to an orchard one month, or a grinder and different grains along with recipes and the ingredients to bake bread at another time.

Lofts or other climbing apparatus support children's need for large-muscle movement (especially for the younger ones) and can also incorporate an "alone" space underneath a slide or on top of a loft. A large cardboard box will also do for an alone space.

Pets are an important part of the learning environment for preschoolers. They can learn about the pets and their habits and develop responsibility by caring for them. Class pets can be as modest as a hermit crab or as ambitious as a family of white mice. When selecting a pet, consider animals that would be happy in a classroom environment and what is involved in caring for them. Have a class pet only if it will be well taken care of when school is in session as well as during holidays and over the summer.

Young School-Age Children

A major shift in thinking happens during these years. Children begin to think in logical ways about concepts, such as number, distance, and size. Rules and consistency matter much more now than they did for younger children. Developing self-confidence, identity, conscience, and a greater ability to control emotional expression are important tasks during these years. Friendships with peers are very important.

The learning environment for young school-age children is in many ways similar to the environment for preschoolers. The same activity areas are appropriate, but the materials in them and the work that goes on differ in complexity and depth. Children still work at tables in small groups and need a group meeting area. Art and woodworking, reading and dramatic play, blocks and pets are still a part of the curriculum and the environment.

Young school-age children need space to work and places to keep their materials. The individual desks commonly found in primary school classrooms are not the best kind of furniture for the school-age classroom. The purpose of a desk is to have a place for one child to work and keep her materials. If one of your curriculum goals is to encourage small-group cooperative work and sharing of materials, a better arrangement is tables and chairs with common places to keep materials where everyone can find and use them. Desks that do not have seats permanently attached to them can be arranged to create a table by putting the open ends together. Desks with seats attached can also be put together. Several rows of two or three desks each will create a larger area to work on and take up much less space than individual desks.

The group meeting area needs to be somewhat larger for school-age children than for preschoolers. Rather than sitting on the floor, taking up lots of space with knees and elbows and their larger bodies, sitting on simple wooden benches (that double as seats at work tables) often works better for school-agers. Chairs can be used for meeting, but they will take up more space and putting them close together often means pinched fingers.

Certain activity areas become more important with young school-age children than with preschoolers. The small manipulatives area becomes a very important part of the space, as math games and materials, such as pattern blocks, tangrams, and attribute blocks are added. Science and nature study are often a large part of the curriculum and need an activity area devoted to them. The art area offers many of the same materials as for preschoolers, but the materials will be explored and used in different ways, and the resulting creations will be more realistic and representational.

Knowing that public appreciation of art creations is important to children's developing sense of confidence and competence, Charlotte (a second grade teacher) has set up a long narrow table just outside her classroom door to display the finished sculptures, building constructions, and mosaic patterns her children have made. Signs (written by the children) describe each work and give the artist's name. Inside the classroom, a short set of shelves serves as the display area for other 3-dimensional works in progress, while finished collages hang at child's-eye level around the room.

Writing becomes increasingly important to these children. An area for writing, separate from the art area or adjacent to it, works well. This area is for storing writing tools, like paper and pencils and pens, as well as each child's writing journal. Placing a basket or bin in the writing area for recycled paper conveys an important message on ecology to children. The reading area needs a wide variety of books, from simple stories to long chapter books, and multiple copies of books that children can read together. It will also include reference books, such as dictionaries and children's encyclopedias, as well as books that children have written and published themselves. If your classroom has a computer, place it where two or more children can use it together (to encourage cooperation).

Dramatic play for school-age children moves from role-playing to the acting out of plays written and directed by children on social themes. Marriage is a popular theme for younger school-agers. Older children may create plays related to aspects of their curriculum, such as reenactments of historical events, like Rosa Parks' refusal to move to the back of the bus and the events that followed. Props and costumes are created by the children and supplied by the teacher on request.

Families

As Judy Leonard sets up the activity areas in her preschool classroom, she decides to share some of her thinking about the environment with children's parents and other family members. She makes a series of signs showing what activities will be offered in each area and how they promoted children's learning. She hangs these signs at adult height in each area. Here is an example of one:

Guide to the Art Area

- What activities will be offered? They include:
  - easel painting
  - drawing
  - creating collages
  - using clay
- Why offer art activities? They encourage children to:
  - express and explore their feelings
  - relax and enjoy themselves
  - explore color, texture, shape, and size
  - feel good about creating something

Of course, some people never even notice the signs. But several comment that the signs help them better understand what the children do all day long. One father says he never realized how important art is and that he will begin doing art activities at home with his son. Another child's grandmother asks if there is anything she can bring in for the art area. That prompts Judy to add this category to the sign:

• What do we need for the art area?

    natural materials such as pine cones and seashells

    fabric scraps

    containers such as baby food jars or margarine tubs

Exercises

Children's families find the signs helpful and so does Judy. She refers to them during conferences and parent meetings when she talks about curriculum and how children learn.

Her experiment is a success. Throughout the year, Judy updates the signs to inform families about new activities and materials they can contribute. The signs become a regular part of her environment.

1. Looking at the space you work in from a child's-eye view will help you understand how children might experience it. Imagine you are a child and mentally walk through your classroom (or your home or whatever setting you work in). What is at child's-eye level? Where are the pathways? What can you see from each area? What is at adult-eye level (too high for children to notice)? Think about what you can change to make your room easier for children to move around in.

2. Think about all the kinds of activities and opportunities for experience you want children to have. Make a list of ten or so. Now think about the space you work in. Is there at least one place in the room to do each activity on your list? Do some have more than one place? Is there an activity on your list with no place to do it in your room?

3. If you are like most people who work with young children, you probably do it in a space that you think could be improved upon. You can redesign your space, on paper, with a little work. You will need graph paper, a ruler, a measuring tape, heavy paper (like an index card), small post-its ("sticky" note paper), markers, and scissors.

   You are going to create a scale model of your room on graph paper with labels for activity areas, and moveable models of the furniture and equipment in it.

   • First, carefully measure your room—the width and length. Measure the width of doors and windows. Draw out the shape of your room on the graph paper, putting in the doors and windows and anything else that is not movable (like a sink). Use an easy scale that will allow your room to fit on the paper—like four squares on paper equals one foot.

- Next, on the post-its, write out the name of each activity area you want in your room. Place them on the drawing. Evaluate the room arrangement, thinking about traffic patterns, light, heat, noise, number of children in an area, areas that should be together or separate. Rearrange the area labels as many times as you need to until you have an arrangement you like.

- Then carefully measure the length and width of each piece of furniture and equipment in your room. Using the same scale you chose for drawing your room, draw exact models of your furnishings on the heavy paper. Cut these out and arrange your new room on paper. When you are satisfied with your arrangement, move the real objects around in your room, referring to the plan you have made.

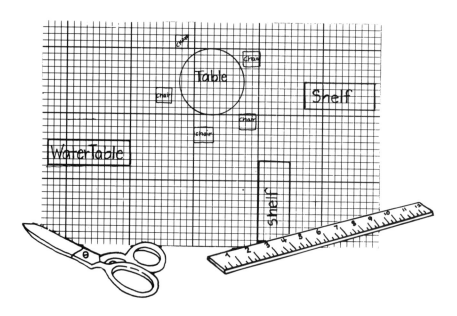

Resources

Aronson, S. (1991). *Health and safety in child care.* New York: Harper Collins.

Child Care Information Exchange is a magazine for directors of early childhood programs available from Exchange Press, PO Box 2890, Redmond, WA 98037-9977.

Greenman, J. (1988). *Caring spaces, learning places: Children's environments that work.* Redmond, WA: Exchange Press.

Greenman, J. (1991). Designing family day care environments. In *A marketing kit for family day care providers.* New York: National Council of Jewish Women.

Jones, E., & Prescott, E. (1978). *Dimensions of teaching-learning environments: Focus on day care.* Pasadena, CA: Pacific Oaks College.

Kritchevsky, S., & Prescott, E., with Walling, L. (1977). *Planning environments for young children: Physical space.* Washington, DC: National Association for the Education of Young Children.

Mitchell, A., with Altman, R. (1991). Indoor movement activities for young children. *Head Start Bulletin, 37.* Washington, DC: U.S. Department of Health and Human Services.

Moore, G. T., Lane, C. G., Hill, A. B., Cohen, U., & McGinty, T. (1979). *Recommendations for child care centers.* Milwaukee, WI: University of Wisconsin at Milwaukee, Center for Architecture and Urban Planning Research.

Moore, G. T., Lane, C. G., & Lundberg, L. (1979). *Bibliography on children and the physical environment.* Milwaukee, WI: University of Wisconsin at Milwaukee, Center for Architecture and Urban Planning Research.

National Association for the Education of Young Children. (1991). *Facility design for early childhood programs: Resource guide.* Washington, DC: Author.

Prescott, E. (1984). The physical setting in day care. In J. T. Greenman & R. Fuqua (Eds.), *Making day care better: Training, evaluation, and the process of change.* New York: Teachers College Press.

Weinstein, C. S., & David, T. G. (Eds.). (1987). *Spaces for children: The built environment and child development.* New York: Plenum Press.

Resources for equipment and materials

There are far too many sources for good materials and equipment to list all of them here. However, many national distributors offer catalogs, and another good source is a local school supply store.

About the Authors:

Anne Mitchell, M.S., is an early childhood policy researcher at Bank Street College, where she did a national study of public schools as providers of programs for children under six and then developed the Early Childhood Curriculum Project. She has taught Education Policy and is the founder of Bank Street's masters program in Early Childhood Leadership. She has been a trainer and consultant with early childhood teachers and family day care providers and was the director of two child care centers where she worked with toddlers, preschoolers, and children with special needs.

Nancy Balaban, Ed.D., is director of the Infant and Parent Development program at Bank Street College. She advises students and teaches the course Educating Infants and Toddlers. She is the author of Starting School: From Separation to Independence—A Guide for Early Childhood Teachers *(1985, Teachers College Press).*

5 ‖ The Group Process

Each child who enters your program is part of many different communities. For example, each is a member of a family, a cultural and ethnic group, a race, a socioeconomic class, and a neighborhood. Over time, through your efforts, children can reap the benefits of joining another community—that of your group.

Group process is what we call the method of creating a sense of community—a sense of belonging—among the children you work with. As children grow, they become increasingly aware of and influenced by their peers. By nurturing a sense of community, you help children benefit from the rich opportunities that come with being a member of a supportive community.

Trust is essential to creating a sense of community. When children trust, they feel accepted for who they are, and they know that their early childhood setting is a place where it is safe to express themselves. They are confident they will be listened to and that their needs will be addressed.

You build trusting relationships with children when you listen to a crying infant and respond to what her tears are saying. You build trusting relationships when you protect children's work by reminding a preschooler to lay his collage flat on a shelf so the glue will dry and the shells he worked so hard to arrange will not fall off. And you build trusting relationships when you sit down with two school-age children and encourage them to tell each other how being teased makes them feel. Trusting you helps children to learn to trust themselves and, with your guidance, each other.

Because trust takes time to grow, so does a sense of community. It develops gradually as children live their everyday lives together. Participating in daily routines such as preparing snack and cleaning up, working together to turn a refrigerator box into a spaceship, and collaborating to solve problems, they learn about themselves and about each other. They learn what it means to share and cooperate, to communicate and listen, to contribute and receive. In other words, they learn about the give-and-take that is part of being a member of a group.

In this chapter, we are going to look at why group process is important and how to implement it. Then there will be exercises you and your colleagues can do together to evaluate and develop your community-building skills.

What is group process?

Why implement group process?

By creating a sense of community, you provide children with skills and a background that will enrich their lives now and prepare them to live and work in the future as members of families and communities and as citizens.

Let us first consider the present. Being a member of a group provides children with two conditions essential for learning: a sense of security and opportunities for social interaction.

When children are accepted and respected members of a group, they feel safe and secure. This allows them to take risks. They are more likely to explore and experiment, as they must in order for learning to take place. Here are some examples of how this works with children of different ages:

- Carla, 7 months, has a trusting relationship with Willa, her family day care provider. Through countless daily interactions, such as listening and responding to Carla's babbling, cheering her attempts to eat with a spoon, and being there to give her a hug, Willa has won her trust. Knowing she can depend on Willa helps Carla feel safe in child care. A new crawler, she is comfortable about moving off her blanket to go check out a "fill and dump" can sitting a few feet away. As she dumps and picks up small blocks, she explores the meaning of "in and out" and develops her small-muscle skills.

- Rico, 4 years old, is frustrated. He wants to put a puzzle together, but cannot get several pieces to fit. "You do it," he tells Mrs. Greene. "You can get that puzzle together," she says. "Maybe Jin Yung will help you." Jin Yung, a whiz at puzzles, eagerly picks up a puzzle piece and puts it in its place. "C'mon. Like this," he says. Rico watches, tries again, and this time his piece fits. He calls Mrs. Greene to come take a look. "I knew you could get this puzzle together," says Mrs. Greene as she takes a good look. "Where do you think this piece goes?" Knowing his work will be respected, Rico is encouraged to keep trying to complete the puzzle. His efforts are fueled by the accepting responses of Jin Yung and Mrs. Greene.

- By the age of 6, children are very conscious of what it means to express themselves in front of a group. When Larry explains in class that he sometimes skips over an unknown word and goes back to figure it out after reading the entire paragraph, he is concerned that others might make fun of him for not knowing the word. But they do not. Larry's teacher has set up ground rules that call for children to listen carefully to each other and to ask questions and disagree without hurting each other's feelings, Larry's teacher promotes the sharing of ideas and feelings. Because of these rules, children are more likely to share their ideas and feelings. This will help them clarify their thinking and feel more confident about expressing themselves.

Children spend much of their time interacting with you and their peers. As you foster a positive sense of group, the children will learn about getting along with other people. But that is not all. As we discussed in the chapter, "Principles of the Bank Street Approach," all areas of a child's development—and thus, of a child's learning—are interdependent. As children begin to identify themselves as members of a group, their cognitive, emotional, and physical development is enriched through the stimulation and challenge of working and playing with others. Here are some examples of how this works:

- When you respond to a crying infant, you are doing more than changing a wet diaper or feeding a hungry baby. You are teaching that infant that he is competent—he can make his needs known. You are also teaching him that he is valued and that he can trust people to respond to him—each a crucial lesson for a child just beginning to develop a sense of self.

- By providing an environment that encourages 4-year-old Donna and 3-year-old Kyle to look at each other's work and talk together about what each is painting, you open the way for each child to learn from the other. Kyle may learn the name of a color; Donna may decide to add some curvy lines to her painting after seeing Kyle's art work. Both children will benefit in ways they could not if you insisted on "quiet" and "pay attention to your own work." As adults, we know that some of our best work is the result of collaborating with peers. Why, then, do we so often insist that children work on their own?

- The respect you show children will be reflected in their interactions with each other. On Friday morning, everyone in Mr. Vasquez's classroom helps to put away the blocks used during that week. As buildings are dismantled, the blocks are stacked in rows of five so they can be counted and then easily carried to the shelves. Week after week, Frank, 6 years old, who is unsure of himself about math, has seen and heard Edward, also 6, count up to 100 blocks by fives confidently. Today he begins counting"5...10...15...16...17" as Edward listens. "No," Edward says. "5...10...15...20...25." Slowly he runs his finger across the stacks of blocks. "You count too," he encourages Frank in a tone of voice that sounds a lot like Mr. Vasquez. This is no accident. Mr. Vasquez purposefully treats children the way he wants them to treat each other. His respect for children sets the stage for this interaction, in which children learn from each other about numbers; one child learns how it feels to know something and communicate it, and the other learns how it feels to be supported as he tries out a new skill.

Looking to the future, being members of a diverse group can benefit both the children you work with and our society. Typically, groups are created along lines of similarities, such as class, gender, race, culture, and interests. By creating a sense of community in a diverse group, you are teaching children how to accept and feel comfortable with differences. Children discover that their group is stronger and richer because of their differences. This has tremendous implications for relationships between different races and cultures.

When toddlers help make fruit salad that everyone will share for snack, when preschoolers collaborate to build a block tower, and when young school-age children take turns watering the wheat seeds they have planted as part of their study about bread, they all experience a collective purpose. They learn there is more to life than their individual needs. On a global level, we hope these early lessons will foster the development of adults who are able to deal collectively with complex problems, such as caring for our natural resources.

If our democratic society is going to flourish, we need citizens who know how to relate to other people, how groups work, and how to be productive members of a group. This is what children in your program are learning as you create a sense of community.

How can you create a sense of group?

There is no recipe for how to create a sense of community among children. How you go about it will depend in large part on your children's ages as well as on the character and personality of the individual members of the group. But here are some principles that can guide you:

- You are your most important resource. By being trustworthy and modeling respectful behavior, you say to children that you value these behaviors and encourage them to follow your lead.

- Your role in shaping a community changes depending upon the age of the children you work with.

To help infants and toddlers grow into people who can be members of a community, you must know each child as an individual. By developing relationships in which you value each child's uniqueness, and by responding to each child's needs, you help children to develop a sense of trust in others and to learn how it feels to be in a respectful, responsive relationship. These are the first steps in creating a community.

By the time children are preschoolers, they are beginning to develop friendships and spend a lot of time playing with their peers. Though knowing and responding to individual children is still a large part of your work, children need you to help them learn how to get along with each other. Your focus begins to shift towards balancing the needs of the group and individuals.

Relationships with peers become increasingly important for

young school-age children. As their teacher, you will need to be aware of your role in guiding the life of the group. This means being there, but stepping back and encouraging children to interact with each other. For example, by sitting quietly with two children in the playground as they discuss the rules of their ball game, you serve as an anchor which encourages them to explore and communicate their feelings. In building a sense of community among your children, keep these points in mind:

Think about the language you use.

What you say in your everyday interactions with children, parents, and co-workers can help you build a sense of community. You are teaching how to make group life work when you caution a toddler, "Watch where you are walking so you don't bump into Jill"; when you suggest to a preschooler, "Maybe Sandy could help you carry that big pillow across the room"; or explain to school-age children, "We are responsible for each other. If you see someone's paper on the floor, please pick it up."

Remember your sense of humor.

Laughing together enhances a sense of group. Whether you laugh with an infant during a peek-a-boo game, share a funny story with preschoolers, or come to the understanding that you and the young school-age children you teach can say to one another "we need to tell some jokes" when a breather is needed, humor is an important part of your group's life.

Create an environment that reflects children and responds to their needs.

This not only shows respect but also helps assure that children will feel at home in your setting. Like adults, children are better able to reach out and get to know one another when they feel comfortable. Places to safely store special belongings; bulletin boards covered with children's paintings, stories, and murals; shelves filled with books that touch on children's issues and interests—from saying goodbye in the morning to how a seed grows—all contribute to helping children feel at ease and, thus, to the development of a sense of group.

Use your curriculum to promote a sense of community.

Experiencing everyday routines within a home-like environment is the essence of infant/toddler curriculum. As you live your daily lives together—as you button coats, change diapers, eat snack, and help children take naps—you can promote a sense of community by being responsive to the needs of individuals. As children get older, individual needs must still be considered but, in addition, there is a common focus on content. Children work together to explore. They go on field trips together. They share ideas and information through building, drawing, writing, and discussions. This promotes a sense of "We are the group studying the neighborhood."

Provide times to come together during the day.

Snack and lunch are group times for infants and toddlers. In addition to these occasions, preschoolers and school-age children have meetings in which everyone comes together to talk in the morning, during transitions, and throughout the day to plan, discuss a project, or solve a problem. During these times, you can promote a sense of community by encouraging children to communicate their ideas, listen carefully, and respond to one another.

Help children be in touch with themselves—their physical selves as well as their feelings.

This is important because groups are made up of individuals. Each child has an impact on other children and thus on the group. Explaining to an infant that now you are going to pick her up and change her diaper, suggesting that dancing toddlers move away from each other to avoid someone getting accidentally bumped, encouraging a preschooler to tell his friend why he is angry, and explaining to young school-age children that laughing at someone's idea during group will hurt that person's feelings—these are all ways that you can promote group life by helping individual children tune into where they are, how they feel, how another person feels, and the impact of their actions on others.

Invite children to problem solve about classroom issues.

Helping find solutions encourages children to become contributing and invested members of their community. Children feel a sense of responsibility and experience themselves in relation to others. Inviting toddlers to help wipe up spilled apple juice so no one slips, discussing with preschoolers how to decide whose turn it is to sit in the popular rocking chairs, and figuring out a strategy with young school-age children for how to balance the need for quiet with the need to talk with peers during writing time—all of these are examples of problems children can address.

Help children learn to resolve personal differences.

In any group of people there are bound to be conflicts. Children need your guidance to learn how to deal with them.

As a caregiver of infants and toddlers, you will sometimes have to step in directly to help them stop hitting, biting, or scratching. At other times, children may need you to step back and give them the opportunity to practice their growing self-control. A reminder—"Tell Dennis you are angry"—can be enough to help some toddlers use words to settle a dispute.

By the time they are preschoolers, children's developing sense of self and language gives them new tools to use in their relationships. Your role shifts from being the chief negotiator to encouraging children to handle their own affairs. You can support their efforts by offering strategies such as, "You have to tell someone how you feel because they may not know" or "When you are each pulling on the doll, it is hard to talk together. Put the doll down and then talk."

When 7-year-olds Sheila and Valerie will not let Michelle play with them, your presence will promote discussion. By reflecting on what is said with comments such as, "Michelle says it hurts her feelings when you tell her to go away" or "Sheila doesn't like that you always want to change the game she and Valerie are playing," you can help children tune into feelings and come up with ways to resolve their conflicts.

Putting group process skills into action

Infants and Toddlers

Sarah cares for children from several different cultures in her family day care home. Lucien Calabi is from France and Yin Shu is from China. Though the children are still very young, she feels it is important that group life in her setting reflect and respond to their many cultures. To this end, Sarah decided she needed to learn more about each child's culture. She met with each family and asked them to share their ideas about how children should be raised. She was surprised when Lucien's mother shared how uneasy she was with the idea of "terrible twos." "When I was two," she told Sarah, "I was expected to sit at the table with my family and to eat with a spoon and fork. I listened to my parents and did what they told me." Since then, Sarah and Mrs. Calabi have had many discussions about what each expects of Lucien's behavior. They have agreed to be consistent on some of the most important issues; on others, they recognize that they differ. For example, Lucien is free to explore and be "messy" at Sarah's, where the environment is more child-centered than at home.

To help children feel safe and secure, Sarah tries to provide continuity between home and day care. She finds out about children's schedules and routines at home. In addition, she asks each family to make a tape of a story and songs in their native language. These are the tapes children request most and are played often.

"My goal," explains Sarah, "is to develop a program that respects each individual. If these children are going to grow into people who can live successfully in a diverse community, they need first to feel good about who they are. I hope I can give them a good start."

Preschoolers

Paula, a preschool teacher, uses daily routines and the physical environment to promote group life. Here are some examples of ways she does this:

- By allowing children to decide where to sit at snack and lunch, Paula creates the opportunity for relationships to develop. Yesterday, she heard this conversation about friendship between Rachita and Elena: "I sit next to you. My blueberries are next to your blueberries. That's because we're friends." "Yeah!"

- Because the loft parents helped build in her room can safely hold three children, there is a classroom rule that only three people can play on it at one time. This provides the opportunity for problem solving when more than three want to play, as well as a special space for small groups of children to play and get to know one another.

- Paula invites children to help with tasks that require group effort and cooperation, such as moving the table to make a tent, unrolling the exercise mat, and carrying a big bag of balls out to the playground.

- Paula knows it is hard work for young children to spend all day in a group. She believes children will get more out of group life if they can take an occasional break to think, rest, read, or just watch what is going on. In arranging her room, Paula was sure to include "private spaces" by curtaining off the area under the loft, building a window seat, and providing two bean-bag chairs in a protected corner.

Young School-Age Children

In the play yard is a stack of large metal triangles that children love to climb in, around, and over. They are heavy. The children have discovered that they cannot lift and move a triangle by themselves. Over time, a ritual has developed. When a child wants to move a triangle, he chants, "team work . . . team work . . . team work." Other children respond by coming over and taking hold. When there are enough children, the cry of "no more help" sounds across the yard.

Families

During a family conference, Mrs. Jilson, a family child care provider, is surprised to hear Dennis and Lisa Simon describe their 3-year-old, Lois, at home. According to them, Lois is a "baby" who eats in a high chair, sleeps in a crib, and rides in her stroller as she accompanies her parents on neighborhood errands.

Mrs. Jilson has a very different picture of Lois. She sees Lois as a competent, involved member of the group of children she cares for. For example, Lois not only eats in a chair at the table with other children, but she helps prepare snacks and lunch. She is proud of being able to get up off her mat when she wakes up and get a book to read while the other children sleep. On trips around the neighborhood, she has learned to hold hands when crossing the street and loves carrying small bags of groceries home from the store.

Feeling that the Simons would benefit if they saw Lois as a contributing, involved member of the class, Mrs. Jilson encourages the Simons to stay as long as possible at the beginning and end of the day, and to come by for lunch whenever they can. She observes with them to help them see how competent Lois is and how much she learns by taking part in daily routines. She shares stories of Lois' day, telling, for example, about how excited and proud Lois was to shell peas for snack. Mrs. Jilson has also suggested the Simons talk with other parents and read a book from the parent library to learn more about who 3-year-olds are.

One afternoon, Lois' mother comments to Mrs. Jilson that Lois is growing up right in front of her eyes. And she adds—to Mrs. Jilson's amazement and pleasure—"We feel like we have another member in our family. It's great for all of us."

Exercises

Here are exercises you can do and other resources you can use to learn more. The exercises will help you sharpen your group-process skills. They can be done with a colleague or group of colleagues. Remember, creating a sense of trust and group means being aware not only of the children in your room but of yourself. It takes time. So does developing these skills.

1. Thinking about some of your own experiences as a member of a group can help you be more aware of what children may be experiencing and ways you can foster a sense of community in your room.

   Answer the questions below and share your responses with a colleague.

   - What groups are you a member of?

   - How does being a member of a group make you feel?

   - What do you like about being a member of a group? What do you not like?

   - What have you learned about yourself through being a member of a group?

   - What have you learned about other people?

2. By establishing trusting relationships with children and colleagues, you set the stage for developing a sense of community in your program.

   Begin this exercise about trust by thinking about someone you trust. What qualities does this person have that invite your trust?

For example, you may think of qualities such as honesty, genuineness, and responsibility. What things does this person do to encourage your trust? Listening to what you have to say and being your friend even when you disagree about something are examples of behaviors that promote trust.

- Think about yourself. What qualities are there about you that invite children and colleagues to trust you?

- Over the course of a week, list examples of things you do to let children and co-workers know you are trustworthy. For example, comforting a crying infant, offering a preschooler a sponge to help wipe up spilled paint, and writing a note on the board with Janine, 6 years old, that says "Find a book about whales" and doing it during library time are behaviors that invite a child's trust. Being on time and following through with commitments, such as remembering to order art supplies, tell a colleague you can be trusted.

- Share your responses with a colleague and discuss the importance of trust.

3. Feeling at home in an environment encourages interaction by helping children feel safe and secure. You can help children feel at home in your space by being sure it reflects who they are, their individual and collective interests, needs, and work. A collection of rocks everyone has helped find, Sylvia's crutches propped in the corner where she can find them, and a class book about a trip to an apple orchard say to children, "This space is yours. You belong here."

   Take a colleague on a tour of your space and explain how it reflects the children who live there. Discuss other ways your environment can reflect and respond to the children in your group.

4. People are not a group just because they are in the same space, but because they share experiences and ideas with one another. Group meetings are vital to establishing a sense of community because it is during meetings that children have the opportunity to share their ideas, feelings and interests with one another.

   Like many teachers, you may be working on how to make your meeting times work better. In this exercise, you will have the opportunity to gain a new perspective on your meeting times and consider ways you might want to change them.

   Begin by considering these questions:

   - What are your goals for meeting times? What group skills do you want children to learn? What are specific examples of ways you promote these skills?

- What are your expectations of children's behavior during meetings? How have you communicated, for example, that you expect children to listen when someone is speaking?

- How does your physical environment influence your meeting times? Consider, for example, the size of your meeting space and how seating is arranged. A space that is too small and confusing leads to inevitable pushing and shoving.

- What are some examples of meeting topics? If there is going to be discussion, topics must be interesting to children. Some topics for lively meetings include, "Where does a letter go after you put it in the mailbox?" and "What is a family?"

- What kinds of questions do you pose to encourage children to talk with one another? For example, "Can you tell us more about that?" and "What do you think about what Regina just said?" are questions that encourage communication between children.

After reflecting on your meeting time, arrange for a colleague to observe a meeting you have with children. Ask him or her to focus on the questions above, as well as any others on your mind.

Then get together to exchange your perceptions of meeting times. How is what you both see the same? How does it differ? Discuss what you have learned. Make a plan to implement any changes you may want to try. Arrange a time to come together again in a few weeks to evaluate how things are going.

5. Working together to solve problems is an important way of promoting a sense of community. Problem solving is filled with opportunities for children to learn about expressing their ideas and feelings, listening to others, making compromises, and sharing. Helping to find a solution will foster children's feelings of responsibility and pride.

In this exercise, you will plan and implement a strategy for helping children see themselves as members of a community who are able to work out problems together. Follow this series of steps:

- List five examples of problems that your children can help solve. To guide you, think of issues that have a direct bearing on children's lives. For example, it makes sense to invite toddlers to help you take care of a dangerous situation by moving a giant pillow into the middle of the room to create a safe jumping space. You can involve preschoolers in preventing disputes about whose turn it is to hammer at the woodworking table by devising a strategy, such as creating a sign-up sheet. You can offer young school-age children the opportunity to figure out how to resolve arguments about rules of a ball game.

- Decide how you will present the problem to the group in a respectful way.

- Consider how children can realistically be involved in coming up with a solution. Remember, there is usually more than one way to resolve a problem.

- After trying out the solution, meet again to review how things are going. Make necessary changes.

Resources

Cohen, D. H. (1988). *The learning child.* New York: Schocken Books.

Greenspan, S., & Greenspan, N. T. (1989). *First feelings: Milestones in the emotional development of your baby and child.* New York: Viking Penguin.

Provence, S. (1967). *Guide for the care of infants in groups.* New York: Child Welfare League of America.

Wolf, D. P. (Ed.). (1986). *Connecting: Friendship in the lives of young children and their teachers.* Redmond, WA: Exchange Press.

About the Author:

Amy Laura Dombro, M.S., headed the Bank Street Infant and Family Center from 1976 to 1983. She is now a consultant with Head Start Parent Child Center programs. She is the senior author of The Ordinary is Extraordinary: How Children under Three Learn *(1989, Fireside) and* Sharing the Caring: How to Find the Right Child Care and Make it Work for You and Your Child *(1991, Fireside).*

6 ‖ Discipline and Management

What comes to your mind when you read the words *discipline* and *management*? Like many teachers and caregivers, you may find yourself feeling anxious associating these words with controlling children's behavior and punishment.

This chapter offers a different perspective. We are going to think about discipline and management as ways to guide children's behavior and help them begin to learn to make their own decisions and control their own actions.

Discipline is what you do and say to teach an individual child acceptable behavior and guide him or her to practice that behavior. *Management* refers to techniques teachers and caregivers use to guide the behavior of a group of children.

Over time, as you guide their behavior, children begin to identify with what you say, your behaviors, and your expectations. They internalize your messages and make them their own. This process leads to the development of self-control.

In this chapter, we are going to look at why discipline and management are so important to children's well-being. Then we will discuss concrete suggestions for positive ways to discipline and manage. Finally, there is a series of exercises for you and your colleagues to do together.

What are discipline and management?

Discipline and management will help you meet three very important goals in your work with children:

Keeping Children Physically Safe

Young children are impulsive. They often move and respond without thinking about the consequences of their actions. When Asata, 15 months, dances around the room waving a scarf, he needs your management to define a dancing space so he does not bump into other children. Older children, too, need your help to keep safe. When 7-year-old Ricky gets carried away telling jokes and begins roughhousing during a field trip to a bakery, he needs a reminder to calm down so that he does not hurt himself or others and so that everyone can listen to what the baker has to say.

Promoting Children's Developing Sense of Self

In the course of defining themselves as separate people, children test limits. Knowing you are there to set limits when necessary lets

Why guide behavior with discipline and management?

children feel safe, because they do not have to be afraid of losing control. It is as if you are the guard rail as they drive over a high bridge on an unknown road. Though she cries, "No!" 3-year-old Shaquandra depends on you to insist that she hold your hand when crossing the street. Knowing that she can count on you to set limits lets her feel safe, which encourages her to explore her independence.

Teaching Children to Develop Self-Control

Helping children develop self-control is important for these reasons:

- People with self-control feel good about themselves. They feel competent and proud to be in control of their own actions.

- Having self-control allows people to make their own decisions about how they should behave. They are not at the whim of what someone else tells them. This is especially relevant in today's society when we want children to learn to say "No" to drugs or abuse.

- People with self-control are more responsible members of a group. They take responsibility for their own actions. They are able to voice their own opinions and beliefs and, at the same time, respect those of others.

Developing self-control takes a long time. Young children are just beginning to develop the set of beliefs and values that they need to help them decide how to behave. Though they have a sense that it is important to respect other people, the 7-year-olds Mr. Burks works with rely on his group-time rules to remind them not to laugh at someone else's ideas. Over time, as their self-control develops, they will not need Mr. Burks or his rules to keep from laughing. They will be able to stop themselves because they believe that is the right thing to do .

How can you discipline and manage?

Here are some suggestions for how to guide children's behavior in ways that will help you to meet the goals outlined above:

Match your expectations of behavior to children's developmental level.

- **Infants** can seem very demanding. The reality is that they need what they need when they need it. When Shawna, 3 months, cries her "I'm hungry" cry, she needs you to feed her even though it is not lunchtime. Do not worry. You will not spoil her. By meeting her needs promptly, you are helping her trust her world and herself. This foundation of trust is a prerequisite for self-control.

- **Toddlers**, like Daimere, are learning to be their own people. To do this, Daimere needs to be assertive and practice saying "No," no matter how difficult it makes life for you. He is not trying to "get you," though it may feel that way at times. He is saying, "I am me." Toddlers are impulsive. They act on their feelings. When Jeremy feels angry or overwhelmed, for example, he may hit, kick, or bite another child. You cannot let toddlers "fight it out" because they can hurt one another. Jeremy needs a caregiver to be there to help him control his behavior by picking him up or moving between him and the other child. Some toddlers, some times, may be able to control their behavior with a verbal reminder. Toddlers are just beginning to learn about possession. While you can encourage sharing, do not expect them to share. Provide several of the same toys to prevent squabbles.

- **Preschoolers** are beginning to understand rules such as "Clean up your toys when you are finished playing with them," and "Tell someone you are angry instead of hitting." Their growing abilities to use language, to reason, to understand cause and effect, and to understand another person's feelings allow them to govern their own behavior more than they could as toddlers. Remember, though, that this ability is unstable. Preschoolers often give in to impulse and temptation, especially when they are under stress, such as when they are hungry, tired, excited before a holiday, or upset when a parent leaves.

- **Young school-age children** are increasingly more capable of self-control. They understand why there are rules and can generate their own rules. However, they sometimes need to be protected from their own rigid standards, as when Harry suggested that Dia never be allowed to go to the library again because he forgot to return a book. In comparison to younger children, school-age children's aggression is often more verbal than physical. They will call each other names or tease; they need your help to learn that this behavior is hurtful and not permitted.

Remember, however, that every child is an individual and some are further along than others in developing self-control.

Know children as individuals.

Children's behavior is affected by their temperaments and approaches to learning, as well as by events in their lives. Knowing, for example, that 5-month-old Tyler is fussy because he is tired, you can offer him a nap. After observing that Eddie, 4 years old, gets overwhelmed and begins pushing other children when the room gets too noisy or busy for him, you may decide to take him and two other children to the kitchen to help prepare snack. Knowing that 6-year-old Carmen's need to be active is behind her disruptive behavior, you can make sure she has time to run and play in the gym or outdoors every day.

Evaluate your curriculum.

Some behavior problems arise when children are bored or find tasks too difficult. If your preschoolers are constantly dropping puzzle pieces on the floor, are the puzzles too hard for them? If older children are constantly distracting and pestering one another, have they lost interest in the activities you offer?

Show children respect even though you may not approve of their behavior.

How you discipline and manage tells children not only about their behavior, but about themselves. Take care never to attack a child's self-esteem, even when his or her actions are inappropriate, disruptive, or dangerous. You may say, "I don't like your behavior when you throw things," but never say (or imply), "I don't like you."

Be aware of the language you use.

Consider the messages your words and tone convey. You can show respect for children and give them helpful information as you guide their behavior. When Rachita's caregiver says, "Please climb off the table. Tables are for eating on, not walking on," she is respectful and gives Rachita information about tables as she addresses a behavior she wants to change.

Use your physical environment to guide behavior.

Put your favorite vase on a high shelf to keep it out of the hands of an active toddler. Make sponges available so preschoolers can wipe up spills at the water table. Arrange the wood-working area in a protected space to limit the number of school-age children who can work there at the same time.

Give children manageable tasks.

Children are more likely to do an activity they feel they can accomplish. Ask preschoolers to "please pick up the pop beads" rather than "please clean up the living room."

Offer alternatives.

If an infant is chewing on the rug, you can say, "Here is your teething ring. You can chew on it." If a toddler is pouring his juice on the floor, you can say, "If you want to pour, let's go over to the water table and you can practice pouring water."

Help children understand others' feelings.

Recognizing how their behavior makes others feel will help children begin to learn to control their own behavior. Explain, for example, "Jason is upset because you hit him," "Megan is angry because you won't let her play with you," and "Gary appreciates your helping him figure out those words."

Involve the entire class in problem solving.
For example, say to preschoolers or school-age children, "We have a problem. The library area is disorganized and everyone's complaining they can't find books. What can we do?" Children might suggest putting books neatly back on the shelves when they are finished reading them or making a sign-out sheet to use when someone borrows a book overnight. If they do not come up with any reasonable suggestions, you offer possible solutions.

Help children see the consequences of their actions.
Helping children to realize the impact of their behavior is a first step in teaching them to be responsible for their actions. "We can't read a book when you tear it. Let's get some tape and fix it."

Remind children of rules in positive language.
"Before you go to the water table, remember that water sometimes spills. What do we do when water spills on the floor? Why do we do this?" or "Before you go upstairs to do your research, let's remind each other about how to behave in the library."

Use alternatives to time-out.
Time-out is a strategy used by many teachers and caregivers. When a child has done something the adult in charge does not want or like, the child is made to sit in a time-out chair for a designated amount of time. The idea is that sitting apart from the group can help children pull themselves together. The danger is that time-out is often overused and misused. Children are forced to sit longer than is appropriate, or for many times during the day. There are other ways to help children pull themselves together that are not as restrictive. For example, a toddler can have one-on-one time with a special caregiver to sing a song or read a book. Sometimes a child may need a chance to be active. Pounding playdough may be just what a wiggly 3-year-old needs, or maybe the entire group needs to go on a march around the room. You can say to a preschooler or older child, "You need some time by yourself. You can sit at the table and look at a book until you are ready to rejoin the group."

Acknowledge children's positive behavior.
Your smile, nod, or brief comment of encouragement will go a long way to promoting desirable behavior: "I like the way you two decided who was going to paint the airplane on the mural."

Guide children to solve their own problems.
The world can be a big and overwhelming place for young children. Helping solve problems promotes self-esteem and a sense of competence, which eventually leads to children's being able to solve problems on their own. Together, Patty, 2 years old, and her caregiver

Library

Who is next
Josey
Alberta
Nicky

decided that when Patty felt cranky, sitting and reading a book together would help her feel better. The preschoolers in Mr. Gonzalez' room helped settle their continuous arguments about whose turn it was to play on the loft by deciding that Mr. Gonzalez would list children's names on the chalkboard. School-age children in Mrs. Benson's room were able to work out the problem of sharing two very popular rocking chairs on their own by devising a sign-up system.

Teach by example.
Behave towards children, co-workers, and parents the way you want children to behave towards each other. What do you say and do when, for example, a parent forgets the extra clothes he has been promising to bring in for two weeks, or a co-worker says something that makes you angry? What does your behavior tell children about how they should handle their differences with other people?

Encourage children to talk about their feelings and frustrations.
Listen to what children's words and actions tell you about how they feel. Acknowledge their feelings. Offer children words to name their feelings as you suggest appropriate ways to express them. "It's okay if you are angry at Carmen, but I cannot let you bite her. It will hurt. I will help you tell Carmen you are angry." "I know it hurts your feelings when Jessie calls you 'stupid.' Why don't you tell him, so he knows?"

Figure out ways to deal with your feelings and frustrations.
Face it—there are going to be times when you feel upset at a child or group of children. It may be a behavior that sets you off. Or you may find a child touches off deep feelings in you that are left over from your own childhood. Regardless of the reasons, it is helpful to think about ways to deal with your feelings. Here are some suggestions:

- Step back and count to 10.
- Explain to a child how you feel. "It makes me angry when you tease Nicky."
- Ask a co-teacher (if you have one) to deal with a child or situation that touches you off. "I can't deal with Danielle's whining today. Will you try to find out what it is she wants?"
- Discuss a bothersome situation with a colleague.
- Reduce stress by exercising—with children during the day or on your own after work.

Keep your sense of humor.
A joke, a silly song, or a funny face can give everyone a much-needed sense of perspective when things get tense.

Be aware of how you deal with diversity.

Do you find yourself encouraging girls to keep clean and do quiet activities while cheering boys on as they climb trees or make mud pies? Do you allow children to get away with behaviors such as teasing or not doing homework because they are disabled? Do your ideas about children's capabilities vary, depending on the language the children speak? If your answer is yes, it is likely your biases are getting in the way of your seeing children for who they are as individuals. Only by becoming aware of your prejudices will you be able to put them aside and respond to children as the unique people they are. (See the chapters "Observing and Recording Children's Behavior" and "Valuing Diversity" for additional information and suggestions.)

Be aware that who you are can influence your expectations and responses to children's behavior.

Your childhood experiences, your personality, and your beliefs about how children should behave can influence how you respond to children. Regina and her brothers were expected to be seen but not heard when they were growing up. As a new caregiver, Regina found herself constantly telling children to "be quiet," until a colleague pointed out her behavior and helped her see the connection between what she expected from children and what her parents had expected from her.

Communicate your philosophy about discipline and management to parents.

Often, parents, like many caregivers and teachers, equate discipline with punishment and control. Here are some ways you can help parents understand that guiding children's behavior lays the foundation for self-control:

- Model positive discipline. Encourage parents to adopt your behaviors, such as treating children with respect even when you disapprove of their behavior, and offering children alternatives.

- Discuss discipline at parent meetings and during parent conferences.

- Offer parents reading materials, such as *Helping Children Learn Self-Control* or *Love & Learn: Discipline for Young Children* by A.S. Honig, which are brochures available from the National Association for the Education of Young Children. (See Resources at the end of this chapter.)

Because you guide children through transitions and group time every day, these events deserve a closer look. Here are some strategies to help you make them easier for everyone.

Transitions

Transitions are by nature unsettling because they are times of change. Children need your guidance to learn how to handle these "in-between-activity" times.

Set a calm tone.
Use both words and actions to steady children. For example, sit down on the bench next to children who are struggling to pull on their boots and say something like, "Those boots look tough to get on. Maybe it would be easier if you hold them this way."

Explain to children what is going to happen next.
"After you get your coats on, we'll walk to the store to buy some apples for snack."

Be responsive to individual needs.
Transitions are harder for some children than others. Offer Tony, who finds transitions upsetting, the opportunity to help you set the table instead of sitting with the group to wait for lunch.

Be organized.
Checking ahead to be sure there is a good supply of toothpaste and paper towels will make brushing teeth and washing hands after lunch smoother.

Set up your environment to anticipate and meet children's needs.
Providing individual hooks for children to hang up their coats or a step stool in the bathroom to help children reach the sink will help children feel more competent and in control.

Provide a routine that children can count on.
Sing the same "before lunch" song to let toddlers know it is time to come to the table. Institute coming together in the meeting area to let preschoolers and school-age children collect themselves between activities. Doing a fingerplay with preschoolers, singing a familiar song with 5-year-olds, and playing a game of 20 questions with 8-year-olds will give children a comforting sense that "now we are a group again" before they move on to their next activities.

Ask yourself, "How can I make transitions more manageable for children?"
When Mrs. Phillips and Mr. Lee discussed their lunchtime procedures, they realized it did not make sense for Mr. Lee to be responsible for all the children after lunch while Mrs. Phillips cleared the tables. They decided to let the tables wait and for Mrs. Phillips to help small groups of children brush their teeth while Mr. Lee and the

others chose before-nap books. As a result, there was less confusion and adults were available to give each child more individual attention.

Group Times

Group times refer to those times when preschoolers and school-age children come together for a common purpose, such as talking about a book, planning for a trip, or solving a classroom problem. Here are some suggestions about ways to manage group times to make them meaningful experiences:

Encourage children to participate as much as possible.
By providing a "Morning Meeting" chart that tells about the day's events, Mrs. Jensen makes it possible for her second graders to take part in morning meetings. Children feel proud and competent as they take turns reading items on the list, including the date, greeting, and announcements.

Use language in ways that help children manage.
Every time he wants children's attention, Mr. Turner says "Eyes and ears on me." Hearing these familiar words helps children collect themselves and turn their attention to Mr. Turner.

Guide behavior through the physical environment.
You can eliminate the pushing and shoving that often occurs when a group of active children try to fit into a small space by assigning places to sit, on benches, pillows, or a rug. Arranging the seating in a circle so children can see each other as well as you helps each child feel like part of the group and encourages participation.

Offer children a choice of an optional activity if they are having a hard time managing in the group.
"You can join in the discussion or go read a book." If a child cannot make up his mind, you might continue, "I gave you a choice. You have to decide or I'll decide for you. Think about how you'll feel if I make the choice." Offering a choice lets children choose a situation in which they can succeed. It also means you can focus on the group rather than on the one or two children who are being disruptive.

Ask yourself the same question you asked about transitions—"How can I make group time more manageable for children?"
When Anita Jones asked herself this question, she realized that children were often distracted by the antics of George, the classroom guinea pig, whose cage was next to the meeting area. By slightly shifting George's cage, she eliminated a distraction and made it easier for children to focus on the business at hand.

Putting discipline and management into action

Infants and Toddlers

"You sure tell these babies 'no' a lot," observes 11-year-old Charlene, who is spending a day of her school vacation as her mother's assistant. Her mother, Regina, a family child care provider, is about to answer, "That's ridiculous," when Kathy, 10 months old, pulls on a lamp cord. "No, don't do that!" Regina calls out as she hurries across the room to pick up Kathy. A few minutes later, Michael, 15 months, grabs the red fire engine from Germaine, 16 months. "No, no," says Regina. "Maybe you've got a point," she tells Charlene.

Over the next few days, Regina listens to herself. She hears more "nos" than anything else; in fact she writes down every time she says "no." She calls on two friends, also care providers, for help. They both suggest that she rearrange her physical environment so it will guide children's behavior.

One evening, Regina, her friends, and Charlene sit on the floor looking at the living room from a child's perspective. They discover a dangling lamp cord that calls for a child to pull on it, one bright red fire engine that is the cause of many disputes, and unorganized, cluttered toy shelves that make it hard for children to help clean up. By taping the lamp cord to the wall, providing two more fire engines, and clearing off and labeling the shelves, Regina decreases the number of times she has to say "no." At the same time, she promotes children's self-control and, therefore, increases their self-esteem.

Preschoolers

Four-year-old Jason is having difficulty managing group time today. He insists on calling out and pushing the children sitting next to him. Mrs. Greene considers "time-out" and then remembers it is no longer allowed by her program's director. When Jason pinches a neighbor so hard she begins crying, Mrs. Greene knows she has to do something. First, she says, "That hurt. Pinching is not allowed. If she was in your way, you could have asked her to move." Then she offers Jason a choice: "Would you like to sit and listen or go read a book in the library corner?" By now, Jason is too frazzled to make a decision. "It's hard for you to decide today. I'll make a choice for you. You can come here and sit next to me. We'll listen together to what children are saying." Everyone—especially Jason—is relieved. By being clear, firm, and respectful, Mrs. Greene promotes self-control. She lets children know they can be decision makers while reassuring them that when they need help, she will be there for them.

Young School-Age Children

"Sandra, a second grader, is driving me crazy. She uses profanity, provokes others, and then smiles at me sweetly." Ida Jackson shares her frustration at a staff meeting. "I need help with her." "I know how you feel," comments Mr. Ellis, who teaches down the hall. "I had a kid who really got to me last year. You're not alone." "Thanks," says Ms. Jackson. "That helps—a little."

It is decided that Mrs. Carlson, the program's director, will observe in Ms. Jackson's room. After a few days, they meet.

"I noticed that when you speak with Sandra, your voice is critical and judgmental rather than clear and direct, as it is when you speak with other kids. Do you feel that way?"

"No," responds Ms. Jackson. "Well, maybe. Sandra seems so adult in the things she says, in what she wears. When I was her age, my father punished me if I cursed, and my mother picked out most of my clothes. I would have never dreamed of acting out in school. I was taught to be good."

This was the first of many conversations. Over time, Ms. Jackson realized that, while she disapproved of Sandra's behavior, part of her was envious of Sandra's willfulness and willingness to try out roles and test limits. Separating her own issues from Sandra's allowed Ms. Jackson to be more objective and to acknowledge Sandra's strengths. It allowed her to be there for Sandra in a way she could not before.

Families

"Be a good boy," says Mrs. Tyler, as she kisses her toddler, Dennis, goodbye on his first day at child care. "If he's bad," she says to Mrs. Lewis, his caregiver, "smack him!" She's out the door before Mrs. Lewis can respond.

Mrs. Lewis believes children should not be hit. Over the next few weeks, Mrs. Lewis tries to encourage Mrs. Tyler to think of alternatives to hitting by modeling positive discipline and commenting on what she is doing and why whenever Mrs. Tyler is around. Every day, Mrs. Tyler's last words are "... smack him!"

Mrs. Lewis sends to NAEYC for pamphlets that talk about discipline as a way of promoting self-control. She distributes them to all the parents after a meeting on the topic. Mrs. Lewis and Mrs. Tyler spend several evenings on the phone talking about who toddlers are and how to respond when they do things you do not want them to do. Mrs. Lewis explains why she does not hit children.

One afternoon, Dennis protests more than usual about putting on his coat. He hits and kicks at his mother. "Stop that," she yells. As she lifts her arm to smack him, she catches Mrs. Lewis' eye and stops herself. "What should I do?" she asks. Mrs. Lewis steps in. She says firmly to Dennis, "It's cold outside. You need your coat on." He looks at her. "Your mother is ready to go now. I'll help you put on your coat. Which arm do you want to put in first?"

She helps Dennis put on his coat. "Toddlers can be a handful," she says to his mother. "Let's talk tomorrow about other things we can do when Dennis doesn't want to get dressed at the end of the day." She waves goodbye thinking, "It's a beginning."

Exercises   Here are some exercises that you can try with colleagues to help you think about ways you can discipline individuals and manage a group in ways that promote children's self-control.

1. Reflect on your childhood experiences of discipline. Describe a few times you were disciplined. How did the adults make you feel? How do you think your past experiences influence your interactions with children?

2. Arrange for a colleague to record what you say to children as you manage and discipline. Read aloud what you have said. Do your words promote self-esteem? Do you offer choices? Do you give children information to help them guide their own behavior in the future? Jot down what you might say to children in the following situations. Remember that your words should guide behavior at the same time that they promote self-esteem.

   a. An infant is crying in her crib.

   b. At lunchtime, you encourage a toddler to eat. He screams "no" and pushes his plate of food on the floor.

   c. Two preschoolers refuse to let a third child play with them and call her "dodo head."

   d. A school-age child refuses to wait for the group and runs down the hall and out on the playground before the rest of the class is ready.

3. Evaluate your physical environment to figure out ways it can guide children's behavior. Look at your environment through a child's perspective. Sit at a child's level. Imagine you are a child you work with. What do you see? Are there potentially dangerous situations you can anticipate and correct? Does the environment make it easy for children to take part in daily routines? If not, what changes could you make?

4. Discuss discipline with a parent. How are your approaches similar? How do they differ? How can you effectively communicate your belief that discipline should promote self-control?

5. Ask yourself, "Is there a way I can make transitions easier for children to manage?" Discuss your response with a colleague. List any ideas and incorporate them into your daily practice. Evaluate how they work and adapt them as necessary.

Resources   Galinsky, E., & David, J. (1991). *The preschool years: Family strategies that work from experts and parents.* New York: Ballantine Books.

Honig, A. S. (1989). *Love & learn: Discipline for young children.* Washington, DC: National Association for the Education of Young Children.

National Association for the Education of Young Children. (1986). *Helping children learn self-control.* Washington, DC: Author.

Riley, S. S. (1984). *How to generate values in young children: Integrity, honesty, individuality, self-confidence, and wisdom.* Washington, DC: National Association for the Education of Young Children.

Stone, J. G. (1978). *A guide to discipline.* Washington, DC: National Association for the Education of Young Children.

About the Author:

Amy Laura Dombro, M.S., headed the Bank Street Infant and Family Center from 1976 to 1983. She is now a consultant with Head Start Parent Child Center programs. She is the senior author of The Ordinary is Extraordinary: How Children under Three Learn *(1989, Fireside) and* Sharing the Caring: How to Find the Right Child Care and Make it Work for You and Your Child *(1991, Fireside).*

7 | Valuing Diversity

Diversity means the range of differences among people that we need to take into account if we are to work effectively with children, families, and communities. The concept of diversity includes the perspectives of multiculturalism and nonsexist and antibias education. Diversity encompasses children's individual interests and capabilities, racial and cultural differences, age and gender differences, and language differences. It also includes the social realities that affect children and communities, including availability of economic resources, access to technology, health and safety concerns, demographic make-up, and locale.

Think about the concept of "family," which is a universal human experience, and consider the diverse meanings it may have for children:

- For one child, "family" may mean a mom and a dad and siblings; for another, "family" may mean the grandmother and aunt who raised her; for a third, the two dads who adopted him.

- "Family" may be a mom or a dad, or two households where a child divides his week—mom's house some days, and dad and his new wife's house other days.

- In some situations, "family" may include a person who is hired to care for a child when parents travel or work away from home; in others, "family" may describe three generations who live in the same building and speak a language other than English.

Knowing and recognizing the diversity of family experiences affects the way in which caregivers and teachers make decisions in planning appropriate programs. Some decisions may affect how you think and relate to the children and families in the program; others may affect the content of the curriculum choices. To value these diverse family experiences, you need to think about:

- when and how to speak to children about families;
- which households should receive school notices;
- how, when, and with whom to plan family conferences;
- in what language to communicate with the children's families;
- how families prefer to describe themselves to their children and others;

- how to interpret children's play, especially around family themes

- how to select materials that reflect different kinds of families.

Diversity represents the richness and uniqueness of human life. It is something we want to value and share with the children we work with.

Why include diversity in early childhood?

There are many reasons to include consideration of diversity as a central theme in early childhood programs. When you value diversity, you maximize the positive impact of your program for all your children by:

- building children's positive self-esteem *(when you do this you give them the confidence to reach out to new learning experiences);*

- affirming children's identities with regard to race, ethnicity, gender, religion, handicapping conditions, class *(when you do this you pave the way for children—who are ever fascinated with how they are alike and different from one another—to appreciate human differences as a natural part of life);*

- strengthening ties with families *(when you do this you promote families' involvement with their children's early childhood programs).*

Further, when you include diversity in your work with children, you are preparing them for citizenship in a society where people speak different languages, practice different customs, and embrace different values. By starting in early childhood, you will be helping individuals learn to work together, communicate across their differences, and value just and fair treatment for all. You will also be preparing children to fight bias and discrimination directed toward themselves or other members of society. Preparing children for active participation in a democracy is one of the educational goals proposed by Dewey and early Bank Street leaders (as discussed in the chapter "Principles of the Bank Street Approach").

Making consideration of diversity a major part of your program is particularly important in early childhood because it is during this period, and especially between the ages of 2 and 5, that children become aware of gender, race, ethnicity, disabilities, and other differences among people. Because young children are aware of diversity, you need to be prepared to address it in your work with them. You need to treat their questions and comments seriously and respectfully, just as you would if they were expressing curiosity about nature or other phenomena. Young children also acquire attitudes and values from their families and society about which differences are positive and which are not. How you respond to the ideas they express will influence the feelings and judgments they will form.

When you value diversity, you too become a learner. You learn about the children you work with and the communities they live in. You may also learn about the educational theories, practices, and policies that will strengthen your program's response to diversity. For example, you might choose to learn about second language acquisition or legislation pertaining to low-income or handicapped children. As a teacher or caregiver, you need to be aware of the laws that challenge unequal practices and policies and promote equal educational opportunity.

If you work with children and families from diverse cultural and linguistic backgrounds, the opportunities for valuing diversity in the curriculum may be quite apparent. But if you are working with children from similar backgrounds, you also need to address diversity in the curriculum. You may need to counter stereotypes or misconceptions they have. All children need to be exposed to new experiences and broaden their understanding of how people live.

There are many ways for caregivers and teachers to help children learn about human differences. Margarita, a teacher of 4- and 5-year-olds, encounters chronic illness for the first time in her class. Two children have diabetes and three others have severe allergies. At first, she worries about how to remember who can eat or drink what kinds of things. She thinks of her curriculum and how she can incorporate these aspects of diversity into the children's learning experiences. She begins with a class discussion of favorite foods; she writes down children's responses on a chart "Our favorite foods." Then she leads the children into further discussion about their eating habits, and from these emerge other charts: "Snacks some of us should not have" and "Snacks we can all have." The charts are put up in the room for all to see and are a reminder of the similarities and differences in this group of children. With these charts as a beginning, Margarita develops a curriculum study around health and nutrition, helping the children learn to take good care of themselves and each other.

Underlying a commitment to diversity is a set of beliefs and values. Caregivers and teachers like Margarita share these:

- a sense of trust in others;
- a sense of justice;
- a belief in cooperation and shared learning;
- a belief that all children can be competent;
- a belief that all children can be proud of their culture and heritage;
- a belief that all children can be curious about and learn to accept human similarities and differences;
- a sense of the individuality of each child;

• a sense that a group of children is a small society where there is fairness, opportunity, caring, and satisfaction for all its members.

When you value diversity, you are addressing the needs of the "whole child" and promoting both affective and cognitive development. You are recognizing that children live in diverse social and physical environments. You are imparting a sense of shared humanity.

How can you incorporate diversity into early childhood?

First, you need to spend time thinking about your own beliefs, behaviors, and knowledge about diversity. Next, think about the lives and experiences of your children and their families and communities. Then you will be ready to plan curricula that expand your own vision, capitalize on children's experiences, and provide new learning experiences. Finally, you need to consider your role as a policy maker and how the policies in your program respond to issues of diversity.

You as Caregiver or Teacher

There are many ways to begin thinking about how to incorporate diversity into your early childhood setting:

- For some caregivers and teachers, gender difference is a comfortable starting point. They think seriously about how boys and girls are influenced by teaching decisions, by the arrangement of the environment, and by new experiences that encourage initiative and competence in both sexes.

- For others, the starting point may be their understanding of racial and economic differences. They might choose experiences that help balance and strengthen educational opportunities for children of different racial, cultural, and economic backgrounds.

- Others count on their knowledge of different languages to help all children learn other languages and about other cultures.

- Many teachers wish to understand more about diversity because they feel a strong desire to foster fairness, interdependence, and peace among individuals. They wish to have those values influence their work with children.

- For yet others, the starting point is the challenge of understanding and nurturing different learning styles. As a result, they might find it more comfortable to begin by learning how to observe, document, and assess learning from this perspective.

No matter where you begin, you will have to think about the beliefs and attitudes about human beings that you want to promote in your program. Related to this, is the necessity of assessing your own behavior and looking at what you say and do to communicate to children that you value diversity. Children look to you as a model of how they should act toward others. Here are some guidelines:

- Monitor the language you use to describe situations so that your words carry a message of inclusion, knowledge, and acceptance of others. You might say, "speakers of another language" rather than "non-English speakers," or "we teach children who come from many places" rather than "we teach immigrants."

- Explicitly counter prejudice and bias. Young children do notice differences. When a 4-year-old says his Chinese friend talks "funny," explain, "Mark is learning English. He also speaks Chinese because his family does. That's why he sounds different. Maybe he can teach us some Chinese words." Think about how to intervene when you hear a remark like, "I don't want to sit next to you because your face is black." Make it clear that prejudiced remarks or discriminatory behavior hurt other people's feelings and are not allowed in your group.

- Study anti-bias curricula which can expand your understanding of stereotypes and racial, gender, and cultural differences and similarities. They can provide you with ways to develop anti-bias materials and change discriminatory behavior (Derman-Sparks, 1989; Williams et al., 1985).

The way you are treated as a member of a racial or ethnic group, as a man or woman, is likely to affect how you treat others. It is important, then, to become aware of ways in which your own individuality and diverse experiences are valued. Ask yourself:

- What kinds of practices and policies at work or elsewhere are supportive of me? What other opportunities would I like?

- Where do I myself encounter discrimination or bias? What can I do to change it?

The Children
Ask yourself if children find their images, interests, or experiences reflected in your program and its environment.

- Do boys and girls feel free to play and work in all the areas of the room? If you have children of diverse economic backgrounds, is their range of experience represented in the curriculum? In a study of families, for example, you can ask children, "What is your favorite part of where you live?" which emphasizes the child's use of space, rather than, "How many rooms are there?"

- Examine your selection of books, pictures, tapes, and stories. Do they represent diverse cultures, races, ages, and the interests of the children in your group. Do they avoid stereotypes?

- Does your study of the community include services and institutions used by people of different socioeconomic levels, such as free medical clinics and used clothing stores, and those used by people of different cultural backgrounds, such as bodegas and synagogues?

Think about what you know about your children's styles of learning and expressing what they know. Providing opportunities for learning, and for demonstrating what is learned, in diverse ways is the essence of educating children, as individuals and as members of a group.

Do you know which children engage with learning by approaching materials first, which children engage first with other children and usually undertake tasks with a friend, which children need to spend a little time with you or with another adult before joining in? It is important to observe and document a child's strengths and interests and build on them as you lead him to new learnings. When you recognize that one child learns best through music and movement, that another child newly arrived in the United States is fascinated with the airplanes that transported him, and that a child in a wheelchair is a leader in the class, you can build individually appropriate curriculum. (You can read more about observational techniques in the chapter "Observing and Recording Children's Behavior.")

Consider the individual circumstances of the children's lives as you plan ways in which your program can nurture them. You may confront such issues as overindulgence, complicated divorce arrangements, lack of adult supervision, and over-scheduling. Your sensitivity to the different circumstances and needs of the children in your program can be reflected in numerous ways:

- In some cases, nurturing comes from a daily bag of fruit and cheese you may have in the class; in other cases, it is the extra rest time for the child who does not get enough sleep at home.

- For another child, the nurturing may come in reassuring him which day of the week it is, and to which household he goes on that day.

- Perhaps you will lend one child a book from the class library to keep him company at bedtime, or send a note home to say that the child lost a tooth today and it is in an envelope in the backpack.

Apply your knowledge of child development to help children learn about and appreciate diversity.

- **Preschoolers** are interested in their own emotional lives and have the capacity to empathize, although from an egocentric perspective. They comfort a friend who is crying or offer a stuffed animal to a sick parent. Preschoolers cannot understand the socioeconomic and political causes of homelessness, but they can understand how people might feel when they do not have a place to live or put their belongings.

- **Young school-age children** are better able than preschoolers to understand people who differ from them. They may be interested in the scientific explanation of different skin colors and fascinated with different ways of speaking and writing. Issues of fairness and justice in the classroom, on the playground, and at home engage the young school-age child's capacity to think in logical and nonegocentric ways. This ability can serve as a basis for exposing 5- through 8-year-olds to social conditions that give rise to discrimination, inequity, and injustice. In discussions, you follow their lead, using their questions or events in the classroom as a springboard for further exploration. For example, when a 7-year-old observes that it is not fair that some people do not have enough to eat, you use this as an opportunity to explore and extend children's thinking about social issues. Keep in mind that young school-age children are still limited in their ability to understand complex cause-and-effect relationships and abstract notions.

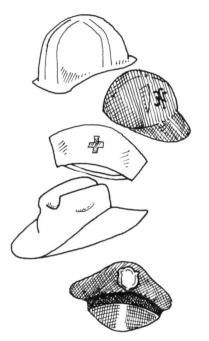

The Family and the Community

Think about what you know about the social influences in your children's lives. What is their community like, and how can you incorporate it into your curriculum?

- **Work**. It is important to find out about the work your families do, since it shapes their experiences and their lives. Children need to learn that all kinds of workers—lawyers, seamstresses, computer programmers, migrant workers, secretaries, doctors, clergymen, pilots, bus drivers, construction workers, sanitation workers, nurses, teachers, butchers—make a community that serves everyone.

- **Demographics**. In the last ten years, there have been demographic changes that have made many communities more diverse. Knowing about population changes in your students' communities helps you think about different languages, different traditions, different family structures, different experiences with schooling, and different expectations about the relationships between families and teachers. In some cultural groups, for example, school and home relationships are more formal than those common in America, and there is no expectation that home and school should create partnerships in making school decisions. If you are unaware of these cultural

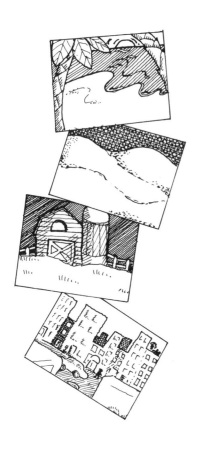

differences, you may misunderstand parents' seeming lack of involvement in their children's lives in school.

- **Urban, suburban, and rural locales.** Every location has its advantages and disadvantages. The urban teacher longs for children to be able see chickens being born and crops picked each season. The teacher of migrant children wishes for trips to museums, airports, and high bridges. The suburban teacher struggles with finding activities that are less homogeneous and predictable in order to immerse her children in a very different experience. All these teachers who are eager to offer something different are on the right track. Begin by understanding what you do have, and capitalize on the learning value inherent in your own community, and then continue your search for the live chicks, the museums, and the unpredictable subway ride as means for expanding everyone's world.

- **Economic conditions.** Issues of poverty, neglect, abuse, and poor health are of major import in many programs that serve young children. These concerns, largely economic in origin, are also part of sensitivity to diversity: all children, at whatever economic level, require careful educational decisions and a curriculum that enables them to feel confident and competent. They need access to toys, books, and age-appropriate materials that will stimulate them and help them learn; for some children, such access may come only in their early childhood education setting. Broken toys, torn books, and pencils that do not write convey the message "you are not valued." As a caregiver or teacher, you need to be aware of socioeconomic conditions as you work with parents or other family members who care for the children, and as you think of the services which may be available to them within or outside of the school.

- **Holidays and celebrations.** The ideas in this Guide discourage the use of holidays as the main source for curriculum decisions, and encourage you instead to select content that includes looking at diversity within the context of a study. For example, if the children are making books about themselves as part of a study, you might suggest that they give the books to their families on a special day of their choice. One child might give the book as a Christmas present; another may choose a birthday; a third may select Father's Day; and yet another may select Chanukah. You can also discuss holidays with children to explore their understanding of why they do not have school or why a particular day is important to some people. These discussions can be part of "social studies" or "study of people," and can help balance the misinformation, commercialization, and media hype that surround most holidays. They also deal with the "here and now" concerns of the young child: "Why is there school tomorrow?"

Another strategy for dealing with holidays and celebrations is to focus on seasonal changes as a way of including and responding to diverse traditions. In the fall, a Harvest Fair can include different traditions centered around this time: baking, canning, sharing meals, dancing, reading scary stories, singing harvest songs, raking leaves, making prints, moving to another migrant community, and making warmer clothes. A winter celebration may include a cluster of traditions that focus on the changes brought in by the cold, the shortest day of the year, winter sports, and family celebrations of many sorts. In spring, the sense of renewal and rebirth can be a catalyst for other celebrations and give rise to studies related to natural sciences, such as the hatching of chicks and the preservation of resources and the environment. These ideas can serve as the basis for including holidays and celebrations in your curriculum; however, it is important that you adapt them to serve the individual needs, values, and traditions of your program and your community.

You as Policy Maker

Think about what you know about cultures, languages, races, geographic influences, history, literature, and art that are different from your own experiences.

- Be aware of what you know and what you do not know. This is the first step in finding out what kind of help and resources you may need in order to serve diverse populations of children. This important step will highlight your own strengths, and it will help you decide when to turn to your community, your families, the library, a film, or a resource book to provide new knowledge you may need to expand the children's possibilities—and your own. Gathering resource materials will also allow you to build a reference library to help you make decisions about many issues related to diversity.

- Invite others to come to your program to share their knowledge and experiences. This, too, is a good starting point because it teaches the children that all people have something to offer, and it provides *you* with an easy way to learn.

- Share ideas with other caregivers and teachers who work with children from similar linguistic and cultural backgrounds. In this way, you will be expanding the resources available to you and creating a community of learners. After a series of staff meetings to discuss curriculum ideas for migrant school children in their classes, one of the teachers said, "I just realized that we have no local people to pick the crops, so we'd better be less prejudiced about the migrant laborers. I now appreciate how important they are to all of our lives." As you deal with issues of diversity, you may also find that you are struggling with issues of economic, social, and educational equity, as these teachers did.

Think about policies in your program and think about how they serve your families needs. The following examples will help you think of and examine other policies in your own programs.

家庭
My Family MI FAMILIA
הַמִשְׁפָּחָה שֶׁלִי
MIO ZAMIGLIA

- **Family conferences**. Most teachers and programs plan conferences with parents. Yet, in many cases, other adults, such as grandparents or aunts, may be involved in raising the child. It is more inclusive and respectful of diversity to plan "family" rather than "parent" conferences. Think about how you set up family conferences. Are they scheduled at convenient times? Will families need to make special work or child care arrangements to meet with you? Can you offer a choice of schedules?

- **Home language**. Parents may need—or want—to speak to their children in the language and manner native to their culture. If your program uses a language of instruction different from the children's native language, it is important to encourage families to be natural and authentic with their children and to communicate in ways they find comfortable. Reassure them that knowing two languages is not only possible but desirable, and will come in time.

- **New families**. Each program has its own system for entering newcomers. When you have new families, do not assume that their previous experience was in a program similar to yours. Encourage visits before enrolling, collect pictures of your program in action, prepare tours or information sessions about your program. When you work with families who are new to your community, prepare information packets and encourage their participation in field trips, which will help them learn about places to take their children in the future. In some cases, families new to the country may need guidance in relation to community resources, such as doctors, jobs, community services, language courses, recreational facilities, and transportation.

- **Children with disabilities**. Legislation—and good educational practice—requires that children with disabilities be placed in the "least restrictive environment" that can still provide them with appropriate education. How you think about children with special needs is important in your acquiring the knowledge and seeking the resources to help them gain the competence, pride, interest in learning, and respect that are the right of all the children in the program. Understanding a specific disability, and knowing the educational practices that are most helpful in addressing it, might affect the way you arrange your program materials or classroom, the conversations you will have with other children when their curiosity gives rise to questions or comments, and how you go about obtaining the parental input that is required for making individualized educational plans for special needs children.

Valuing diversity is a challenge. It requires attention to who you are as a caregiver or teacher, who your children, families, and communities are, and what your program is like. It offers opportunities to learn about yourself and to help children value themselves and others.

Infants and Toddlers

Anna Walters and Susan Fein work in an infant-toddler center located in a suburban hospital. They care for children of hospital staff, many of whom come from other countries with diverse child-rearing practices and languages. Anna and Susan plan ways of learning about these differences, about how children and families communicate, and about how to make this knowledge explicit and public so that the families can learn about each other.

They first ask the families to write down the words their children use when they need something. They want to ensure that they can understand the children and respond to their needs. Anna and Susan post a chart in the room with this information on it:

Putting what you know about diversity into action

Our children's favorite words when they need something:

Lucy:	"No tete"	means "no bottle"
Paco:	"Oto"	means "otro" or "another one"
Katie:	"Uppy"	means "pick me up"
Lin:	"Sto"	means "stop" and "no more"
Scott:	"Baba juice"	means "bottle of juice"
Andy:	"No pamper"	means "I am going to the potty by myself"

Later on in the year, they continue this practice by collecting information on the children's favorite music, stories, and toys. All this is written down on charts for the caregivers and families to see. By the end of the year, they have learned a great deal. Lucy started using the cup when she came to the center. Paco's mother is a pediatric nurse who works with Spanish-speaking families; she uses Spanish when talking to Paco to foster his bilingual development.

Katie has several older siblings who love carrying her around. Lin is from Taiwan and her father will work at the hospital for two years before returning to Taiwan. Scott loves taking his juice from a bottle and other liquids from a cup. Andy stopped using diapers last summer, before coming to the program.

They have also learned that some of the families take long airplane trips to return home for important holidays. So the center has toy airplanes and pictures of families going on trips. Anna and Susan help prepare the children for these trips by talking about them. They take photos of all the children, the room, and themselves and put them in a small album for the departing child to take on the trip. They have learned that some of the families address them (the caregivers) by their first names, Anna and Susan, while others, coming from more formal traditions, call them Miss Walters and Mrs. Fein. They have also learned to work with families to make labels for the classroom materials and to write notices in several languages.

In this infant/toddler program, valuing diversity means building close ties with families. It all started with the teachers' invitation to the families to "Tell us what it means when we don't understand your child." To the families new to the community and the program, this said, "Welcome, we think that your language, ideas, and lifestyles are important to share with us and with others."

Preschoolers

In her classroom of 3- and 4-year-olds, Akiko has children from several cultural backgrounds, some born in the United States, some from other countries. They have been studying their families, and talking about whom they live with, what they like to do at home, and the kinds of foods their families eat. Discussions about younger siblings and visits by babies to the program have provoked a lot of interest. Akiko has decided to collect a variety of clothes (including kimonos and dashikis), dolls, and baby clothes for the dramatic play area. She has also put up magazine photos of families from many parts of the world.

Zack and Cindy are involved in their favorite activity, playing "Mommy and Daddy." Zack places two dolls in a backpack and puts it on. Cindy wraps a scarf around her head and another around her hips. She looks at a photo on the wall, as if to make sure she has got the placing of the scarves right. Then she unties the scarf on her hips, places a doll inside, and ties it up again. She and Zack put a few more dolls in the baby carriage and push it toward Akiko, who comments, "Isn't it great how parents carry babies in so many different ways!" Zack smiles and says, "I really like the backpack. My daddy has one for my little sister." Cindy adds, "I like scarves for *everything*. I'm going to get one to put around my neck!"

Akiko smiles, seeing that the children's play reflects their understanding of diversity. She feels she has worked hard to include materials and to arrange the room in ways that encourage many kinds of play. She also knows that with children of this age, the best place to begin is with their interest in families and their own experiences.

Young School-Age Children

A first grade teacher, Jean-Marie, thinks about the characteristics of her group and her community as she plans the direction and content of the curriculum study of libraries and bookstores. The program is located in a suburban community which has several bookstores, a town library, and a community college with a library and a store that sells secondhand books. She plans activities that will differentiate between the concepts of making books, borrowing books, and buying new and used books.

Jean-Marie plans to help the children read, express their ideas through illustration and writing, classify different types of books, and learn about bookmaking, printing, and illustrating. But she also decides to include the diverse language experiences of her students and to build on their individual strengths in drawing, writing, and bookmaking. As she develops the curriculum, she comes up with the following activities:

- having a meeting with the children to ask them what they know about libraries and bookstores, and what new things they may want to know *(this helps the teacher learn what previous experiences with books the children have had and to determine what they understand about libraries and bookstores)*;

- organizing the classroom library to include books written in the native languages of some of the children, and books in English that depict children of diverse cultural or racial backgrounds *(this helps reinforce a sense of belonging for all class members)*;

- asking parents to take dictation of stories in their native languages when children are writing *(this recognizes that all children can express their thinking best in the language they are most familiar with)*;

- asking family members to share a story they heard or read when they were children *(this includes oral as well as written traditions, and expands everyone's understanding of stories)*;

- taking field trips to libraries, bookstores, secondhand bookstores, and developing trip-boards to record these experiences *(this offers common experiences for the whole group and fosters group life)*;

115

- having children work in teams of writers, illustrators, and bookmakers in order to have children share each other's different strengths *(this allows each child to contribute his or her skill and experience)*;

- inviting book sellers, writers, and librarians to come and talk about their different jobs *(this provides opportunities to talk about different careers and the skills and training needed for each job)*;

- building play libraries and bookstores in the block area to understand the concepts of borrowing and selling, and the use of money and library cards *(this integrates several curriculum areas)*;

- collecting fairy tales from different cultural traditions and finding their similarities and differences *(this emphasizes the common humanity portrayed in folk literature)*;

- making charts to illustrate where books were printed or the languages in which they are written *(this fosters understanding that books are made in many parts of the world)*. The chart might look like this:

Name of Book	Author's Last Name	Language Written	Place Printed
Joseph had a Little Overcoat	Taback	English	Colombia
Toad is the Uncle of Heaven	Lee	English	Japan
The Giving Tree	Silverstein	English	UnitedStates
El Cuento de Ferdinando	Leaf	Spanish	United States
El Gusto	Rius and Puig	Spanish	Spain
Le Prince et la Souris Blanche	Coulibaly	French	Cote d'Ivoire

Jean-Marie also considers what kind of culminating activity would be appropriate. She thinks that sharing the classroom library with other first graders would give her children a sense of accomplishment and expose the others to cultural and linguistic diversity in literature.

Families

Mr. and Mrs. Clark have just had a conference at their children's school, where the reading/writing process and invented spelling are part of the curriculum. They are very concerned, because this curriculum approach is new to them and so different from the way they were taught in school. They wonder whether their children are learning what they need to know to succeed in school and later in life. The Clarks know that their children, Nicky, 5 years, and Jason, 7 years, are interested in reading. They see them reading cereal boxes, sports books, cassette labels, and birthday cards at home. They want to understand better what the teachers are telling them about the curriculum. The school has suggested that all parents talk to their children about what they read or write in school. The teachers have also suggested that parents call or send a note if they have further concerns.

During the next few weeks, the Clarks ask Nicky and Jason to tell them about what they are writing in school. Nicky explains that he sometimes just writes down his ideas the way they sound. At other times, he dictates to a teacher or into a tape recorder, which later he transcribes into in his writing book. Jason, who is in second grade, describes how his class dictated a letter to the lady at the museum who had shown them the fossils. He says,

> The teacher wrote down what we said on the chart. When she was finished, she told us that the names of people and places begin with capital letters and that thank-you letters are important to send to people who helped us. She also asked us to pick two words from the thank-you letter and put them in our writing book to remember them later. I picked the words "fossil" and "subway" because they both have "s" sounds, like the one in the middle of my name, Jason.

Mr. and Mrs. Clark intend to continue to ask the school about their sons' work, but they are beginning to understand what the teachers mean about children finding ideas that are interesting to them and expressing them in letters, stories, and tapes. They are impressed with Jason's knowledge about thank-you letters, capitals, and "s" sounds.

The teachers are trying to communicate with all parents about the different ways they teach literacy. The school recognizes how important it is to keep the dialogue open between parents and teachers if they are to succeed at educating children.

Exercises

Here are some exercises for you to do by yourself or with colleagues to help you apply what you have learned about diversity and young children.

1. Ask yourself which is your preferred mode for learning. Do you have to be actively involved and then read about it, or do you gather a lot of reading material first and then apply it? Do you like trying new things by yourself, or with a peer, or with a group of people? Think about your favorite part of your own teaching day. Is it when you read stories to children, or do you prefer the walks

to the local park when the children ask questions about nature, or do you thrive on the type of logic they use to settle an argument? Do you look forward to the quiet time when they write, or the outdoor time when they hang from their feet on the jungle-gym? Now summarize what you know about your own preferred way of learning and teaching.

2. Now ask yourself similar questions about the children with whom you work. Which parts of the day and what kinds of activities do individual children prefer? Do you tend to notice the children who are more like you or different from you? Use this information to think about your group and about your curriculum. Is it flexible and varied enough to offer opportunities to foster initiative and competence?

3. Next, shift your focus to your school, program, and community. Is there any aspect of diversity that makes your program different from most others? Consider family types, cultures, economic issues, languages, health concerns, and access to technology. How do the mission and the policies of your program respond to different aspects of diversity?

4. Think about experiences outside of school that will foster a respect for diversity. Plan field trips that will help you create common experiences. Trips to museums or radio stations and access to magazines, like *National Geographic*, or newspapers in different languages can validate experiences for some and expand horizons for others.

5. Review the reasons why valuing diversity is important. Make up your own list of why you want to incorporate diversity in your early childhood setting. Brainstorm with a colleague.

6. Keep informed on advances in technology that provide you with access to information, or resources that will enrich your knowledge about other fields and their impact on education.

7. Think about your own experiences and the times when you could express your individuality. Then, recall the times when you felt that you were not respected or that you were being stereotyped. Were you able to alter the discriminatory behavior? Reflecting on our own experiences helps us empathize with children and respect their individuality.

8. Be vigilant about the ways in which you model behavior or affect others. How do your behaviors, attitudes, curriculum choices, and use of resources demonstrate respect for children, as individuals and as members of groups? Share your insights with a colleague, and together think of ways to broaden your own understanding and appreciation of diversity.

Banks, J., & Banks, C. M. (Eds.). (1989). *Multicultural education: Issues and perspectives*. Boston: Allyn & Bacon.

Comer, J. (1989). Racism and the education of young children. In F. Rust & L. Williams (Eds.), *The care and education of young children: Expanding contexts, sharpening focus*. New York: Teachers College Press.

Cuffaro, H. (1975). Reevaluating basic premises: Curricula free of sexism. *Young Children, 30,* 469-478.

Derman-Sparks, L., & A.B.C. Task Force Staff. (1989). *The anti-bias curriculum: Tools for empowering young children*. Washington, DC: National Association for the Education of Young Children.

Dewey, J. (1956). *The child and the curriculum and the school and society*. Chicago: The University of Chicago Press.

Gardner, H. (1983). *Frames of mind: The theory of multiple intelligences*. New York: Basic Books.

Grant, C. (1989). Equity, equality, and classroom life. In W. G. Secada (Ed.), *Equity in education*. London: Falmer Press.

Moll, L. (1990). Creating zones of possibilities: Combining social contexts for instruction. In L. Moll (Ed.), *Vygotsky and education: Instructional implications and applications of sociohistorical psychology*. Cambridge: Cambridge University Press.

Ramsey, P. G. (1987). *Teaching and learning in a diverse world: Multicultural education for young children*. New York: Teachers College Press.

Williams, L. R., & De Gaetano, Y. (1985). *Alerta: A multicultural, bilingual approach to teaching young children*. Menlo Park, CA: Addison-Wesley.

About the Author:

Maritza B. Macdonald , M.S., is a faculty member in the Graduate School at Bank Street College. She directs the Preservice Program and teaches curriculum courses for teachers and administrators. Mrs. Macdonald is a doctoral candidate at Teachers College, Columbia University. Her professional interests include issues of diversity, accountability, and bilingualism.

8

Creating Curriculum in Early Childhood

What is curriculum?

At Bank Street, we think of curriculum not as a series of recipes for activities, but rather as the opportunities for experience you offer children that help them deepen their understanding of the world. The curriculum is the sum of those opportunities and it is created through a dynamic process of planning and decision making.

When you plan curriculum, every decision you make affects what children learn and how they feel about themselves as learners. Every day, you make important decisions about how children use the physical environment, materials, and time, and about how they work with each other. In doing that, you are developing your curriculum. These decisions are based on your understanding of how children grow and learn, and on your special knowledge of the individual children in your class or program. Let us look at some examples of the kinds of decisions you make:

- The physical space of your program is the laboratory for children's learning; it is where you help them ask and answer their questions and work out their thinking. Decisions you make about room arrangement can support children's learning. For instance, Luis, a kindergarten teacher, has learned from experience that putting the art supplies across the room from the sink makes it difficult for children to assume responsibility for a project from beginning to end. Inevitably, spills and messes occur during clean-up. By placing the art table next to the sink, with painting supplies on clearly labeled shelves close by, Luis teaches children to be in charge of their work, which includes clean-up.

- The materials you decide to make available are tools of the curriculum. Materials children can touch and move like blocks, playdough, paint, collage, clay, sand, and water provide children with opportunities to re-create and symbolize their observations of the world. Such materials can be used by children of varying ages, although they will be used differently. Thus, blocks can be used by 16-month-old Martha to load and empty a "fill and dump can," by 4-year-old Jenny to construct tall buildings, and by 6-year-old Marcus to recreate the airport visited earlier in the week.

- Decisions you make about the daily schedule also shape curriculum. For example, in her family day care home, Sandra

alternates active and quiet times during the day; after the playground time, she reads stories to the children and plays soft music. Mrs. James, teacher of a multi-age group of 5- and 6-year-olds, knows that children this age benefit from a long, uninterrupted work period to explore materials. Therefore, she plans an extended work period from 9:15 to 10:45 a.m. each day, during which children may choose several activities. (You can read more about physical environment, materials, and schedule in the chapter "The Learning Environment.")

- Helping children develop social relationships is also part of curriculum planning. Rose, a preschool teacher, knows that working in small groups enables 4-year-olds to handle both taking turns and their emerging friendships. For this reason, she invites a parent volunteer to help out with small-group cooking activities on Thursday mornings. (You can read more about social relationships in the chapter "The Group Process.")

All of these decisions are curriculum decisions. In this chapter, we discuss why a dynamic approach to curriculum planning is important and how you do it, and then give you some examples of curriculum experiences for different age groups. There are exercises for you to do with your colleagues to help you understand better how to develop curriculum.

Why is it important for you to be a curriculum planner?

You and the children both benefit from a dynamic approach to curriculum development. By dynamic, we mean an approach that allows you to change and modify your plans easily in response to things that happen in the course of the day—an unexpected question that can lead to an interesting discussion, an opportunity to have a parent share a special skill with the children. This approach allows you to look carefully at children and create a flexible program that meets their needs.

Like many caregivers or teachers, you may have to work within curriculum structures based on federal, state, or local mandates. The framework we provide will help you tailor prescribed curriculum to the needs of your program and individual children. As curriculum creator rather than consumer of pre-packaged curriculum materials, you can feel good about curriculum decisions you make because they will be based on your knowledge of the children in your program and will thus be appropriate for them.

Because you observe the children, you are able to make subtle changes in your program to meet individual or group needs. Consider these examples:

- A caregiver of toddlers, wanting children to feel competent and knowing that they often get impatient waiting for a turn to pour juice, provides several small pitchers at snack time.

- Noticing that the children have lost interest in dramatic play, a preschool teacher introduces new props, thus extending their ideas for play.
- A teacher of young school-age children plans a second trip to the bus station because the children are trying to accurately construct, in the classroom, a bus station made of crates and cardboard.

These are all curriculum decisions, facilitated by the flexible framework of a dynamic approach.

A dynamic approach to curriculum development forces you to think about what you do and why you do it, rather than simply following a prescribed series of activities. You make your curriculum decisions on the basis of what you believe is important about children at this stage of development, the individual children in your program, learning, and the function of education in society. You alter or modify your plans on the basis of what actually happens in the classroom. Assuming the role of decision maker enhances the sense of purpose you feel about your work.

Bank Street has always viewed the caregiver or teacher as a curriculum developer. When you assume a leadership role in developing curriculum for your program, everyone benefits—teaching is more exciting for you, and children's learning is deeper and more exciting for them. Carefully planning your work with children makes you a better teacher.

How do you develop curriculum?

Curriculum development is guided by what you know about how children grow and learn. This includes knowing how children develop, knowing that social influences affect them, that children learn by active exploration, that certain content is particularly engaging for children of a given age, and that emotional development plays a central part in children's growth and learning. It also includes listening carefully to the children themselves. Children's questions are what enliven and give direction to your curriculum. Many of these questions may be thought of as leading to investigations in the social studies curriculum. Later on, we describe how social studies can be used to integrate other learning experiences. Let us look at how your knowledge of children's growth and learning shapes curriculum decisions.

Curriculum planning must be based on your knowledge of child development.

Laura, a family day care provider, knows each child in her group is behaving appropriately for his or her age in the sandbox when she observes Jason, age 2, filling and dumping sand in a pail, while 3-year-old Tory imitates two 4-year-olds busily making "blueberry pies," and Josh, also 3 years old but not yet aware of the consequences of his actions, happens to push his truck right through the middle of everyone's play. Laura also knows that children develop at different rates. Although both Tory and Josh are 3 years old, Tory is beginning to engage in cooperative play, while Josh continues to play alongside others, but is not yet capable of sustained interaction.

Caregivers and teachers provide opportunities for learning, knowing that children's ability to make sense of the world is different at each stage of development. For example, 5-month-old Pete experiences the world through his senses and bodily movements as he grasps, sucks, and pats the soft blocks his caregiver has placed on his blanket in front of him. Ricky, 4 years old, clarifies and refines his ideas about the world in his play. After a visit to the pet store, he builds a store out of blocks and pretends to be the "man who sells fish and puppies." Eight-year-old Becky, guided by her teacher, first molds plasticene in a pan and then pours water in, observing how islands exist beneath the water. At her stage of development, Becky can begin to think in logical ways; she decides to "test out" how a volcano can form an island.

Knowing that social influences affect children in your program helps you plan curriculum that is sensitive to their personal experiences and interests.

Social influences affecting children include family life, cultural background, and community issues and concerns. For example, Margaret, a first grade teacher, knows that 6-year-old Celia, recently arrived from the Philippines, is homesick for family and friends. A conversation with Celia's mother about holidays in the Philippines helps Margaret make a plan to welcome Celia's family into the classroom. Celia's mother will come to school on the Patron Saint's Day in the family's hometown to make Suman (a rice treat) with the class. Think about the children in your program. What are their cultural backgrounds, languages, and family structures?

By observing, listening, and questioning, you can learn about children, their lives, and their families, and use that knowledge to make curriculum decisions that engage children's interests. For example, Ms. Burton spoke with Ramon's father yesterday about Ramon's work in the classroom and learned that next week, Ramon will visit his grandfather in Puerto Rico for the first time. Because of this, at story time she reads a book about a boy taking a plane trip.

Children's daily lives are an important factor in curriculum decisions. The locale of your program affects your planning. When they wake up in the morning, do children in your program hear sirens, traffic, or birds chirping? Children's interests and concerns come from what they see and hear each day.

As you make curriculum decisions, think about children's everyday experiences as these teachers did: Wanting to show children how print is used in the environment, Janice takes her class of urban first graders to observe and photograph traffic signs on the busy street outside their school, while Margie, teaching in a suburb, takes children from her second grade class to a nearby railroad station where they study train schedules and billboards. (To learn more about the social influences that affect children, you can read the chapter "Valuing Diversity.")

Knowing that children learn through firsthand observation, play, and direct experience influences decisions you make about curriculum.

Children need to take hold of an idea and make it their own. For example, Brenda is a teacher in an interage class of 5- through 7-year-olds in a nongraded elementary school. She knows that children learn best when they first observe, and then, through dramatic play, painting, construction, and discussion, re-create and reveal what they know and what they are confused about, thereby suggesting next steps for curriculum planning. For a study of the marketplace, Brenda plans a trip to the apple orchard nearby. On the trip, children talk with workers, pick apples, and bring several baskets full of apples back to school. Afterwards, they choose their own ways of recreating the experience. When they do this, children engage in active thinking about what they have seen. Some children reconstruct the orchard trip with blocks, using different colors of plasticene for apples and cardboard for trees; others paint a colorful mural. Small groups of children take turns making applesauce. Brenda plans some additional cooking experiences so that they can think more about how cooking affects apples.

As children learn about their world through concrete experiences, they discover how things and ideas relate to each other.

This happens best when you plan experiences that build on each other. While on a neighborhood walk, Mr. Rosco and his preschoolers see a letter carrier transferring letters from a mailbox to her truck. The children ask many questions such as "Where are you taking the letters?" "Are there any magazines there?" and "Is there a letter for me?" Back in the classroom, Mr. Rosco and the children discuss what they saw. He records all the children's questions about the letter carrier and the mail on a chart. Then he plans a visit to the post office so children can gather firsthand information to answer their questions. Following the trip, the children use hollow blocks to recreate the post office, with Mr. Rosco providing props (a plastic mail carrier's hat, a mailbox, and some mailbags) to stimulate their play. He has placed many kinds of paper, envelopes, stamps, and ink pads on the writing table so that the children can "write" letters with scribbles and invented spelling to mail in their post office. Taking the spontaneous experience of seeing the letter carrier, Mr. Rosco ex-

tends it so children can ask new questions, make discoveries, and construct meaning out of the connections and relationships they see. Thus, out of the children's questions and interests, their teacher has developed a social studies unit.

Addressing children's emotions is also part of curriculum development.

Young children have very strong feelings. By observing children and listening to them as they talk with you and their peers, you can begin to understand how they feel inside and identify their questions and confusions. You can use this information to figure out how to be sensitive to children's emotional lives in your curriculum.

Young children do have fears. No matter how much you wish you could shelter them, children encounter frightening scenes as they watch TV and walk down a city street. Their fears may center around experiences they have had or someone they know has had. Some fears may be imagined, although nightmares and monsters seem very real to young children, who cannot always distinguish fantasy from reality. They may be frightened of bad weather, racial unrest, or death.

Curriculum includes discussions about why the class guinea pig has died, what a hurricane is, or why people go to war. Preschoolers and young school-age children may want to talk about what makes friends angry at each other and ways they can deal with their feelings. They need opportunities to express their concerns through dramatic play, story writing, art, and other areas of the curriculum. When one of their classmates is hospitalized, a group of 4-year-olds begin asking questions about hospitals and why people get sick. This is the time for their teacher to think about taking a field trip to a hospital, inviting parents who work in the health field to talk with the class about their jobs, and adding a doctor's kit and related props to the dramatic play area.

Children's emotional lives also include moments of joy, excitement, and exuberance. It is important to build these into your curriculum, for example, by celebrating a new baby in a child's family, talking about an impending trip, or creating a dance to show how a puppy walks. When first graders cannot stop talking about the warm spring weather and the "greening" of the drab winter landscape, you may decide to plant seeds indoors or outdoors and study seasonal changes.

Throughout early childhood, children are learning about themselves and their social world.

The following overview of children's interest and abilities at different ages will help you develop curriculum that engages them in learning. (This information will be familiar to you if you have read the chapter "Child Development.") These general descriptions of infants through 8-year-olds can serve as a guide to planning curriculum, supplemented by knowledge of your individual children and their relevant experiences.

- **Infants** are learning through their senses—seeing, hearing, tasting, smelling—and through their physical activity. Their initial activities, such as sucking on their fingers and kicking their feet, are focused on themselves. In a few months, more of their activity is directed toward the external world as they reach for things and smile at familiar people. As they become independently mobile—crawling and eventually walking—they explore the world even more. They are learning all the time, as they go through the daily routines of sleeping, eating, and diapering, and as they establish trusting relationships with adults.

- **Toddlers** demonstrate increased autonomy and mobility, as well as beginning language and abstract thought. They explore their immediate environment in active, physical ways. They use their large muscles to climb and run or explore materials by splashing water, pounding playdough, or drawing big circles. As toddlers get older, the world of self expands to include other things and people—the neighbor's dog, the shop where snack is purchased, a favorite cousin. Familiar activities may be expressed in pretend play. Daily routines and primary relationships continue to be at the core of their learning and constitute the essence of their curriculum.

- **Three- and four-year-olds** focus many of their interests on the world they know best—their family relationships. They take on family roles in their play, pretending to be a parent at home or at work, a baby, or a grandparent. They are interested in learning about what families do, how they shop, cook, get around, and have fun. They are interested in the work of adults, such as the fireman, hairdresser, librarian, or bus driver. They work hard to make sense of the world, based on what they already know. A 4-year-old tells her teacher that on the way to school she saw a nurse. When her teacher asks how she knew the person was a nurse, she replies, "She was wearing white shoes." This explanation makes sense to the child, who had recently visited a hospital where she saw many nurses wearing white shoes. Preschoolers' questions concern everyday life. They use their senses to examine and investigate, as they observe the environment piece by piece. Through their play, they try out roles, express their concerns, and clarify their ideas. It is helpful to think of the child's expanding world in terms of concentric circles; as the circle gets wider to include more people and more relationships, earlier interests still remain important.

- **Five-year-olds**, pleased with their competence, are curious about work—how people and things work. They are eager to explore the working world of their neighborhood in systematic, planful ways. Studies of stores, farms, transportation, post offices, and police stations are some ways 5-year-olds begin to understand how people do their work. The blurring of reality and fantasy, characteristic of 3- and 4- year-olds' role play, gives way to more realistic and accurate depictions. Their block buildings are visual reconstructions of what they see, feel, and think about. Block building is early geography. Think about how you might incorporate the 5-year-old's interest in jobs and workers in the community into your curriculum plans.

- **Six-year-olds** think about how things fit together, the interrelationships of workers and jobs, machines and workers, and services and people. For example, a class of suburban first graders are studying their neighborhood. First, they look at all the services people need to live in the town. They find out who does these jobs by taking trips and interviewing workers. Later, when they build a model of their city, they decide to include the street lights using batteries and bulbs. This leads to a study of the electric company. Some of their questions are: why the streets need lights, how you decide where to place street lights, how the lights work, and how electricity gets from the electric company to the street light in the neighborhood. They make maps of the neighborhood, the city or town where they live.

- **Seven-year-olds**, more flexible in their thinking, look at what is familiar and gradually think about the past. Concrete experiences help them answer their questions. For instance, a group of 7- and 8-year-olds make personal timelines of their lives, recording one important event to mark each year. Their questions about the past include: "Were there cars when our grandparents were little?" "When were computers invented?" "What were schools like in the past?" They interview parents, grandparents, and other older relatives or neighbors and create timelines of *their* lives. Comparing the lengths of the timelines helps them visualize "long ago." The children write stories of the childhood memories they learned about in the interviews and, in this way, gain knowledge and answers to their questions about life in the past, as well as insights into the historian's methods.

- **Eight-year-olds** learn about "distant and long ago" still linked to "here and now." Gradually moving from concrete to more abstract thinking, 8-year-olds might begin a study of environments by thinking about environments they have visited and creating dioramas of these places. Next, they might create homes for snails or other small creatures they could keep in their classroom. As they move on to a study of the people in a particular area long ago, they are already deeply engaged in thinking about environments. They can gather information from museums, myths and stories, diaries, timetables, maps, and pictures. Through crafts, construction, and plays, they can make generalizations and abstractions about new ideas.

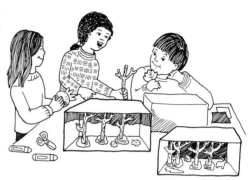

All these factors—child development, social influences, active learning, engaging children's interests, listening to children—are elements in curriculum planning. By using a dynamic approach to curriculum development, you can take each of the factors into account and create a program that builds on what children know, what their interests are, and what you know is important for them to learn. In this way, you engage them as active and eager learners.

Infants and Toddlers

Putting curriculum development into action

Joan, a family day care provider for infants and toddlers, knows her children learn from events that occur during the daily routine. She takes advantage of a learning opportunity on the day the paper towels run out. Two-year-old Sandra comes running over to Joan, saying, "No towels!" Joan kneels down to Sandra's level and responds, "The towels are all gone. We will have to get some more from the pantry. Shall we go?" Hand in hand, they go off down the hall to get more towels.

Once in the pantry, Sandra points to the box of paper towels and Joan reads the label to her. They return to the kitchen and Joan pulls over a chair for Sandra to climb on; together they replace the towels in the paper towel holder. By involving Sandra in solving a problem, Joan has helped her gain a sense of order about how things work. She is also supporting early literacy, helping Sandra make a connection between print and what it stands for.

Preschoolers

Preschoolers, curious about their immediate world, use materials in the room to recreate their experiences. A group of 4-year-olds uses cardboard boxes, chairs, and some blocks to re-create and dramatize their recent visit to a car repair shop. Carla, their teacher, supports their play by providing some props: coveralls and some child-sized tools. Some children create a sign, using scribbles and invented spelling, to label their shop.

Carla observes Daryl and Tanya as they change a tire on a make-believe car made of several chairs pushed together. Wanting to extend their play, she suggests they jack it up with some tools and reminds them of the jacks they saw on their trip. The children go off to find something that will work to jack up their car. They return with some long blocks which they push under one chair leg. Their play continues. Meanwhile, two other 4-year-olds have put on dresses and are having a party right beside the car repair shop. Carla comes over to them and asks, "Did your car break down on the way to the party? Do you need a ride home?" In this way, she supports their ideas while engaging them in the work of the other children.

Young School-Age Children

Don, a teacher of 6-year-olds, knows his children are interested in reading and creating stories, but have different levels of skills. He has helped children feel comfortable with their abilities by providing many different reading and writing choices.

During reading/writing workshop, the following activities take place in the room, indicating that all children are participating at their own levels: Don listens to Rico read his story written in invented spelling. Two small groups of children sit nearby at tables using markers and pencils; they are drawing and writing in writing folders, helping one another with invented spelling and listening to each other's work. In another part of the room, a group of children uses props to act out a story they have written collaboratively and will perform later for the class. Curled up on pillows, four children read picture books and several others read chapter books. (For more information on how to help children work in small groups, see the chapter "Discipline and Management"; the chapter "Literacy in Early Childhood" describes ways to promote children's interest in reading and writing.)

Families

Sarah works in a day care center where many children are transported on the bus provided by the program. As a way of helping parents understand her curriculum and feel a part of what is happening in the classroom, she takes pictures of the children at play and includes these with the newsletter she sends home every month.

Sarah makes frequent home visits to the families. Her conversations with parents during visits are similar to the informal chats she might have with them if they were able to bring and pick up their children each day. Once a month, the staff at Sarah's center hosts a parent breakfast from 7:15 to 8:15 a.m. Sometimes the breakfasts are purely social; at other times, there is a brief meeting or workshop planned.

Sometimes, Sarah also arranges to ride the bus back and forth. This gives her a chance to observe the children in a context outside the classroom and stimulates her to think about how to incorporate the bus ride into her curriculum planning.

Our goal in this chapter has been to offer you a framework for thinking about curriculum. We encourage you to look carefully at your children and plan your program accordingly. Collaboration with colleagues is both helpful and supportive as you create curriculum. It provides opportunities for shared perspectives, other opinions, and new ideas.

Here are some exercises that you can try with colleagues to help you think about a dynamic approach to curriculum planning:

Exercises

1. Observe a child for at least five minutes and record your observations. Look over your observations and think about what the child was doing. What experiences could you provide for that child to extend his or her learning?

2. Imagine that a child in your program has told you that her older sister is having a baby. You can tell from her comments that she is very interested in and curious about the upcoming event. What are some ways you might help her (and her friends, with whom she has also discussed this event) answer her questions. Depending on the age of the child, would a story be best, props for dramatic play, a visit from the sister, or perhaps a class discussion in which children could share common experiences?

3. Have a conversation with a parent in your program. Ask questions about the family's culture and how it is a part of their family life. Think of some ways you can incorporate what you learn into the program. Share the conversation with a colleague and see if you can come up with more ideas.

4. Observe three different children doing a similar activity during a work/play time. From the way each of them does the activity, what can you tell about their interests, their abilities? Are there ways you can build on each child's experience with the activity?

5. Think about an upcoming event or holiday that is recognized or celebrated in different ways by families in your program. Find pictures, objects, stories, and books to have in your classroom that represent the differences (and highlight similarities). Plan ways you can share these materials with children.

Resources

Bredekamp, S. (Ed.). (1991). *Developmentally appropriate practice in early childhood programs serving children from birth through age 8* (rev. ed.). Washington, DC: National Association for the Education of Young Children.

Christensen, D., Feeney, S., & Moravcik, E. (1987). *Who am I in the lives of children?* Columbus, OH: Charles E. Merrill.

Derman-Sparks, L., & A.B.C. Task Force Staff. (1989). *The anti-bias curriculum: Tools for empowering young children.* Washington, DC: National Association for the Education of Young Children.

Dewey, J. (1956). *The child and the curriculum and the school and society.* Chicago: University of Chicago Press.

Duckworth, E. (1987). *"The having of wonderful ideas" and other essays on teaching and learning.* New York: Teachers College Press.

Goodlad, J. I., & Anderson, R. H. (1987). *The non-graded elementary school* (2nd rev. ed.). New York: Teachers College Press.

Katz, L. G., & Chard, S. C. (1989). *Engaging children's minds: The project approach.* Norwood, NJ: Ablex.

Pratt, C. (1984). *I learn from children.* New York: Simon & Schuster.

Ramsey, P. G. (1987). *Teaching and learning in a diverse world: Multicultural education for young children.* New York: Teachers College Press.

Scales, B., Almy, M., Nicolopoulou, A., & Ervin-Tripp, S. (Eds.) (1991). *Play and the social context of development in early care and education.* New York: Teachers College Press.

Seefeldt, C. (1989). *Social studies for the preschool-primary child* (3rd ed.). Columbus, OH: Charles E. Merrill.

Williams, L. R., & De Gaetano, Y. (1985). *Alerta: A multicultural, bilingual approach to teaching young children.* Menlo Park, CA: Addison-Wesley.

About the Author:

Judy R. Jablon, M.S., is a curriculum consultant who works with teachers in Head Start and public school programs. She has been a primary grade teacher in public and private schools, including Bank Street School for Children. She has taught courses in curriculum development at Bank Street College.

9 | Planning for Infants, Toddlers, and Threes

As you plan for infants, toddlers, and 3-year-olds, remember:

- It is often difficult for young children to spend the day away from their families and homes. They need the chance to express and deal with their many deep feelings about separation.

- Feeling safe and secure frees children to explore and learn.

- Young children learn about their world and themselves as they take part in daily routines and play.

How do you feel when you have to say goodbye to someone you love? Sad? Angry? Scared? Excited? Like you, the children you care for have many deep feelings about saying goodbye to their family members.

For example, they may feel upset that their mommies and daddies are leaving and wonder if they will return. They may feel angry, too, that they cannot go to work with their parents or to school with their older siblings. Or they may feel overwhelmed by the rush of getting ready to leave their home and go to child care, leaving no time for play.

Helping children express and learn to cope with their feelings about separation is the core for your curriculum. Here are some ways to do this throughout the day.

Encourage family members always to say goodbye to children.
Though "sneaking out" may seem easier, it should be avoided. The reasons why become clear when you see through a child's eyes. Imagine how you would feel if you looked up from a puzzle you were doing to find the most important people in your world had disappeared. You might feel unsafe in a world where people vanish with no warning or you might always be on the alert, unable to get involved in play, trying to keep track of your parents' comings and goings. By letting their children know when they are leaving, parents encourage trust. Their children know they can count on them to say when something important is going to happen. In addition, saying "goodbye" gives children the opportunity to express their feelings about separation, which means you and their families can better support them.

Helping infants, toddlers, and threes with separation

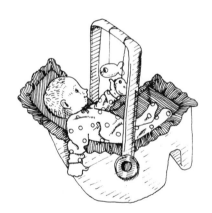

Encourage children and families to develop "goodbye" and "hello" rituals.

Having a set pattern, such as walking a parent to the door or waving goodbye at the window, gives children a sense of control and comfort when it comes time to part. Rituals such as taking time to read a book together or sharing a glass of juice can also help ease the transition at the end of the day when families and children reunite.

Listen and acknowledge how a child feels.

Carl, 18 months, cries when his grandfather says goodbye. When Rachel, a caregiver, holds Carl on her lap as she gently rubs his back and listens, she is telling Carl that he can share his feelings, no matter what they are, and that she will be there for him. By asking, "Are you feeling sad?" she gives him words for his feelings.

Offer experiences with expressive materials.

Paint, playdough, markers, crayons, and blocks give children the opportunity to explore and express their feelings.

Encourage children to bring a favorite toy or blanket from home.

These items are special. They are comforts from home and should not have to be shared.

Make family pictures available.

Hang them at child's-eye level on the wall. Put them in a scrapbook or in a basket so children can carry them around. Cover the pictures with clear contact paper to protect them.

Recognize how children use play to cope with their feelings.

Games of peek-a-boo and dramatic play about mommies and daddies going to work are examples of ways children gain a sense of mastery about the "hellos" and "goodbyes" in their lives. You can support this by offering children the space, time, and props they need.

Offer books about families, saying goodbye, and beginning school to help children understand their feelings.

There are many good books, such as *Goodnight, Moon* by Margaret Wise Brown (Harper & Row, New York, 1947) and *Are You My Mother?* by P. D. Eastman (Designer Books, Random House, New York, 1960), translated in 1967 to *¿Eres tú mi mama?* You can also write your own hello and goodbye books with children.

Be aware of your own feelings about separation.

What memories and feelings do you have about your own childhood separation experiences? How do you feel each morning when children and parents say goodbye? How do your feelings color your responses to parents and children in your program?

In order to have fun and learn, children need to feel protected and comfortable in child care. Here are some ways you can help children feel at home in your setting.

Helping children feel safe and secure

Create a partnership with families.
Families and caregivers each have different kinds of information about children. A child's family, for example, knows that she is allergic to strawberries and likes to sing "The Eensy Weensy Spider" before naptime. You, on the other hand, know a lot about young children and running a program. You know, for example, that children develop language at different rates and you know how to get a group dressed and out the door for a walk to the park.

Build bridges between the two worlds of home and early childhood setting.
Knowing from her parents that Willa, 3 months, likes to lie on her stomach and have her back rubbed when she is upset means you can better soothe her and make her experience in day care more "home-like." Knowing from you that their son will one day be out of diapers can release some of the tension that has been building around toilet training in a toddler's household. Working with families, you can figure out the best way to support children. Ask them, for example, "What can we do to help Jamie feel more comfortable in the morning?" When parents make a suggestion such as, "Let him carry papers around, like his Daddy does at work," go ahead and give it a try. When it no longer works, brainstorm with the family (and with the child if old enough) for other ideas. (You can read more about family-teacher interaction in the chapter "Working with Families.")

Know and respond to children as individuals.
Every child in your group is a unique person with his or her own personality, likes, dislikes, and needs. Here are some suggestions to help you meet the individual needs of each child in your group:

- Observe on a regular basis. Look through children's eyes to try to understand what they are feeling and what they are learning about. Share it with families at the end of the day. Use this information to make curriculum decisions. (See "Observing and Recording Children's Behavior" for suggestions on how to observe.)

- Think creatively about how to find additional staff. An extra adult means children can have more individualized attention. Recruit parent volunteers. Call local colleges and high schools that have early childhood programs. Janey, a family child care provider, found an older man who was happy to come in and be the "group grandfather" three mornings a week.

- Plan small group activities to give children and adults an opportunity to talk and be together. For example, arrange for a caregiver to take two children on a walk or to run an errand. Divide up so some children can help make snack while others have free play time. Seat children in small groups at meal time so you can have conversations, much like a family at home.

Be aware of who children are developmentally.
Knowing about children at different ages will help you meet their changing needs and plan your day accordingly. For example, young infants eat and sleep on their own schedules throughout the day. By the time they are three, children can eat and nap together at set times.

Knowing about children at different ages will also help you understand their challenging behaviors. This is especially important with toddlers. For example, when 2-year-olds declare "No," they are working on defining a sense of self—not being bad. They are saying, "I am me." When they scream, "It's mine," and refuse to share, they are not being selfish. Rather, they are still learning what their personal boundaries are and what ownership means.

Build trusting relationships with each child.
Knowing they can count on you to be there for them makes child care or school a safe place for children. You can foster trust by:

- listening and responding to what a child says: "I know you miss Grandma. She'll be back after nap";
- following a regular schedule: "After I change your diaper, it will be time to go outside";
- keeping promises you make: "Here is the picture of the cow I said I would show you";
- laughing together: "That is a silly face";
- giving children space and time they need to explore: "Jackie is really concentrating on shaking the rattle. I'll wait until she is done before I change her diaper";
- acknowledging a child's feelings: "I know you are tired. Let's sit in the rocking chair together";
- being honest: "I can't open this jar of applesauce. Let's see if Mrs. Winston can help";
- talking about children's families and things they do at home: "Do you help your Grandma make soup?"

- reading familiar books: "Do you remember what the caterpillar ate next?"

- showing your pleasure in children's achievements: "That's good pouring. All the juice went in the cup."

Create an environment where children can feel at home.
For infants and toddlers, this means making your setting as much like a home as possible. If you care for children in your house or apartment, you have it made! In centers, a soft comfortable chair where an adult and child can read together, pictures hung at child's-eye level, and pots and pans stored under the kitchen sink for play can all help children associate your setting with home and its feelings of safety and security.

An environment for threes should be comfortable and manageable. Cubbies labeled with children's photographs, clearly labeled shelves so children can find what they need, and a pet or plants that children help care for gives them a sense that the space is theirs. (See the chapter "The Learning Environment" for more about setting up your physical space.)

Help children feel competent.
Children naturally want to be capable. Jeremy, a new pourer, showed how strong this desire is. When his caregiver offered to help pour the milk he was spilling down the side of his cup, he replied, "No thanks. I can spill it all by myself." She agreed, but also gave him a sponge to wipe it up. You help children feel competent when you:

- Give them real opportunities to contribute to group life. (We will come back to this when we talk about everyday routines.)

- Set up the physical environment to help children be effective. For example, you can provide infants with mobiles to bat and kick as a way of letting them have impact on their world. Provide child-height hooks so children can hang up their own coats and clearly label shelves with pictures and words so children can easily find and put away toys. Although 3-year-olds cannot yet read, they can recognize pictures and match them to real objects.

- Encourage relationships between children. Having friends gives older 2- and 3-year-olds the sense of strength and comfort that comes with feeling connected to another person. Let the children know they are important to one another and that the group matters. When Rico was sick, his caregiver explained to the other children, "Rico has a bad cold so he has to stay home until he feels better and can play with you again." The group decided to send him some of their drawings.

Supporting children's learning

Everyday routines and play are direct sources of young children's information about the world. Getting dressed after nap, preparing snack, walking to the hardware store to buy a hook to hang up the bird feeder in the backyard of a family day care home, working with playdough, painting, and reading books are the kinds of experiences that should fill children's days.

Because a program based on daily routines and play is a new idea for many people, we are going to take a look at the rich learning opportunities of each. Then we will consider the daily schedule and your role in guiding young children's learning.

Everyday Routines

Here are some reasons why daily routines should be an integral part of your program.

Everyday activities offer children the firsthand experience they need and want about how the world works.
Here are some daily activities you may want to highlight as part of your program:

- dressing
- toileting
- brushing teeth (for 2- and 3-year-olds)
- cooking
- eating together
- neighborhood walks to the park, store, mailbox
- running errands
- caring for pets

Perhaps the best thing about daily routines is that they happen over and over again.
The repetition, which can be boring for adults, gives children a sense of competence and mastery as they figure out, for example, that you must put your socks on before your shoes and that cleaning up after lunch "signals" that it will soon be naptime.

As children grow, the same experience takes on new meaning.
For a 2-month-old, being dressed is primarily a sensory experience as the cloth touches her skin and she hears the sound of her caregiver's voice. When you begin pulling a shirt over a 6-month-old's head, she closes her eyes. She has already learned to anticipate what will come next. As a toddler, she will learn to pull on her own shirt. She may also use dressing as an opportunity to practice making choices, insisting on wearing her orange shirt with the blue balloons on it. As a 3-year-old, she may use her knowledge about dressing and clothing as she dresses a doll and says, "You have to bundle up. It's cold outside."

Everyday activities afford children the opportunity to feel capable and proud as they contribute to group life.

Carrying a bag of pears home from the grocery store, putting the paper towels away under the sink, scrubbing carrots for snack, wiping up spilled juice, and hanging up their coats are all examples of legitimate, valuable contributions children can make. You need to allow the extra time it takes children to accomplish these tasks and praise their efforts, imperfect as they may be. It takes lots of practice for children to learn how to pour without spilling, throw their napkins and cups in the garbage, and stir the batter for biscuits.

Play

Play offers children the opportunity to explore new ideas, practice making choices, feel competent and in control, interact with others, and fine-tune new skills.

All play is an opportunity for language learning. Here are several examples of activities you might offer children:

- **Art activities** such as playdough, painting, and collage help develop small muscle skills and eye-hand coordination, as well as color recognition.

- **Block building** offers math experiences such as categorizing, comparing, and patterning.

- **Playing at the water table** allows children to explore science concepts such as filling and emptying, floating and sinking, and evaporation.

- **Listening to stories and singing** invites children to enjoy language and appreciate books—prerequisites to reading and writing.

- **Dramatic play**, a favorite of 3-year-olds, allows children to explore themes, events, and feelings from their daily lives as well as to engage in make-believe and fantasy.

As children develop, so does their play. Chances are good that a young infant will put a block in his mouth. In a few months, he may experiment with dropping it off the edge of his highchair. As a toddler, he likes to put blocks in a can and dump them out. By 3 years, his play is more organized and purposeful. He might construct a zoo cage with hay for the elephants to eat.

The Daily Schedule

Meeting children's needs requires a flexibility that is only possible when you have an overview of what is going on. A daily schedule will give you and children a sense of order. Here is a basic schedule for a full-day program that you can adapt to meet the needs of the children you care for:

Arrival	7:30–9:00
Free Play	arrival–10:00
Snack (preparation and eating)	10:00–10:30
Outdoor Time	10:30–11:30
Lunch	11:30–12:00
Nap	12:00–2:00
Free Play	2:00–3:00
Snack	3:00–3:30
Outdoor Time	3:30–4:30
Free Play	4:30–5:00
Departure	5:00–6:00

Your Role

As a caregiver and teacher of young children, your role is to "shape" and "guide" children's daily experiences and play to enhance their learning. Here are some ways to do this.

Talk with children about what is happening.
Comments such as, "Now I'm going to fasten your diaper" or "The cup is filled with flour. Now you can pour it in the bowl," help children learn about the world.

Share your curiosity and enthusiasm.
Smiling at Kevin, 4 months, as he bats at the fish mobile over the changing table and commenting, "You are making those fish move," can encourage him to continue practicing his new skill.

Introduce "experience extending" materials.
Observing, for example, that 3-year-old Ronny is getting bored with the eight-piece puzzles can lead you to offer him the challenge of a more complicated puzzle. Shaquandra's restaurant play may be enriched if you offer her a pad of paper and a pencil to write down orders.

Encourage children to think.
Ask questions that call on a child to recall or predict something, such as, "What do you think will happen when you drop the cork in the water?" Do not worry if children do not have the right answer or any answer at all. You can continue by saying, "Let's see what happens. Oh, look, the cork is floating. Now let's drop the leaf in the water. Do you think it will float or sink?"

Teach directly at times.
Being told, "First you put your toe in, then pull the sock over your heel," can be helpful to a new dresser.

Know when to step back and give children the space and time they need to explore and try out new skills.

Stepping back to let an infant solve the problem of getting a rattle that has slipped away or giving 3-year-olds an opportunity to talk through a conflict is as important a teaching skill as knowing how and when to intervene.

Be alert and aware of what is going on so you can step in immediately if needed.

When Denise, 3 months, begins crying, Shawna, 8 months, begins reaching for a lamp cord, and Greg, 2-1/2 years, is about to bite Ron, you need to be there. Children's safety is always your first consideration.

Encourage children to use one another as resources.

Both children benefit when Nick shows Sam how he flattens play-dough with his palm and Sam shows how he uses a rolling pin.

Let us take a look at snack time and how it is experienced, first by infants and toddlers, then by a group of 3-year-olds.

Snack Time for Infants and Toddlers

"Time for snack," calls Ellen, a caregiver.

After washing their hands at the sink, children and caregivers come over to the table.

"We're having bright yellow bananas today," says Ellen. Jerry, 18 months, repeats the words "yellow bananas." Ellen also notices, "Jerry, you're wearing a yellow shirt." Ellen asks, "Who likes yellow, yellow bananas?"

"I do," says 2- year-old Laura as she begins crawling up on the table. Ellen reminds her, "Chairs are for sitting on. Tables are for eating on." When Laura sits down, Ellen asks, "Would you like to peel your own banana?" Ellen hands Laura half a banana. Laura's forehead wrinkles with concentration as she works to remove the peel.

Sally, 14 months, and Lester, 12 months, are each trying to climb into the same chair. After Sally nudges him away, Lester climbs down. Ellen helps him find another chair.

Betty, Mary, and Louis, 2-year-olds, talk with Ellen. They shake their heads "no" when she asks if people eat banana peels. "Oranges have peels," says Louis remembering snack from yesterday. "Me no like oranges," says Mary. Betty adds, "Drink orange juice for breakfast."

Eating bananas for snack holds many lessons for these children, lessons they will learn over the course of many snack times:

- Washing hands before eating introduces children to a healthy habit.

Seeing a program in action

- By regularly choosing healthy snacks such as bananas, carrot sticks, mashed potatoes, green beans, or cottage cheese spread on crackers, caregivers convey a message about nutrition. Serving chocolate cookies and lollipops would say something else. Their message is getting across. Children in this group often "serve" each other carrot sticks when they play house.

- By saying, "yellow, yellow bananas," Ellen shares her enjoyment of language, encourages children to communicate, and sets the stage for reading and writing. She is also "teaching" the color yellow and gives children another color lesson by calling attention to Jerry's shirt.

- By reminding Laura that chairs are for sitting in, Ellen is saying, "There is a certain way people behave at the table." Ellen knows it is not easy for a 2-year-old to sit still. She also knows that over time, with gentle reminders, Laura will learn society's meal-time rules.

- Sally and Lester are experimenting with basics, such as how to climb into a chair and how much space they take up. Toddlers do not automatically know that two children cannot fit in one chair. Ellen decided to give them a few minutes to try to work things out. She would have stepped in immediately if she thought either child was in danger.

- Betty, Mary, and Louis are learning about peels. They are beginning to form categories: fruit with peels and fruit without peels.

- The three 2-year-olds are also learning about themselves and about how people differ. Mary does not like oranges. Louis does. Betty makes the connection between drinking orange juice in the kitchen at home and eating oranges at school.

Snack Time for Threes

How 3-year-olds experience snack is colored by who they are. Although snack holds many similar lessons about nutrition, language, and etiquette for threes as it does for infants and toddlers, snack becomes primarily a social experience for the older children. Interested in each other, they are learning to form relationships. Their caregiver or teacher, though important, is no longer the center of attention as she was at the table of infants and toddlers.

Here are some "social" experiences snack time offers a group of 3-year-olds:

- Threes can choose whom they want to sit next to.

- They have conversations with one another that can range from "Please pass the juice" to talking about the falling snow.

- Children can practice social skills such as passing a plate of crackers or sharing a banana.

- Snack offers the chance to develop problem-solving skills, which are important in any group. When Lynn finishes the juice and passes Maria an empty pitcher, Maria has to decide what to do if she wants more juice. For example, she can ask an adult for more or she can borrow a pitcher from another table.

- Threes can also think about what "juice" is. Perhaps prompted by a teacher's remark, such as, "How is orange juice made?" conversation can lead to what other fruits produce juice to the kinds of juice at home to "Let's make our own juice!" This remark prompts the teacher to think about a trip to the grocery store to buy oranges to squeeze into juice for snack.

- Throwing away their cups and napkins when they are finished with snack gives children a hands-on experience with taking responsibility for their space.

By building a program based on who young children are and how they learn, you help assure that their first steps into the world outside their families are successful. As a "supporter," "encourager," "guide," and "shaper" of children's learning through everyday routines and play, you are helping them develop not only skills but a positive sense of self as a learning person. You give them a sense of "I can do it!"—a feeling about themselves that will serve them well as they face new experiences and challenges throughout their lives.

Exercises

1. One of your major goals is to help children feel at home in your setting. Only when they feel safe and comfortable, are they free to do the experimenting and exploring that are necessary to learn. Think of ways you can use each of these areas to help children feel safe and secure:

   - physical environment;
   - knowledge of families and the community;
   - everyday routines;
   - materials; and
   - your relationship with children.

   Share your responses with your colleagues. You may also want to share some of your findings with parents at a meeting or in a newsletter to help them recognize this important aspect of your work.

2. In this exercise, you and your colleagues will do an everyday activity you do with children, such as take a walk around your neighborhood or make a fruit salad for snack. As you do the

activity, think of a child in your program and try to look at what you are doing through his or her eyes. Ask yourself the following questions:

- What might _____ learn about himself?
- What might _____ learn about other people?
- What might _____ learn about how the world works?
- How could I keep _____ safe during this activity?
- What kinds of things would we talk about?
- How could I promote _____'s learning?

3. Every day, perhaps without realizing it, you make countless decisions that shape children's experience in your program. You make decisions, for example, about activities to offer, what to say, where to sit, and how and when to divide up the group. Over the next week, pick three half-hour periods and try to jot down all the decisions you make, big and small. Exchange lists with colleagues. Are you amazed at how many decisions you make and how much the smooth running of the day depends on your decisions?

Resources

Balaban, N. (1985). *Starting school: From separation to independence—A guide for early childhood teachers*. New York: Teachers College Press.

Dombro, A. L., & Wallach, L. (1988). *The ordinary is extraordinary: How children under three learn*. New York: Simon & Schuster/Fireside.

Gonzales-Mena, J., & Eyer, D. W. (1989). *Infants, toddlers and caregivers*. Palo Alto, CA: Mayfield.

Greenspan, S., & Greenspan, N. T. (1985). *First feelings: Milestones in the emotional development of your baby and child*. New York: Viking Penguin.

Johnson, H. M. (1972). *Children in the nursery school*. New York: Agathon Press.

Miller, K. (1984). *Things to do with toddlers and twos*. Marshfield, MA: Telshare.

Miller, K. (1984). *More things to do with toddlers and twos*. Marshfield, MA: Telshare.

Provence, S. (1967). *Guide for the care of infants in groups*. New York: Child Welfare League.

About the Author:

Amy Laura Dombro, M.S., headed the Bank Street Infant and Family Center from 1976 to 1983. She is now a consultant with Head Start Parent Child Center programs. She is the senior author of The Ordinary is Extraordinary: How Children under Three Learn *(1989, Fireside) and* Sharing the Caring: How to Find the Right Child Care and Make it Work for You and Your Child *(1991, Fireside).*

10 ‖ Integrated Curriculum for Four- through Eight-Year-Olds

At Bank Street, we call the work children do to understand their world "social studies." Social studies means seeing connections between self, family, and community. Using social studies topics as a framework, teachers provide opportunities for experiences that help children learn concepts about the social world and master important skills. It is through the social studies that you build an integrated curriculum, one that helps children use the skills they are learning throughout your program in a meaningful context.

Most often, skills are taught in isolation. Using an integrated approach to curriculum helps children see the direct application of these skills in their learning. For example, as the 7-year-old writes down how many and what kinds of workers she observes at the produce market, she employs writing and math skills in a useful context.

Social studies topics range from a study of families to the study of a river, depending on the age and interests of children, where they live, and the skills and concepts you want them to master. The constant element within any study is that children have experiences in art, movement, building, cooking, science, reading, writing, math, dramatics, and music. Experiences planned in an integrated way help children make sense of their world.

With infants, toddlers, and 3-year-olds, the question of teaching "subjects" does not come up in the way that it does in later childhood. As children mature, however, they are increasingly ready and need to learn skills and disciplines that traditionally have been compartmentalized into discrete areas or subjects, such as the three "Rs." Yet children 4 through 8 years of age need to continue to learn from organizing experiences in their own, more holistic ways.

Experiences are meaningful for children when they build on each other and lead to new experiences and further learning. We have found that the most effective way for children to understand how and why the human and physical world works is to allow them to act upon this information in their own way. Children need to experience things first. Then they gather meaning from what they have experienced by re-creating it. This re-creation includes discussion, dramatization, and construction. As a caregiver or teacher, you need to provide a wide variety of opportunities for children to re-create and

What is an integrated curriculum?

Why use an integrated approach to curriculum?

process what they encounter in the world around them.

An integrated curriculum supports children's learning because it provides ample time for experimentation, speculation, and discussion in order for children to become deeply engaged in content. This way, over time, they see subtle relationships and make connections. In-depth thinking does not happen when children gather disconnected bits of knowledge or learn in compartmentalized packages.

Children are motivated to learn when content is interesting to them. Cohen (1972) says that children "mix science, math, poetry, body movement, and feelings with total ease in the examination of problems that concern them." When the content of a study is rich, it will engage your interest as well as theirs. You can have satisfaction seeing children master meaningful content from a study you created.

In an integrated curriculum, you integrate:

- a variety of curriculum experiences, including music, reading, writing, math, dramatics, and art around a core study of a social studies topic;

- all aspects of children's development—physical, social, emotional, cognitive;

- firsthand experience with opportunities to re-create them;

- children's experiences at home and in the world with their work in the early childhood setting.

How can you integrate curriculum?

In this section we offer a framework to use as you develop an integrated curriculum. Do not think of this as a rigid system, but rather as an outline to help you with your planning. As you read this section and consider the examples, keep in mind that there are many ways to approach every study; each teacher is different and every environment and group of children suggest rich and creative possibilities. At the end of this section, we suggest techniques some teachers use to integrate curriculum. The following is a guideline for planning; each step will be described in detail:

- Think of a study in relation to the children in your program.
- Consider concepts.
- Learn about the subject.
- Gather resources.
- Plan opportunities for experiences.
- Involve families.
- Plan a culminating activity.
- Evaluate the study.

Think of a topic for study.

You select a topic for an integrated study based on what you know about the children in your program—their age, their interests, where they live, and what they see each day. A good topic provides opportunities for the children in your program to make sense of their immediate world, their families, and their communities. Choose a study that offers variety—you want it to appeal to the different interests and talents of children in your program. At the beginning of the study, children's questions may appear superficial, but as they gather information and spend time with projects, their questions become deeper and more subtle.

- Be sure the topic challenges children's thinking but does not ask too much of them. When we ask 4-, 5-, even 6-year-olds to study a place different from where they live—a group of children in a large city studying farm animals, for example— the study has less meaning for them. It would be more meaningful for urban children to study transportation, or apartment buildings, or stores in their neighborhood because of what they see and use each day.

- Emphasize tangible experiences connected to the children's lives. Four-year-olds are deeply interested in their own families, the foods they eat at home, and the ways their families celebrate holidays. This could be the basis of a rich study around Thanksgiving. A focus on the historical facts is inappropriate for this age group. On the other hand, 7- and 8-year-olds can study the historical story of "the Pilgrims and the Indians" and use it as an opportunity to evaluate stereotypical portrayals of these groups. You can also broaden their knowledge of other celebrations related to harvest and fall activities. (You can read more about holiday celebrations in the chapter "Valuing Diversity.")

- Select a topic that offers children many possibilities for investigation. For instance, a study of their city by a first grade class might include visits to a bus station, police station, firehouse, hospital, harbor, and sanitation department. Follow-up activities include block building, dramatic play, sketching and painting scenes from their trips, and reading and writing stories.

  The study of the city also demonstrates how a study helps children organize their learning. First, children have chances to observe—to collect information by seeing, handling, smelling and tasting, and listening. After they observe, they re-create these observations. Children use art and drama to symbolize and represent their firsthand experiences. They act on what they have learned. They use movement, art, math, and writing to make connections.

- Think about what books the children can read or have read to them. Although young children learn best from direct experiences, books are an important resource. They help children extend what they have seen firsthand and learn about other people, places, and ideas.

- Choose a topic that offers opportunities for children to talk and think about differences. Through a study of families, for example, 4-year-olds can begin to think about diversity of language, celebrations, foods, family size and structure, and music.

- Be sure the topic appeals to your own interests. You have to be challenged by the subject in order to help the children explore it. For a study to be meaningful to children, you have to put together a great deal of knowledge first, and that takes time and energy.

Consider concepts.

Think about concepts you want children to learn and the big ideas you want them to think about. Concepts are the important questions children will think about—the relationships they can discover. When children put two facts together to make a new fact, they are thinking. They are seeing connections and making generalizations. These generalizations lead children toward further knowledge and promote the ability to think, reason, and solve problems.

Think about what you want children to know *during* the study as well as at the end of the study. Taba (1971) tells us that concepts are the teacher's starting point of a study and the children's ending point—after they have done a variety of activities, had many experiences, posed and answered many questions.

Consider this example: Bart, a teacher of 8-year-olds studying Native Americans of the Eastern Woodlands, brings dried corn and a mortar and pestle to the classroom. He wants the children to think about what kinds of tools the Native Americans used and how they did their work. The children begin to grind the corn. They work each day and by the end of the week, one child observes, "All we have is a tiny bit of cornmeal and it isn't even powder like the cornmeal we bought at the store." Another child adds, "We do not make things from scratch. The Native Americans did. We go to the store and buy flour, butter, and eggs and think that this is baking from scratch. Well, it isn't." These children are learning about many relationships. They discover the relationship between corn, cornmeal, the mortar and pestle, and hard work. Bart understands that by letting the children re-create the Native American experience of grinding corn, the children will draw comparisons between long ago and the present, and they have. Could these children learn and fully appreciate these concepts from reading a textbook?

148

Learn about the subject.

Lucy Sprague Mitchell (1934) says that, as a curriculum developer, you yourself must explore the environment. Take a walk to capture the child's-eye view; look for ways for children to begin to see relationships between people and the environment. Mrs. Alvarez teaches second graders in a fishing town beside a river; her class will study how the river is used by the community. First, she herself takes several walks along the river. She visits the harbor to talk with the fishermen and climb on their boats; she reads the history of the river and learns some of the science and geography about how rivers are formed.

To learn more about the subject, go to your local library for books about your study. Books with vivid pictures are especially helpful. Look for folktales and poems that relate to the topic and are appropriate for your age group. Museums and bookstores can also be a good place to find materials. As you look in card catalogs, computer files, and bibliographies, you may get additional ideas. Or you may discover that you have to rethink your idea because there is not enough appropriate material available.

When, at last, you feel like an expert on the subject, your hardest job is to keep what you know to yourself, allowing the children to make their own discoveries. It is through these discoveries that children learn.

Collect resources.

For the children, the study is an investigation. You provide them with resources and opportunities for experiences that stimulate questions, speculations, and hypotheses, but the discoveries they make and the knowledge they acquire are their own. Having yourself been an investigator, you have greater sensitivity to their questions and to problems they may want to solve.

Think of resources that will deepen, expand, and extend children's knowledge of a topic, and always keep in mind the age of the children in your program. You will want to:

- identify appropriate trips;
- collect props for dramatic play;
- gather block accessories;
- choose books to have in the library;
- find recipes;
- locate pictures, posters, films, and maps;
- gather artifacts;
- find poems;
- invite people who can talk with your class about the topic.

Studies for older children that focus on the past depend more on books and museums as sources of information. Children can use atlases, old diaries, myths, and legends to help them gather information about people. These materials give children raw facts and let them draw some of their own conclusions, whereas encyclopedias and textbooks present conclusions already drawn. Listening to a Native American myth about creation gave 8-year-olds studying "environments" clues about famines, celebrations, and religious beliefs. Pictures from magazines like *National Geographic* provide children with visual details of a culture they cannot observe firsthand.

As you plan the resources of the study, include books and pictures that help children observe differences in ethnicity, color, lifestyles, and gender roles.

Plan opportunities for experiences.

Plan opportunities for experiences that help the study come alive; trips are especially valuable when children can have firsthand experiences relevant to the study. Keep in mind that children's understanding of a topic deepens when they can see it from a variety of perspectives.

Begin a study by asking children what they know about a subject and what they want to find out. This helps you assess your group as well as engage their curiosity.

Trips, in small groups or with the whole group, provide children with firsthand opportunities to observe and question. Experiences children have following a trip help them to relive and process it. Construction with blocks, clay, or other open-ended materials allows the initiative for play and the reconstruction of their experience to come from children. The relationship thinking that children act out in their play can be extended through discussions and stories.

Simple trips, like taking a few preschoolers to the local grocery store to purchase snacks, stimulate discussion and dramatic play. Each environment suggests its own trips. A class of 6-year-olds in a suburban school visits the railroad station where their parents take the train each day to go to work. They bring back train schedules from the trip. They make block buildings and cardboard constructions of trains. They draw clocks.

Trip sheets for 5- through 8-year-olds encourage children to record what they see, as well as directing their attention to a particular part of the trip. Mr. Bickel makes a trip sheet for the 5-year-olds he takes on a neighborhood walk; he has drawn and labeled columns so they can record how many cars, buses, and trucks they see (see Figure 1). They will use this information to make graphs back in the classroom. Ms. Roth helps her third graders, who are visiting the museum, by including some detailed questions about blacksmith tools and a place to sketch what they see.

Kindergarten Trip Sheet

Name: _____

How many do you see?

| Cars | Buses | Trucks |

Figure 1

As you plan opportunities for experiences, think carefully about sequence. The experiences of your curriculum are building blocks of children's learning. Always ask yourself: "Why do I want the children to do this? What learning will take place? What experiences can it lead to? What questions might children ask?" Attention to sequence helps children organize their thinking and fosters in-depth thinking. As the following example illustrates, each experience connects logically to the one that came before and prepares children for the next one.

A group of 4- and 5-year-old children visit a shoe store in the neighborhood. When they return, they talk about what they see. The teacher makes sure that the children take the lead; she listens to what is interesting to them, rather than directs them. Through discussion, she sees what they know and what confusions they have. Several children remark that some stores sell only children's shoes; Tanya adds that she buys her shoes at the same place she buys clothes. Shiwon asks, "Why does the man measure your foot?" Allison thinks he is weighing her foot.

Some children draw pictures and dictate stories about the trip. Their drawings are visual representations of what caught their interest. As they write and converse with each other, they experiment with new vocabulary and concepts. The teacher makes a list of words about the shoe store for the children to refer to. Through constant discussion and play with new language, the children learn words like cashier and merchandise.

Spontaneous play emerges in the block area, where some 5-year-olds build a shoe store and use the block people to act out the roles of salesperson, customer, and cashier. The children make signs for the shoe store. To encourage others to join in, the teacher adds shoe boxes, shoes, and a stool to the dramatic play area.

It is important to use open-ended questions when children have new experiences. An open-ended question has many answers and no

I love this farm.
I am glad I went
And these are
pumpkins.

Eli   Figure 2

We Went
on A hAy
ride. It Was
fun. I heard
birds CrY.

Yuta   Figure 3

single right answer. It allows children to do their own thinking. Before the trip to the shoe store, the teacher asks, "What do you think you will see?" This question helps the children anticipate and lets the teacher know what previous experiences her children have.

You constantly make decisions about when to extend children's thinking. For example, later in the shoe store study, the teacher introduces a foot measurer to the children's shoe store and a series of measurement experiences begin. Think of some other activities you could offer to children to extend the experience of visiting the shoe store.

As you develop curriculum, plan opportunities for the whole group, for small groups, and for individuals. Children learn differently in each of these circumstances. And consider the complete spectrum of learning—have you included activities in your study that let children think mathematically and scientifically? Are there musical and artistic possibilities? Have they cooked? Have they read lots of stories? Have they written or dictated their own stories? (For examples of stories written and illustrated by 6- and 7-year-olds after a class trip to a pumpkin farm, see Figures 2 and 3).

Involve families.

As you plan, think about how you will involve families in the study. At what point should you invite parents to visit? Parents and other relatives can be a wonderful resource for children's learning.

Jenny is 5. Her father works on a boat in the harbor. Jenny's teacher invites him to come and visit the children to talk about his work. The children ask him many questions. After the visit, some of the children make boats to use in the water table.

Nick's grandmother is coming in to make guacamole with his class. Nick is very excited. Nick's teacher has called ahead for the recipe, which she has written on a big chart in the classroom (see Figure 4). Some of the children help shop for the ingredients at a local bodega (Hispanic grocery store).

Sending home weekly or monthly newsletters describing your study lets parents know what is happening in their child's program. In the newsletters, suggest ways for parents to be involved and welcome other ideas. Having an updated bulletin board near the door to your classroom or center is another way to keep families informed.

Plan a culminating activity.

It is difficult to say how long a study should go on. Sometimes a study takes one month and sometimes it takes three. The length of time depends on the age and interest of the children. Children's enthusiasm or boredom can be effective measures of how long the study should continue. It is better to end it sooner than planned than to

Guacamole
(Avocado Dip)

Ingredients:

   2 Avocadoes

 1 Lime

 2 Tomatoes

1 Small onion

 Pinch-salt

1 Bag tortilla chips

Instructions:

1. Rinse the avocadoes, lime, and tomatoes with cold water. Set aside.

2. Peel onion and cut into small pieces. Set aside.

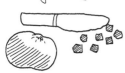

3. Remove stem from tomatoes. Then, cut into small pieces. Set aside.

4. Cut the avocadoes in half lengthwise. Remove the seeds. Scoop out the meat with a spoon, put it in a bowl, and mash it with a fork.

5. Squeeze lime juice into avocado meat. Add salt to taste. Add onions and tomatoes. Mix well. Serve with tortilla chips.

   Enjoy!

6. Plant the avocado seeds and watch them grow!

Figure 4

continue when interest has faded.

However long they last, all studies must have closure. Part of planning is deciding on an ending, a culminating experience for a study. The ending is the organizing experience—the thing that brings all the learning together. Think of the ending as a way for the group to celebrate their collaborative efforts and their cumulative learning. For you as the teacher, the culminating experience is a way of evaluating your work and the work of children. The kind of culminating experience you choose depends on the age of your children and the nature of your study.

Your ending may be a class book, a mural, a play, or the re-creation of a store in the classroom. Preschoolers studying families make a class book with pictures and stories about their families. They have a potluck supper with family members to share their book. Eight-year-olds studying the history of the river in their town make a permanent model, using clay, wood, soil, sticks, and other found materials, to depict life along the river one hundred years ago. The model is the synthesis of the children's learning. They donate the model to the local public library for the community to enjoy. Think about ways you can bring a study to closure. Remember, each of these examples is only one of many possible ways.

Observe and evaluate.

How you observe and evaluate children during a study is another part of the planning process. A content approach to curriculum such as we have described does not lend itself readily to tests or other standard measures of evaluation. These guidelines may be useful:

- Constant observing and recording are essential. As children prepare for the culminating experience, it is important to observe and record what they have learned and also to keep track of misunderstandings that still exist. (You can review the chapters "Observing and Recording Children's Behavior" and "Assessment through the Curriculum" for methods.)

- Listening to the children as they build in blocks, construct a model, or talk to a friend lets you know what they have synthesized and what confusions they still have. Follow up on their confusions with group discussion, individual experiences, or a one-to-one conversation.

- Saving examples of children's work is important. Creating a portfolio for each child allows you to assess growth over time, and is especially helpful in talking with parents during conferences.

Teachers find it helpful, whenever possible, to work with at least one other colleague to plan a study. By working as a team, you can think about ideas collaboratively, ask each other questions, try ideas out, share successes, and ponder failures together. Some questions for you to think about are:

- What are the interests and abilities of the children in the program?

- What resources does our community offer?

- How might we involve parents?

- What special strengths do each of us, as teachers, bring to this study? Sharing materials and resources, as well as dividing research tasks, reduces the amount of work teachers have when they plan studies for the first time.

As you become more experienced with developing studies, you may use different techniques or develop your own to help you conceptualize a study. In the early stages of planning, some teachers find "webbing" an effective strategy for exploring the range of possibilities a study can offer. Even if you do the study independently, do the brainstorming with other people; it will help you extend your thinking. Webbing helps you identify all of a study's possibilities. These are the steps:

1. Write down as many words related to your topic as you can think of on small pieces of paper. Be as inventive as you can. For a study of breads, you might write words such as flour, work, good smells, pizza.

2. Group the words to make categories of similar words and label the categories. Categories might be workers, ingredients, utensils.

3. Transfer your categories to a large piece of paper for a permanent record. For a study of breads, your record may look something like Figure 5.

Large monthly planning calendars can be used to help you plot curriculum plans. Using the steps described earlier in the chapter, think about how and when to begin the study and record it on the calendar. Put in specific dates (or the week) you plan to take trips. Consider the logical sequence of trips as well as when appointments are available. Record experiences and activities you plan as follow-up to the trips. Jot down notes for open-ended discussion questions you will use in group meetings before and after trips and projects. If you have found stories that fit with specific parts of the study, add them to the calendar.

Curriculum wheels help you see that your curriculum is complete. They are divided into subject areas; teachers list possibilities for experiences and activities according to subjects (see Figure 6). Often activities overlap subjects; for example, a graphing experience about favorite types of donuts might be a math activity as well as a writing experience as children record data during a survey and print labels on the actual graph. Although some teachers find using

A Bread Web

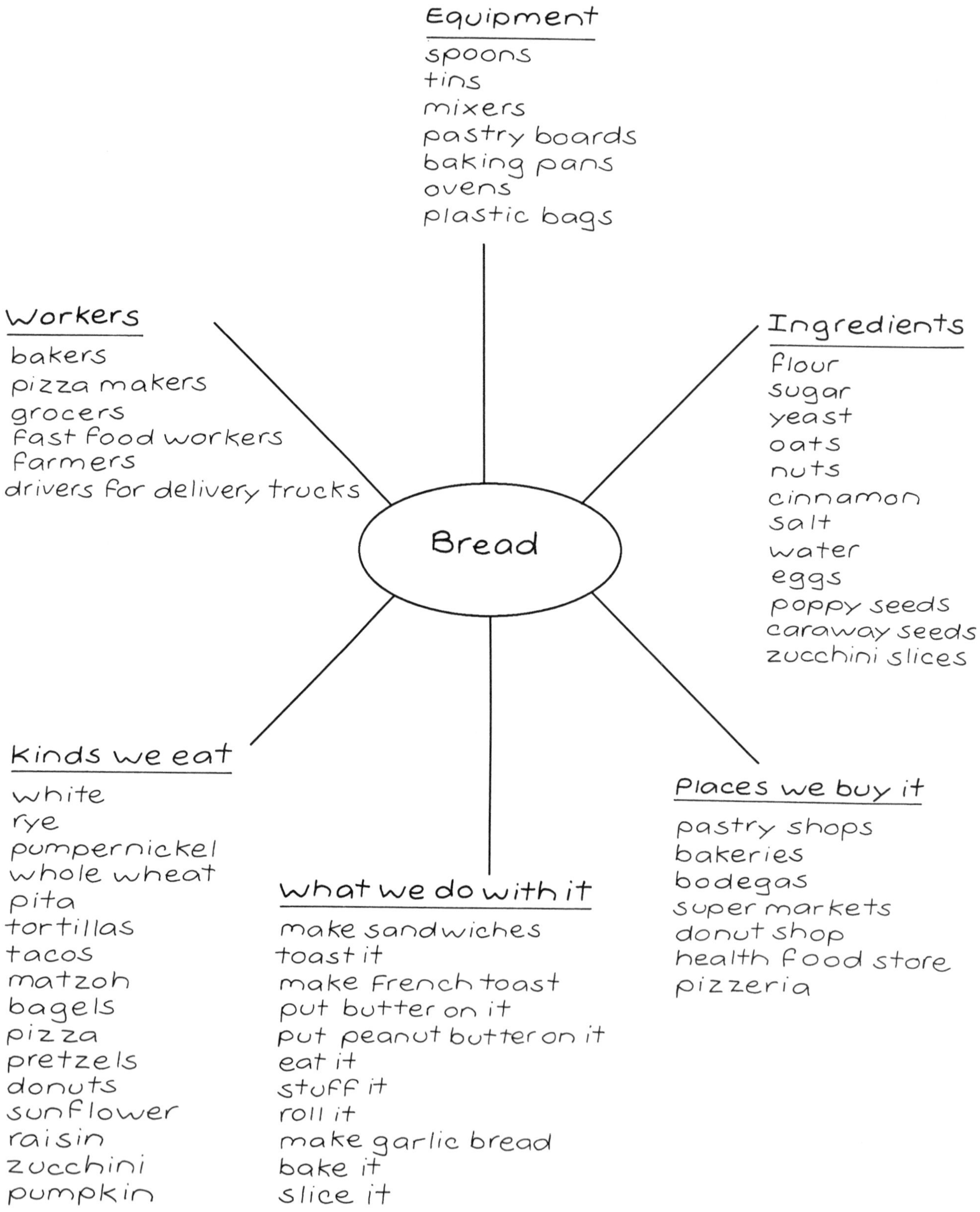

Equipment
spoons
tins
mixers
pastry boards
baking pans
ovens
plastic bags

Workers
bakers
pizza makers
grocers
fast food workers
farmers
drivers for delivery trucks

Ingredients
flour
sugar
yeast
oats
nuts
cinnamon
salt
water
eggs
poppy seeds
caraway seeds
zucchini slices

Bread

Kinds we eat
white
rye
pumpernickel
whole wheat
pita
tortillas
tacos
matzoh
bagels
pizza
pretzels
donuts
sunflower
raisin
zucchini
pumpkin

What we do with it
make sandwiches
toast it
make French toast
put butter on it
put peanut butter on it
eat it
stuff it
roll it
make garlic bread
bake it
slice it

Places we buy it
pastry shops
bakeries
bodegas
super markets
donut shop
health food store
pizzeria

Figure 5

156

A Curriculum Wheel

Study - The School Building
Grade/Age Level - Kindergarten

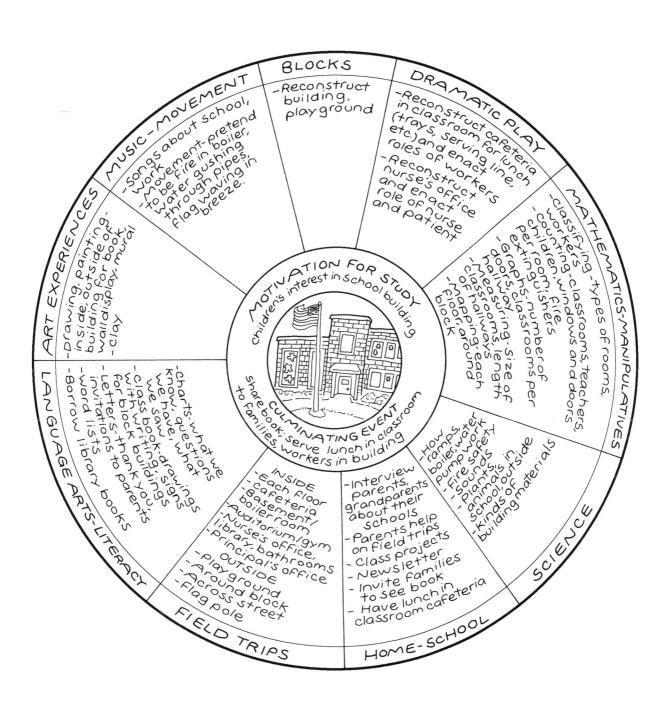

Figure 6

157

curriculum wheels helpful, be careful not to make up gimmicky ideas simply to fill the wheel; be sure the activities you plan really enhance children's learning.

All teachers have different styles, and you will find the technique that works best for you. A good study must be well planned but should also remain flexible to include the spontaneous ideas that come from children, other colleagues, parents, a visitor, or you. In the chapter "A Study of Bread and Bakeries: An Example of Integrated Curriculum," you can read about how a teacher of 5- and 6-year-olds developed a study. As you read it, keep in mind that this is one teacher and one study. There are many ways to develop a study and many topics that are appropriate for each age group.

Exercises

Here are some exercises for you to try alone or with colleagues to help you understand how to integrate curriculum.

1. Think of an idea for a study you might do with children in your program. Is it appropriate for their age, their environment? What are some trips you could take with children to help them gather information about the topic? Think about ways to follow up on children's experiences on the trip. What are some open-ended discussion questions you could use to help children think about the study? Discuss your ideas with a colleague.

2. Imagine you are doing a study of a topic with a multi-aged group of 4-, 5-, and 6-year-olds. With a few other colleagues, create a web about a topic that fits your neighborhood. Think about how the same study can be adapted to meet the interests of each of these age groups in a multi-aged setting.

3. Create a web or wheel for a study of the same topic for three different age groups; each age group will work in its own classroom. How will the study differ for each age group? Does this exercise influence your thinking about Exercise 2? Discuss your findings with colleagues.

4. Make a curriculum wheel for the study you began planning in Exercise 1.

5. Draft a letter to parents about this study, inviting them to share their ideas and participate in some way.

Resources

Cohen, D. H. (1972). *The learning child*. New York: Schocken Books.

Gamberg, R., Kwak, W., Hutchings, M., & Altheim, J. (1988). *Learning and loving it: Theme studies in the classroom*. Portsmouth, NH: Heinemann.

Katz, L. G., & Chard, S. C. (1989). *Engaging children's minds: The project approach*. Norwood, NJ: Ablex.

Mitchell, L. S. (1991). *Young geographers* (4th ed.). New York: Bank Street College of Education. (Originally published in 1934 by The John Day Company.)

Taba, H., Durken, M., Fraenkel, J., & McNaughton, A. (1971). *A teacher's handbook to elementary social studies: An inductive approach* (2nd ed.). Reading, MA: Addison-Wesley.

About the Author:

Judy R. Jablon, M.S., is a curriculum consultant who works with teachers in Head Start and public school programs. She has been a primary grade teacher in public and private schools, including Bank Street School for Children. She has taught courses in curriculum development at Bank Street College.

11 | Literacy in Early Childhood

Research shows that becoming literate—learning the skills of reading and writing and using them to communicate—is a life-long process that begins at birth. Children of all languages and cultures are natural communicators. Nearly all children will learn to read and write between the ages of 5 and 8, if allowed to go at their own pace with the encouragement and guidance of adults. Learning these skills can be compared to learning how to speak. Each requires lots of practice and support from adults who express delight in children's efforts rather than rush in to correct mistakes.

As infants, children communicate through cries, sounds, facial expressions, and body movements. At around 6 months, they begin babbling, which may at first sound like "ba-ba-ba" or "me-me-me" and over time develops into recognizable sounds. By their first birthday, they can say a few words. As they interact with people and things in the course of their daily lives, children develop an ever-expanding vocabulary. And, eventually, they discover another way of communicating—written language.

Print is a natural part of a child's world. It appears everywhere—on the cereal box at breakfast, on tee-shirts, bulletin boards, shopping lists, street signs, and in books at home and in school. As they read stories, see their parents, siblings, and teachers read and write, and explore print in their play, young children learn about how written language works.

Understanding that print has meaning is a first step in learning to read and write. Children learn this by observing that reading influences people's behavior. They might see, for example, a parent stopping the car at a STOP sign or a teacher getting out the flour after referring to a recipe for playdough. Inviting children to help write lists, notes, letters, and books helps them understand that written messages are ways of communicating with other people. You can see that children have made this key discovery when, for example, Amelia, 3 years old, intently reads "Do Not Knock Over" as she runs her finger along marks she has made on a piece of paper, then hangs it on her building in the block corner.

Over time, in an environment where children are safe to explore and practice new skills without fear of "making a mistake," they refine their knowledge about print. They discover, for instance, the direction of a line of print, that words are made up of letters, the names of those letters, and later, strategies for figuring out an

What is literacy?

unfamiliar word. Each discovery is another step towards becoming a capable reader and writer. The charts at the end of this chapter will give you an overview of the major stages of literacy development in early childhood.

In the past, we thought children had to master spoken language before they were ready to read and write, so we didn't teach reading and writing until age 6. Educators talked in terms of children's "readiness" to read and write. We now know that children begin learning about both spoken language and print in their early years (in communities where they are exposed to written language). We know that speaking, reading, and writing are interactive, each one supporting the other's development. Because we see that these skills develop together from a very young age, we now speak of the "emergence" of literacy. Knowing that speaking, reading, and writing are all part of the language development process leads us to use the term "whole-language approach" to describe how we help children learn language.

In this chapter, we are going to explore the importance of emergent literacy and discuss how you can promote the literacy of the children with whom you work. Then there will be some exercises you and your colleagues can do together to apply what you have learned in this chapter to your daily practice.

Why is it important to understand emergent literacy?

You want the children you work with to learn eventually to read and write. Understanding the idea of "emergent" literacy can help you figure out how best to promote these critical skills.

Like many caregivers and teachers, you may find that, as you learn more about emergent literacy, you end up questioning and modifying your approach to teaching reading and writing. Do not be alarmed. This is a terrific opportunity for growth. Your development as an educator and children's development as communicators will be enhanced as you examine your practices in light of what researchers have discovered.

Let us take a look at a few recent discoveries about how children learn to read and write that have led many teachers to reevaluate how they go about promoting these skills:

Children learn about reading and writing through play.
Researchers have found that as children play they become more competent "symbol-users." They also learn about what reading and writing are.

When 3-year-old Gregory picks up a block and uses it as a car, he is using the block as a symbol. It is something that stands for something else. Learning to use symbols is a necessary part of learning to read and write, and making the letters "t-e-l-e-p-h-o-n-e," which are just marks on paper stand for a telephone.

162

As she proudly scribbles on paper, 14-month-old Maritza is trying to use and understand reading and writing, long before she is a reader and writer. By playing with books, paper, crayons, and markers, children learn what reading and writing are and how it feels to be a reader and writer.

These findings can serve to remind you and parents of the value of play in literacy development—an idea that can easily be overlooked by adults who feel pressured to "teach" children to read and write. Offering children opportunities to play is one of the best ways of promoting their emerging literacy.

Children learn about reading and writing throughout the day.
We used to think that children learned to read and write during defined teaching periods of the day. But if we believe children are natural communicators and learn about language—be it English, Spanish, Creole, or Arabic—throughout the day, it no longer makes sense to equate learning to read and write with only one or two specific times. This is not to say that you should eliminate reading and writing periods, but rather be aware of the tremendous amount of literacy learning that takes place as children play with friends, take neighborhood walks, and read an applesauce recipe when preparing snack.

The teacher's role is to nurture children's natural desire to read and write.
Researchers have found that spending time reading and writing about what interests them is what makes children competent readers and writers. Wanting to read and write is more important than mastering mechanical skills. Skills are better learned and remembered as children need and use them.

No matter what age children you work with, they come to you with a certain amount of knowledge about reading and writing. Sam, 13 months, may be learning that a crayon is for making marks on a paper, not for eating. Natasha, 4 years old, may spend long periods of time writing her name and the names of her friends. Cordell, 7 years old, uses invented spelling (spelling out words the way they sound to him) to write a page that will become part of a class book about a trip to a nearby farm.

We have to shift our idea of the teacher's role from developing specific skills, such as auditory discrimination (hearing the difference between sounds), to discovering what children already know and are inquiring about and building a program that moves them forward. Rather than teaching skills in isolation of content, the challenge is to nurture children's desire to explore the world and communicate, and to enhance their sense of competence as readers and writers. The teacher's role becomes that of acting as a model, providing materials, and offering support for children's efforts.

We need a new picture of what teaching reading and writing looks like. Our image of a teacher standing in front of the room must be replaced with a teacher who moves around the room, responding to the needs of individual children and small groups—someone sitting in a rocking chair reading to an infant, or having a conference with a small group of school-age children about how to figure out the meaning of words. In the role of facilitator, the teacher is no longer the sole source of information. He or she helps children become resources for one another so they can share their interests and knowledge as they read and write together. This is not to say a teacher never teaches a skill or addresses a whole class at once—only that this is just one small part of supporting the development of readers and writers.

Children read more when they decide what they want to read.

Literacy researchers have found that when children decide what they want to read, they take more responsibility for their reading. Children need books that reflect their changing interests. They need books that range from simple to more difficult to read. They need books that are relevant to the social and cultural reality of their daily lives and our multi-cultural, multi-ethnic, multi-racial world. Perhaps most important of all, they need books that are not simply stories, but literature—quality books that touch their lives, model rich language, and spark the imagination—books that make them want to read.

This has direct impact on the use of basals in the classroom. It does not mean a teacher should not use basals but that they be used flexibly. Rather than viewing them as a prescribed program to be followed step by step, you may choose to see basals as collections of readings from which teachers and children can make selections based on children's interests and needs. And basals should be only one of many books that are available to children.

Children learn from their mistakes.

Researchers have studied the best ways to help children learn from their mistakes in reading and writing. Instead of jumping in to correct children, they have modeled different responses and encouraged children to find their own solutions. When, for example, a child could not read the word "elephant," she was encouraged to take a guess or use picture cues. When a boy did not know how to write "green," he was urged to invent his own spelling, ask a friend, or look around the room to find the word and copy it.

To the surprise of many, it was found that children were often able to come up with the correct answers themselves. This gave children a sense of mastery and a desire to continue reading and writing.

It was also found that observing children's "mistakes" could help teachers plan curriculum. When they realized that there were many children who did not make full use of picture cues, teachers made it a point to talk about using pictures and modeled using them when reading aloud.

Children benefit when parents and teachers work together to promote reading and writing.

Literacy develops not only at school but at home. As children talk and read in the course of their daily lives with their parents and siblings, aunts and uncles, and friends, their language is enriched along with their understanding of print. The recognition of family literacy means that teachers and parents need to work together to support a child's reading and writing.

Think, for example, how much Sergio, 6 years old, benefits when his teacher and parents discuss such basic information as how children learn to read and write and the neighborhood signs Sergio reads. His parents, upon learning how important it is for Sergio to gain reading and writing experiences that arise naturally from his daily life, might ask him to add a note to the bottom of a letter to Grandma, spelling the words the way he wants—something they had never considered before. Knowing that Sergio always talks about the "Bakery" and "Shoe Repair" signs when he runs errands in the neighborhood with his parents, his teacher can point them out during a walk and encourage him to use signs in his block building by placing slips of paper and crayons in the block area. In addition to enriched literacy experiences, Sergio has the security of knowing that his important adults at home and in school are behind him and value his work and interests.

Perhaps most important of all, knowing about emergent literacy allows you to take advantage of moments that promote literacy by giving children the sense of competence and pride that come with "being the knower." Consider this situation:

Patty, age 3, runs across the living room to Mary, her family child care provider, calling "Mary . . . this is my book about the circus." Mary, with surprise and delight, takes a careful look at what Patty hands her—a folded piece of paper with scribbles. How would you respond?

Because Mary knows about emergent literacy, she can see the importance of what Patty has done—writing a book and reading it. Mary is therefore able to treat Patty's book with the respect and attention it deserves. "What a wonderful surprise. Would you like to read your book to me?"

How do you promote literacy?

The age of the children you teach will determine the literacy activities in your room. But here are basic principles that support the development of readers and writers of any age.

Recognize and respect children's efforts and knowledge.
Literacy development happens within relationships. When you acknowledge an infant turning the page of a book or a toddler turning a picture book right-side-up you are encouraging their interest in literacy. When you listen intently as a preschooler reads you the scribbles she carefully made on a sheet of paper, and encourage a school-age child to explain to a friend how he figured out the meaning of an unfamiliar word, you are helping children feel good about themselves as readers and writers. You are saying, "It is safe here to explore and try something new." You are making reading and writing theirs. By fostering a sense of confidence and competence, you encourage children to read and write more, which will ultimately lead to them becoming better readers and writers.

- **Observe.** When a toddler goes over to get a truck as you read a truck book together, you can see she understands what the book is about.

- **Collect work** of preschool and school-age children. Date the samples so you can keep track of how their interests develop and change over time.

- **Talk with school-age children about what they want to learn.** After noticing punctuation in a book he was reading, Rico told his teacher he wanted to use the same marks in his writing.

- **Have school-age children keep writing books and reading journals.** Writing books (books in which children write about topics of their choice) and reading journals (books in which children record responses to what they read) can reveal children's interests and give you insight into their thinking.

Make reading and writing part of children's life in your room.
Children want to communicate about topics that interest them. There is plenty of subject matter in your room that fits this bill every day. You can encourage even young toddlers to add a few scribbles to a shopping list or a note home. A message about what is going to happen that day, a job chart, class books written by the children about trips and special events, and a recipe board listing the day's snack provide meaningful reading and writing opportunities for preschoolers and school-age children. When a child asks you a question about how roads are made, say, "How can we find out more? Let's look for a book about it." Let children know that books are sources of information and learning. Take regular trips to the library.

How do we get to school?

Ann: I go on the bus.

Miguel: I walk with my father.

Jessica: I ride in the car.

Be a reader and writer.

By reading and writing, you show children that you value these activities. As you read and write with children and on your own, share your pleasure in these skills. You might, for instance, communicate the satisfaction you feel about writing a thank-you note to a class visitor or express your delight in reading a note from home about a child's weekend. As you read and write, give children a behind-the-scene look at strategies you use. Articulate, for example, your thinking about how to spell or pronounce a word. Seeing that you are interested in and enjoy reading and writing, children are encouraged to follow your lead.

Be sure your physical space promotes reading and writing.

Here are some basic steps for creating an environment that invites children to read and write:

- Create a comfortable, protected, well-lit reading area. Though reading should occur throughout your room, this is a place where an infant can snuggle with her special caregiver and listen to a story, or two 7-year-olds can sit uninterrupted and read to one another stories they have written.

- Provide a variety of age-appropriate reading materials around the room. For older children, this includes reference materials, periodicals, newspapers, and reading games. These materials should be displayed clearly so children can easily find what they want to read.

- Provide a variety of writing tools. Supervise toddlers in their use of crayons and markers to prevent tasting and poking. For older children, clearly display these items plus pencils so children can easily find them.

- Display a variety of written materials that reflect children's interests. Be sure to include materials made by you and children as well as those you have purchased. For example, consider making a book for infants and toddlers out of photographs you took during a walk to the park, a box labeled "NAMES" that holds an index card for each child's name (for preschoolers who love to write the names of their friends), and, for school-age children, a list of words that have come up during a study of cities.

- Offer opportunities for reading, recording, and communicating throughout the day. Welcome toddlers into the world of reading by inviting them to help you open your junk mail. Offer preschoolers dramatic play props such as menus, tickets, prescription pads and maps. Keep a supply of markers, pencils, and paper available in the woodworking area so school-age children can record measurements and label their projects.

Read regularly to children. Encourage them to read to one another.
Being read to is one of the most satisfying experiences of life. It is a time of warm, personal interaction between the reader and listener that enhances children's interest in books. Over time, children learn that a story has a beginning, middle, and end. As they learn to write, their work becomes more coherent, resembling stories they know so well.

If you are a caregiver of infants and toddlers or preschoolers, count on reading the same story over and over. Though you may be tired of reading about a bunny that runs away or a hungry caterpillar, repeated readings give children a pleasing, confidence-inspiring sense of predictability.

Here are several recognizable strategies parents, caregivers, and teachers use that are helpful to children (examples for younger children are based on *Goldilocks and The Three Bears*; examples for older children are based on *Charlotte's Web* by E. B. White):

- Prompt responses, asking questions such as: "What is Goldilocks doing in this picture?" to toddlers, and "How does Wilbur feel?" to first graders.

- Model responses for children: "I think that maybe the bears will come home. Let's see what happens on the next page." "I wonder if Wilbur will win at the fair. Let's see what happens in the next chapter."

- Help children relate stories to personal experiences: "Remember the time you tasted your soup and it was too hot? Just like Goldilocks." "Tell us about a time you felt sad like Charlotte did."

- Ask children to predict: "What do you think is going to happen next?"

- Offer positive reinforcement for their comments and questions: "You remembered that the little bear found his cereal 'all gone.' You remember so well." "You remembered a lot of details about what happened at the fair. Does anyone have something to add?"

- In addition to reading to children, encourage them to read to one another. Reading to a friend gives children a sense of pride—a sense that they truly are readers. This is true even for toddlers, who proudly sit with a doll turning pages and retelling a familiar story. Show children you value and respect their reading together by giving them the space and time they need for this important activity.

Infants and Toddlers

When he was about 2-1/2 years old, Andrew could identify "M." Then he was thrilled to discover "W," which he called an "upside-down M." He made up stories about the letters: to him, a "K" looked like someone walking; an "A" he called "mine," recognizing that it began his name. In another six months or so, Andrew began to try to form his own "M" and "K." All along, his parents and teachers encouraged him to write his name (even if it was just a mark) on his paintings and to find an "M" on a page in a book. Soon Andrew was finding his own "Ms"—in the name of the refrigerator at home, in the labels on the shelves at school. Although some of Andrew's classmates knew all the letters in their names before Andrew did, his parents and teachers took their cues from him, knowing that he was learning about letters as they acquired meaning for him. It would have been counterproductive to force him to learn all the letters of the alphabet when he was not interested.

Preschoolers

There is no better way to encourage reading and writing than by giving children the pride and satisfaction of being authors of books that are about their lives. After years of worrying that it would be too complicated a project, Mrs. Benson now regularly writes group books with the 4- and 5-year-olds she teaches. They are about topics of interest to the children—class trips, a special visitor, the guinea pig. Sometimes Mrs. Benson initiates a book idea. Other times, small groups of children decide to publish a book. (The most recent one, *The Fire Station*, was five pages of children's drawings stapled together.)

The first book was written after a trip to a nearby apple orchard. She asked each child to draw and write about his or her favorite part of the trip. Together they punched holes and fastened the pages with metal rings. Then she asked each author to read and tell about his or her page. To Mrs. Benson's delight, the children were thrilled as they read "their book." She noticed that it quickly became one of the most popular books on the shelf. Children asked her to read it aloud, and they read it to themselves and one another.

If you, like Mrs. Benson, feel hesitant about the idea of making a group book, remember that you do not have to do it perfectly the first time. You can learn as you go. Over time, Mrs. Benson refined her book-making techniques by asking children to make a cover and covering the pages with clear contact paper to protect them. It is an activity well worth trying.

Young School-Age Children

One of the ways Louis promotes literacy in the group of 6- and 7-year-olds that he teaches is by incorporating Writer's Workshop into his daily schedule. Writer's Workshop is a time of day during which

From LAUReN219
MA+ARAZZO'S
(on OctoBeR 1 1991
I PickAPUMPKIng
I Pick A MeDiUM

Size PUMPKin
I FeLt tickily
At MA+ARAZZO
FARM I FeLt
Like I HaD ticks

in My BoDy I Saw
THeSe LiTTLE
PLANtS With Big
BugS ontheM
TickLing MeI

ScRatched NY
Face NY Leg AND
NY head I
tried To
ScRatche NY Back

But I couLDn'+
THAT IS THE
END oF
MA+ARAZZO'S
FARM StoRY

Lauren   Figure 1

children are writers. Like all writers, they not only put words to paper but think of a topic and of ways to develop it. Giving children the responsibility for deciding what they will write about motivates them by making writing theirs. (For an example of 7-year-old Lauren's story about visiting a pumpkin farm, see Figure 1.)

At the beginning of each Writer's Workshop, Louis gathers children for a meeting. Sometimes they discuss what went on the day before or techniques to improve their writing. For example, he might read children examples of opening sentences from books in order to introduce a discussion about how authors capture their reader's attention and interest. He encourages children to think about their own opening sentences.

For the next 20 to 30 minutes following the meeting, children work on a piece in their writing folders and consult with one another. During the workshop, Louis moves around the room responding to children's work, helping them, as necessary, to focus on the task at hand. He holds individual conferences with children. During a conference, he invites the child to share part of his story. After "receiving it" (listening carefully and openly), he tells the child what he heard. Often he asks extending questions designed to stretch the child's thinking. He may say, for example, "I liked the part when you and your mother got stuck in the elevator. How did you feel? How could you show the reader how you felt?" This process conveys his interest in what the child is writing about.

Knowing he cannot be everywhere and wanting to give children the satisfaction of becoming more independent learners, Louis encourages children to have conferences with one another. He puts children in touch with others who have similar interests or who may need help. For example, when Jason wants to write about whales, Louis suggests he talk with James, who just finished reading a book about them. Helping one another gives children the sense of pride and empowerment that comes with being the "knower." Louis asks individual children how they can get the information they need to continue their work. For example, he may ask Francis, age 6, "Where in our room could you find the word 'helper'?"

At the end of most days' workshops, Louis calls the children together for a "share" meeting in which they take turns showing their illustrations, reading any text they have written, and explaining their work to the group. He puts a lot of thought and effort into helping children learn how to be positive responders. He sets the tone by modeling respectful listening and questioning. He may, for example, ask the group, "What did you like about the writer's work? What did it remind you of? Have you ever had a similar experience?" Over time, with guidance, children learn how to talk to one another in positive, supportive ways about what they did not understand or what they might have done differently.

Because so much happens during every Workshop, Louis keeps brief notes on what children say about their writing. This helps him decide if, when, and how to intervene. For example, after reviewing his notes, Louis realized how frustrated Harry was. His story about dinosaurs just was not going anywhere. Louis decided to step in and help Harry figure out where he might get the information he needed to develop his piece.

Louis' emphasis is on helping children understand that they have something important to say. Addressing mechanics is secondary. Louis teaches about quotation marks, for example, when children need to use them in their work. When Max writes a story with lots of dialogue, Louis asks if he will share his work with the class. Together Louis and Max write part of Max's story on chart paper. Louis explains that writers use quotation marks to let the reader know who is talking. He does not expect that everyone will begin using quotation marks. He offers the information and leaves it at that. Louis knows it takes time for mechanics to carry over into writing and that worrying about mechanics interferes with children's writing.

Families

Harriet, a new kindergarten teacher, is struck by 5-year-old Robert's seeming lack of language skills and literacy background. He does not speak much. He is not able to sit still, let alone pay attention when she reads aloud. She never sees him pick a book up on his own. Rather than using crayons to draw or practice writing his name, he rolls them around the table on good days and throws them across the room on bad days.

She makes an effort to build a relationship with Robert's mother and grandfather who alternately drop him off in the morning. Over time, a picture emerges. Robert's family clearly wants the best for him. Struggling to meet basic needs, such as paying the rent and buying food, there just is not time or energy to spend talking with Robert about his day, let alone reading aloud to him.

Feeling frustrated and overwhelmed, Harriet talks with colleagues about how to promote Robert's sense of self as a communicator. She comes up with a beginning strategy. She decides she can best support Robert's literacy in the classroom by enhancing his sense of competence in every area. She observes and works to build an individualized "literacy" program based on his interest in cars and trucks. She talks with Robert about vehicles out on the playground, brings in books and magazines with pictures of cars and trucks, and invites him to help her make and label a cardboard box car to add to the dramatic play area.

With the idea of creating a literacy partnership with his family, Harriet continues building her relationship with Robert's mother and grandfather. She offers a welcoming smile and, when they come to drop him off and pick him up, an observation of something Robert said or did. When Robert shows a strong interest in the pictures in one of the magazines, she lets him take it home and keep it. Over time, Harriet hopes to encourage the family to borrow class books. She believes that establishing a sense of trust and caring about Robert must come first, before she talks more directly about reading and writing.

Exercises

1. One of the best ways that we know for teachers and caregivers to understand what children are experiencing as they learn to read and write is to become writers themselves. Consider joining a group of people who meet regularly to discuss their writing. You may want to write for pure enjoyment or use this as an opportunity to write job-related materials for parents or a class you are taking. Sharing your writing with others can put you in touch with feelings children in your class may experience about learning to trust peers, accepting encouragement and suggestions for clarification, listening to other writers' ideas, and offering support.

    You may find yourself feeling shy, even resistant, when thinking of sharing your writing with others. You are not alone. It can be intimidating. But we would like to suggest that you give it a try. Many adults who have tried Writer's Workshop find they have many interesting ideas and begin thinking of themselves as writers.

2. Keeping track of children's literacy development gives you a valuable source of information to use in planning and in your communication with parents. How you record children's progress is up to you. You may want to keep a file of preschool children's writing and of observations of their reading, including information about what they like to read and how they use books. Writing folders and reading journals can help you trace the path of school-age children's literacy development. The key is that you choose a system that you will regularly update.

    To complete this exercise:

    • Create a system (or review a system you have in place).

    • Implement your system and use it for a month.

    • Describe your system and share with a colleague some of the information you have collected. Discuss ways to make your system even better.

    • Make any changes and see how they work.

3. Because it is experiences of reading and writing that make good readers and writers, one of the most important ways adults can promote these skills is by encouraging children. Every day, you have many opportunities to help children feel good about their

developing skills. You may, for example, applaud an infant's ability to turn the pages of a book, ask a toddler to read what he wrote when he offers a page of scribbles, and prominently display a book written by school-age children.

To complete this exercise, list things you do over the course of a week to help children feel good about themselves as readers and writers. As you make your list, take care not to overlook responses such as smiling, placing crayons and paper in the dramatic play area, and taking time to sit down next to a child to hear what she has written. Share your list with a colleague. You may also want to share it with parents as a way of communicating how to promote literacy.

4. When Dennis brought William, his 3-year-old son, to child care, the first question he asked the family child care provider was, "When will you begin teaching him to read and write?" This is not uncommon. Wanting the best for their children, parents often press teachers to "teach" reading.

In this exercise, you will explain the concept of emerging literacy to parents and help them understand what you and they can do to promote literacy. You may want to communicate by using one or all of these suggestions: create a bulletin board display showing samples of children's writing, make literacy the topic of a newsletter, or hold a parent meeting about literacy.

Information found in this chapter and the resources listed below can help you answer the following questions for parents:

- When do children begin learning to read and write?

- Why is learning to read and write like learning to talk?

- How do you promote literacy in child care or school? (Give specific examples. You may want to share the list you made in the exercise above.)

- How can parents promote literacy at home? (Give specific examples.)

5. Everyday life in child care and school is filled with real, purposeful opportunities for writing and reading. Even young toddlers will feel proud to add scribbles to a sign or invitation to parents to come one morning for muffins and coffee.

To assess how you use real-life opportunities to promote literacy, answer these questions:

- What are some of these opportunities in your program? Think, for example, about writing a shopping list, a note home, a thank-you note, or labels for a shelf. What about reading recipes, a note from another class, or a book to find out about caring for a new class pet?

- Do you think you take full advantage of these real-life opportunities to promote literacy? Why or why not?
- How could you involve children even more?
- Discuss your responses with a colleague.

6. In this exercise, you are going to take a good, hard look at the books in your room. Use the following criteria to help you decide if they are the right books for you:

- What condition are the books in? Books that are well cared for say to children that books are to be respected.
- Are the topics of the books meaningful for children?
- Do the illustrations reflect ethnic, cultural, and racial diversity? Are disabled people included?
- Are the books free of stereotypes? Are there, for example, women firefighters and nurturing men?
- Are any of the books predictable? Recognizing a familiar refrain or event helps children feel competent and encourages reading.

7. Writing about their experiences will encourage children to be writers. Writing a book with children is not as intimidating as it may seem at first. Give it a try with the children you teach.

Resources

Calkins, L. M. (1983). *Lessons from a child: On the teaching and learning of writing*. Exeter, NH: Heinemann.

Calkins, L. M. (1986). *The art of teaching writing*. Portsmouth, NH: Heinemann.

Fields, M. V. (1988). *Literacy begins at birth*. Tucson, AZ: Fisher.

Hansen, J. (1987). *When writers read*. Portsmouth, NH: Heinemann.

Oppenheim, J., Brenner, B., & Boegehold, B. (1986). *Choosing books for kids: Choosing the right book for the right child at the right time*. New York: Ballantine.

Schickedanz, J. A. (1986). *More than the ABC's: The early stages of reading and writing*. Washington, DC: National Association for the Education of Young Children.

Smith, F. (1985). *Reading without nonsense* (2nd ed.). New York: Teachers College Press.

Strickland, D. S., & Morrow, L. M. (Eds.). (1989). *Emerging literacy: Young children learn to read and write*. Newark, DE: International Reading Association.

Taylor, D. (1983). *Family literacy: Young children learning to read and write*. Portsmouth, NH: Heinemann.

About the Author:

Amy Laura Dombro, M.S., headed the Bank Street Infant and Family Center from 1976 to 1983. She is now a consultant with Head Start Parent Child Center programs. She is the senior author of The Ordinary is Extraordinary: How Children under Three Learn *(1989, Fireside) and* Sharing the Caring: How to Find the Right Child Care and Make it Work for You and Your Child *(1991, Fireside).*

12 | Mathematics in Early Childhood

To understand the current definition of school mathematics, we have to look first at what it was before. Traditionally, school mathematics was a set of rules and rote procedures taught systematically. Today, it is defined as one way for children to make sense of the world. When they observe patterns, make predictions, estimate, solve problems, and talk about their ideas, children are doing mathematics.

Mathematical thinking in young children emerges naturally when they notice size, shape, and position and wonder about how long, how big, and how much. They discover basic mathematical concepts in everyday experiences as they play at the water table, build with blocks, bake cookies, and count classroom election votes. There are many examples of young children's mathematical thinking:

- Luz, 18 months, likes to play with a sorting box, matching the shapes to the holes.

- Three-year-old Laura notices patterns as she jumps over repeating lines on the sidewalk.

- Tanya and Jack, 6-year-olds, guess how many watermelon seeds are in their slices and then count to check their guess. They are working on estimation skills.

Caregivers and teachers support and extend mathematical thinking when they help children find words to describe their discoveries. Looking at the playdough he has molded, Max runs his finger along the smooth rounded edges. His teacher asks him to describe it. "It's like this," he says, repeating the circular gesture with his finger. Giving Max a label for a concept he knows, she replies, "Yes, Max it's round. It's a circle like the clock." This helps Max learn the language of mathematics. Teachers also extend mathematical thinking when they offer opportunities for children to read and write about math. Four- and five-year-olds who are studying the shoe store make a graph of what size shoes they wear; a first grade class reads today's date during their morning meeting.

In this chapter, we are going to look at why this view of mathematics is important and how you can promote the mathematical literacy of the children you work with. Then there will be exercises for you and colleagues to do together to apply what you have learned in this chapter to your daily work with children.

What is mathematics?

Why adopt this view of mathematics?

Like many adults, you may remember feeling intimidated by the rules and rote of mathematics. We know early experiences in school set a tone for future learning. With the new view of mathematics, the children you teach can feel comfortable about math, which will promote their learning. Active, hands-on math experiences in a safe and trusting environment help children become learners who take risks, think independently, and see math learning as enjoyable.

As a caregiver or teacher, your job is to help children develop the math skills needed for the world we live in—a world of technology, of sophisticated machines, computers, and calculators. This is the information age, which means we have a tremendous amount of information (called data) that must be collected, organized, interpreted, evaluated, analyzed, and communicated to others. To deal with these data, people need to understand and be able to use such mathematical principles as chance, reasoning, form, and pattern. When children have opportunities to work on practical problems and explain their thinking, they begin to develop the math skills necessary for the information age.

This approach to mathematics can open your eyes to the beauty of math. Sharon, a preschool teacher, brings a new appreciation of mathematics to her interaction with 5-year-old Anna, who asks her to look at a completed painting. Although Sharon immediately notices its symmetry, she first invites Anna to tell her about the painting, and then asks if she planned to paint the same wiggly lines and dots on the left as on the right. Once pointed out to her, Anna expresses delight and purposefully uses symmetry on her next painting. Children will come to appreciate the elegance and order in mathematical thinking just as adults do.

How can you promote mathematical literacy?

Traditionally, the mathematics teacher's role was to present children with sets of rules, pages in a textbook, and flashcards. This is no longer the case. Mathematics as a way of thinking is promoted by encouraging children to observe, think, and talk about their observations. You help them to:

- study things ("Look at how much our bean seeds have grown");
- compare them ("Which seeds grew the most?");
- look at their attributes ("How many leaves does each plant have?");
- observe similarities and differences ("Do the bean plants and radishes have leaves that look alike?");
- describe mathematical relationships ("How can we measure how much the beans have grown?").

When you respond to "math moments" in your program—taking attendance, setting the table, or dividing cookies—you show children the importance of mathematical thinking. In addition to math moments and the math learning that happens naturally in children's play, you plan opportunities for children that help them learn specific concepts. Mathematics experiences in your program will vary with the age of the children. Here are some guidelines to help you support the development of mathematical thinking in early childhood.

Encourage children's enjoyment of and curiosity about mathematical thinking.

You are encouraging children's natural curiosity about mathematical relationships when you:

- remark to the toddler playing at the water table, "I see you are doing a wonderful job pouring water from the big container to the little one";

- listen to the 4-year-old tell you which blocks he decided to use to make his building so tall;

- offer the young school-age child materials, such as counters, beans, unifix cubes, or a calculator, to divide 60 crackers among 22 people.

Children's natural curiosity is a powerful motivator for learning. They spontaneously create problems to solve, and by valuing their investigations and helping them see mathematical connections, you encourage them to explore further.

Look beyond what children appear to know to elicit their ideas. Your comments, questions, and suggestions can help children think about mathematical concepts.

Children take pleasure in finding patterns—it is a way of seeing order. You can see this happening when you play hide and seek with a 9-month-old, when a toddler eagerly waits for the repeated phrase in a story, when a preschooler plays a clapping game, or when a 7-year-old figures out that if one bike has two wheels, then 50 bikes have 100 wheels. By helping children notice patterns—in the clothes they wear, on the leaves outside, and in the rhythm of their daily schedule—you are nurturing their mathematical thinking.

Listen carefully to children and observe their thinking.

In order to know what concepts children understand and what they are trying to figure out, observe what they do and listen carefully to what they say. Children reveal their thinking when, for example, a 13-month-old tries to fill his bottle by sticking it in a neighbor's cup of milk at snack, two 4-year-olds stack big plastic pegs to their respective heights and announce who is taller, or a group of 8-year-olds working on probability flip a quarter 100 times and tell you their final score is 55 tails to 45 heads.

- Look at their intuitive insights and listen to their language, rather than simply correcting them. Children learn from their own errors—so let them make mistakes. Three-year-old Carrie continually topples her building each time she tries to balance a large cylindrical block on top of a small square one. She does not center it and the weight is unevenly distributed. Finally, she pauses and looks at the fallen blocks. Then she adjusts the top block, finding the perfect balance point.

- Use their confusions to help you determine what other experiences they need. When you convey to children that you value their thinking, you encourage them to take risks and test out new ideas. Observing 4-year-old Julio counting, "One, three, four, six," as he gathers leaves in the yard, his caregiver decides to offer him the job of putting out juice cups for snack time so he can practice one-to-one correspondence.

- Pose open-ended questions and statements like, "Tell me how you decided to group these objects," "How could we figure out how to measure the height of this wall?" or "What do you think would happen if you flipped the quarter 200 times?"

In these ways, you encourage children to explain their thinking, consider possibilities, and communicate mathematical relationships.

Take advantage of everyday situations to promote mathematical literacy.

Children need active, hands-on experiences to develop mathematical understanding. Take advantage of everyday materials and daily routines to foster emergent mathematical thinking. You can, for example, offer a 12-month-old the opportunity to explore size by giving her a set of measuring cups to play with. You can help a preschooler figure out how many napkins are needed for snack by saying, "Put a napkin at each place where there is a chair." You can encourage young school-age children to practice counting by having them tally the results of a class survey. You can include games in your early childhood setting to encourage math: dice, cards, and chess are favorites of young school-age children.

Use real problems—ones that are realistic for children to solve at different ages—to help children learn concepts. Problems can be presented in different ways:

- You can set up a situation by placing a pattern of colored blocks on the table and inviting children to continue the pattern.

- You can pose a problem: "We have twenty cookies to share."

- You can ask a question: "How can we figure out how many children are absent today?"

You integrate math experiences into the work of your program when you add a scale for preschoolers to weigh fruits and vegetables in the market created in dramatic play, provide 5-year-olds with yarn to measure widths of buildings outside, or help first graders think about building their model city to scale. Important math experiences can emerge from studies your class may be working on.

Encourage children to communicate about mathematics.

Communication is a critical part of mathematical learning. After repeated efforts, Alison, 3, declares that her trike and the tunnel "won't fit!" Delante, 8 years old, explains how, using a ruler, he made a mark for every foot measured and had seven inches left over when measuring the length of his classroom. Alison and Delante are putting mathematical thoughts into words. In this way, they organize and clarify their thinking.

Encouraging children to listen to one another helps them reflect on their own ideas and compare their thinking to that of others. Collective problem solving or collaboration encourages children to talk to each other, to share information, to combine strategies. It teaches children that they have a responsibility to a group, that everyone has to understand, that everyone may have an opinion. In a second grade, four children are estimating the number of macaroni in a jar and then dump the contents on their table in order to count the actual number. Amir randomly splits the pile into four groups, suggests ways that each group member count his or her pile, and then add their answers to get a total. Schuwanza begins to group her pile by tens while Evan counts by ones, losing his place and starting over more than once. Schuwanza finishes first and invites Mr. Gomez over to the table to observe her work. Mr. Gomez encourages Schuwanza to explain her method to Evan. Schuwanza shows Evan the "tens" strategy. With Mr. Gomez's support, these children are learning to work in groups, to help each other, and to combine their ideas.

Reading books about mathematical ideas lets children see how mathematical thinking is all around them. Books about the history of math, cookbooks, books of mazes and puzzles can be added to your classroom library. Drawing and writing about math allows children to find symbolic ways to describe their mathematical discoveries. As they get older, math journals can serve as personal records of their thinking.

Allow enough time for children to pursue learning about mathematics.

Real understanding of mathematical concepts takes time. In the course of a week, 8-month-old Nina explores spaces of different sizes. Her caregivers observe her repeatedly crawling in and out of an empty refrigerator box, trying to crawl under a table that is so low she cannot fit, and squeezing between two pieces of furniture. Four-year-old Japera explores measuring by making trains of unifix cubes that stretch the length of her classroom. Other children become interested in what she is doing and begin measuring book shelves, rugs, and tables. This activity continues for a few weeks and leads to graphing. Two 7-year-olds spend many sessions in the woodworking area building a model plane and making wings of different sizes. Some wings are too big, others too small. Having time for trial and error, they eventually end up with wings that are just the right size. Children of all ages need ample time to work on their math ideas and solve the problems they set for themselves. For caregivers and teachers, learning not to interrupt children or to "rush" them to an answer is as important as learning when and how to intervene in order to extend their thinking.

You offer many different opportunities to explore a mathematical idea and understand that all children do not learn the same things from an experience. And when you demonstrate persistence, children are helped to understand and confront the frustrations of problem solving—sometimes an answer cannot be found right away. Nikki and Raymond, first graders, plan to paint a mural to hang along the bottom of the chalkboard. First they have to figure out how long to make it. Nikki moves a yardstick along the bottom edge of the chalkboard but does not keep track of where the yardstick ends each time. "Six feet," he says. The children measure and cut off a length of paper. When they hold it up, it is too long. Frustrated, they take the paper down. Raymond cuts it again. "That's too short," Nikki says. Both boys are ready to give up. Ms. Samad, the teacher, suggests, "Let's think of other ways to figure out how long the paper has to be." The boys are quiet. Then Raymond says, "I'll count my footsteps." Nikki says, "Okay. I'll use a piece of string and hold it up to the chalkboard." Ms. Samad knows that even after the children have tried out their new methods, they still may not be satisfied. They may need further support and encouragement from her; they may have other ideas of their own about how to measure the paper. She intends to give them the time they need to learn about mathematics from this experience.

Be sure your physical environment fosters mathematical thinking. Create an environment in which mathematical thinking can be nurtured. Materials that can be handled support mathematical thinking.

- Collections of found objects, buttons, dried beans, shells, egg cartons, and orange juice cans are great for sorting and classifying, making patterns, and counting.
- Manipulatives you buy, like unifix cubes, Cuisenaire rods, rig-a-jig, and pattern blocks, are mathematical models that help

children discover patterns and relationships.

- Scales, measuring cups, clocks, thermometers, and other measuring devices should be available for children to use every day.

Repeated experiences with a variety of objects helps children develop mathematical concepts. For example, measuring length with cubes, their own hands, and pieces of string allows children to experience what longer and shorter means and apply their understanding to conventional measures like a ruler.

The same materials will be used differently by children at various stages of development. The tablespoon is sucked by the infant, used by the toddler to stir, and held by the preschooler to measure vanilla when cookies are made. The Cuisenaire rod used by the 6-year-old to add is used by the 8-year-old to learn fractions.

As children become engaged in solving problems, they need to know where to find the right tools to help them. Labeling the math materials and blocks will encourage the children to use them and take care of them.

Provide opportunities for thoughtful and creative uses of technology.

Calculators and computers are tools that support and simplify mathematical work. They do not replace mathematical understanding, but feeling comfortable with their use gives children additional flexibility as problem solvers.

- Nicole, 5 years old, experiments with the computer during choice work time as she did with the typewriter a few days earlier.

- Matthew, 6 years old, uses a calculator to help him predict the height of his bean plant a month from now because he has not learned formal multiplication.

- Rick, 8 years old, uses Logo on a computer to support other hands-on geometry experiences he has had.

In these classrooms, teachers are using calculators and computers in creative ways. They make careful decisions about when and how to include these tools in their programs.

In summary, the National Council of Teachers of Mathematics recommends that educators focus more attention on use of manipulative materials, cooperative work, discussions of mathematics, questioning, justification of thinking, writing about mathematics, problem-solving approaches to skill instruction, and content integration. Less attention should be spent on rote practice and memorization of rules, one answer and one method, use of worksheets, written practice, and teaching by telling.

Putting mathematics into action

Infants and Toddlers

Della, a family day care provider, is playing dress-up with toddlers, Jessie and Lori. Several pairs of adult shoes are in the prop box. Grabbing a pair of slippers, Jessie takes off her own shoes and slips into the new ones. Smiling, she says, "Too big!" and walks across the floor. Della agrees, "Yes, Jessie, they are big, but you are walking in them just fine." Now, sitting on the floor, Della takes off her shoes and tries on Jessie's sneaker, pushing and tugging as if to make it fit. Jessie comes over to take a look. She giggles. Della asks, "Does Jessie's sneaker fit me?" and Jessie says, "No." Lori takes Jessie's other sneaker and discovers that it is too small for her foot. She reaches into the prop box and takes out a pair of boots. Capturing a math moment, Della has helped Lori and Jessie think about big and little.

Preschoolers

Joyce teaches 3- to 5-year-olds in a cooperative nursery school. During a walk in a nearby park, the children collect things in paper bags. Back in the classroom, Joyce puts out small trays on a table. She talks with some of the children about what they found and suggests, "Let's put the things that are alike or go together on the same tray." The children discuss the objects, which include leaves, stones, bottle caps, feathers, and candy wrappers. They decide to put all the leaves and stones together because they are brown and keep each of the other items on separate trays. Joyce asks them to think of another way to group the objects. Shara, almost 5, suggests, "Things from nature and things from birds." Alberto adds, "And garbage." The children push the items around on the trays to create the new groups. Kelly and Shara make a graph of the leaves they found, grouping them by their shape. The objects and the graph become the focus of a group discussion in which children report enthusiastically on how many in each group, which category has more and less, and debate on other possible categories.

Young School-Age Children

Mrs. Graves has been introducing the concept of fractions, whole groups, and parts of groups to her 24 second graders. Knowing that math learning occurs throughout the day, Mrs. Graves uses baking cookies to highlight children's exploration of fractions. When the cookies come out of the oven, she presents the class with the problem: "We have 80 cookies to share with 24 people. How many can each of you have?" She prepares materials, including unifix cubes, counting chips, calculators, paper, pencils, crayons, scissors, Cuisenaire rods, beans, and cups, and asks the children to work in groups of four to solve the problem. The children collaborate to select materials of their choice and come up with methods and solutions.

One group counts out 24 cups, one for each child, and 80 counting chips. The children place the chips in the cups, one by one. Three chips go in each cup and 8 are left. The children stop there. Someone suggests taking the leftovers to the school secretaries. Another group uses a calculator to divide 24 into 80. They get an answer that mystifies them—"3.3333333." One child studies the calculator and remarks, "This says three and something." Mrs. Graves suggests, "See if three and something left over helps you figure out how to share the cookies. The unifix cubes or the Cuisenaire rods might help you." From experience, the children know they can break cookies in half to share. To see if halves will work in this case, they set out 8 unifix cubes, one for each leftover cookie. They then place 2 beans next to each cube to show the two pieces of each cookie. Immediately, they see that they still do not have enough to put one bean in each cup. Frank blurts out, "So, let's cut the cookies into three pieces." They place three beans next to each cube to show three pieces of each cookie. When they count the beans, they discover they have 24, one to put in each cup, or in other words, one little piece of cookie for each child. They run to Mrs. Graves with delight. "You have discovered thirds," she tells them.

Mrs. Graves invites each group to describe how it approached the "cookie" problem. The children argue, defend, and rethink their strategies. The group that discovered thirds explains their findings. Some children hold on to their way of thinking, while others are intrigued with new ideas. Many are delighted with the idea of fractions. The class votes whether to divide the eight leftover cookies in thirds and eat them or bring them to the secretaries. They decide to give them to the staff.

Mrs. Graves builds on this experience during the next several days by writing sharing problems on the blackboard for children to work on in small groups and providing them with many manipulatives for problem solving.

Families

The Smith-Gerstons are concerned that Jason, 7 years old, does not know his times tables. Bonnie, Jason's teacher, explains that he consistently uses effective strategies to solve problems in the classroom. She shares a page in his math journal in which he had been asked to solve this problem: "You have a pile of 40 counters which you have to organize in some way so that your friends can tell how many there are without counting by ones. Find at least two ways." Jason has carefully drawn pictures of the work he did using color cubes. He has one array of four rows of ten cubes and another of five rows of eight cubes. Bonnie explains that since Jason clearly understands grouping and arrays, he will eventually master the times tables as he continues to apply the already learned and more important concepts.

185

Exercises

Here are some exercises for you to do with colleagues to help you apply what you have learned about mathematics to your daily practice.

1. Have a discussion with several colleagues comparing your experiences as math learners. What are some positive and negative memories you have about learning math?

2. Take a survey of the materials in your classroom. Write down what they are and how the children in your program can use them to develop math concepts. Share your list with a colleague. Think of materials you may want to add to your program.

3. Think about the everyday routines of your classroom. What math skills can they promote? For example, putting away blocks on labeled shelves helps children learn one-to-one correspondence. Using attendance charts allows children to see how many are absent and how many are present. Clearly posted daily schedules help children develop a sense of sequence and time. Make a list and share it with colleagues.

4. Look in your local or school library for children's books about math. Think of ways you might use them with children in your program.

5. Observe several children at work or play. What differences do you notice in their emergent math understanding? For example, Jenny and Rina are constructing two separate buildings in the kindergarten block area. At some point they decide to connect their buildings with a bridge. Rina says her building needs to be taller and begins counting to see how many more blocks she needs. She gets distracted and begins counting again. Jenny tells her she can "see" she needs five more and hands them to her. Jenny visualizes the difference in heights whereas Rina relies on counting.

6. Observe how children communicate what they know about mathematical thinking. Record several specific anecdotes of children's actions or comments. Have a colleague do the same and discuss what you observe. Think of experiences you might provide these children to extend their thinking.

7. How are mathematical ideas displayed in your classroom? Do you have schedules posted, a clock, recipes, number lines, charts or graphs? (These will vary greatly with the age of children you teach.)

8. Think of ways children could write or draw about math in your classroom.

Baratta-Lorton, M. (1972). *Workjobs: Activity-centered learning for early childhood education.* Menlo Park, CA: Addison-Wesley.

Baratta-Lorton, M. (1976). *Mathematics their way: An activity-centered mathematics program for early childhood education.* Menlo Park, CA: Addison-Wesley.

Burns, M., & Tank, B. (1988). A collection of math lessons from grades 1 through 3. Sausalito, CA: Marilyn Burns Education Associates.

Clark, C., Carter, B., & Sternberg, B. (1988). *Math in stride 1–6.* Menlo Park, CA: Addison-Wesley.

Commission on Standards for School Mathematics. (1989). *Curriculum and evaluation standards for school mathematics.* Reston, VA: National Council of Teachers of Mathematics.

Harcourt, L. (1988). *Explorations for early childhood.* Menlo Park, CA: Addison-Wesley.

Kamii, C. (1982). *Number in preschool and kindergarten: Educational implications of Piaget's theory.* Washington, DC: National Association for the Education of Young Children.

Kamii, C., with Clark, G. (1985). *Young children reinvent arithmetic: Implications of Piaget's theory.* New York: Teachers College Press.

Kamii, C., & Devries, R. (1976). *Piaget, children, and number: Applying Piaget's theory to the teaching of elementary number.* Washington, DC: National Association for the Education of Young Children.

Kamii, C., & Devries, R. (1980). *Group games in early education: Implications of Piaget's theory.* Washington, DC: National Association for the Education of Young Children.

National Research Council. (1989). *Everybody counts: A report to the nation on the future of mathematics education.* Washington, DC: National Academy Press.

The Nuffield Foundation. (1979). *Nuffield maths.* Essex, England: The Longman Group.

About the Author:

Judy R. Jablon, M.S., is a curriculum consultant who works with teachers in Head Start and public school programs. She has been a primary grade teacher in public and private schools, including Bank Street School for Children. She has taught courses in curriculum development at Bank Street College.

13 | Science in Early Childhood

Science is a way to find out about the world through exploration. Scientists are careful observers. They engage in scientific investigation by forming a theory about something they want to know more about, collecting data about it, and evaluating the data critically. The belief that it is possible to understand things about the physical and natural world by active investigation is at the core of scientific thinking. Scientists understand that knowledge that results from scientific investigation is not static—it is constantly expanding and changing.

Active investigation—experimentation and discovery—is a natural part of children's lives. You can see it when a 4-month-old grabs her toes and puts them in her mouth, a toddler repeatedly drops the cereal box from the shopping cart, a 4-year-old picks up a toad for the first time and squeezes it a little too hard, or two 6-year-olds move forward and back from the edge of the seesaw, noting how they can make it stay up or crash down.

Science is something everyone can understand. Openness to discovery is what matters in scientific thinking; the techniques and tools of science are vehicles that facilitate the process of discovery and can be learned along the way. As caregivers and teachers, when you nurture children's natural desire to investigate, you are helping them develop scientific minds.

In this chapter, we look at why scientific thinking is important and how you can promote scientific inquiry in young children. Then there are some exercises you and your colleagues can do together to apply what you have learned in this chapter to your daily practice.

Why promote scientific thinking?

We live in a time when science and technology deeply affect our lives. Yet many students have developed little scientific understanding by the time they finish school—they may not be prepared, some fear, for jobs that require basic knowledge and skill in science. Studies show that children's weaknesses in science come, not from their inabilities, but from how science is taught and even whether it is taught at all.

People's attitudes about unfamiliar or unknown things are formed at an early age. Infants and toddlers, brimming with curiosity, are engaged in constant investigation and inquiry. As they get older, we want their natural ease with discovery and investigation—with asking questions and analyzing answers—to flourish. When young children have a positive attitude about science as a method of discovery, they approach further training in science with eagerness and pleasure. If they have not been encouraged to explore and discover, they may think that science is incomprehensible and forbidding.

In addition to providing a framework for exploration, scientific investigation enables children to appreciate the natural world. When caregivers and teachers make it possible for an 8-month-old to crawl on grass, a preschooler to hold a bunny (the class pet) and learn how to take care of it, and a 7-year-old to use a magnifying glass to examine sea shells, an appreciation of nature is being fostered.

As children explore, they make discoveries about cause and effect, an important scientific concept. At the water table, toddlers experiment with pouring water into different size containers and making them overflow. Preschoolers make hand prints with finger paints and observe that their hands are different sizes. First graders see what happens when they give water or sunshine to some plants but not to others. Through such positive experiences, children can develop a lifelong enthusiasm for the physical and natural world.

As caregivers and teachers, part of our responsibility is to help children become informed citizens—ones who can say, "We don't know about this problem. Let's find out about it." We want them to feel they can take an active role in understanding and shaping their world. Positive exposure to science is one way to achieve this.

How can you promote scientific thinking?

Children are investigators by nature. You encourage innate curiosity when you say to the 10-month-old squashing some blueberries and putting others in his mouth, "I see you like the way the blueberries feel. Do they taste sweet?" or to the 4-year-old watching his 6-month-old brother being fed, "Why doesn't he eat the same kind of food we do?" You watch the 3-year-old poking his finger in the playdough over and over. By not interrupting his play, you show him you value his interests. You model qualities of an investigator when you respond to 2-year-old Karen's fascination with ants by suggesting, "Let's follow the ant home to see where it lives."

As children get older, their observations and questions become more complex. At the same time, there are specific concepts and skills they need to learn. Rather than providing them with answers or controlling the specific direction of their inquiry, your role as caregiver or teacher is to facilitate, guiding them in ways that keep them in charge of their investigation. Begin with what they know, find out what they are curious about, and extend what sustains their interest. In this way, you shape their investigation by helping them experiment with possibilities, and they maintain a high level of involvement.

Many of the examples in this chapter describe everyday events involving scientific thinking. Some "science experiences" just happen, some you shape, and others you actively plan. Science experiences are different for children at different ages and what you do to encourage their scientific thinking will differ as well. However, there are principles to help you in your role as facilitator of scientific thinking in young children of any age. Here are some of them:

Let children develop and evaluate their own theories.
Through active sensory involvement with everyday things, children form theories. Often their logic seems illogical to adults. Elaine, a family day care provider, shows the children a live crab in a bucket of water. Francisco says, "Let's feed it." He begins to tear up a paper towel and drop it in the water. Elaine is tempted to stop him but instead asks, "Why are you giving him a paper towel?" Francisco answers, "The hamster chews them so I think the crab will like them too." Elaine knows that hamsters use shredded towels for nests, not to eat. She knows the crab will not eat the paper towel, but she believes that Francisco must make these discoveries himself. Later Elaine asks Francisco to show her what he found out about the crabs.

Your role is not to tell children they are wrong or to tell them the right answer, but rather to provide opportunities for them to evaluate their theories. While talking about archaeology and the question, "How do people find out things about long ago?" third graders bury some objects in a terrarium in the classroom to see if they will change or stay the same over time. The children make initial predictions which they revise as they gain new information from their experiments and from trips to the museum to study artifacts.

Class discussions reveal to their teacher that the children have different levels of understanding about the disintegration process. Four months later, one 8-year-old declares that someone has stolen the sheet of newspaper from its buried location because it can not be found when they dig it up. Some children are sure it has disintegrated, while others insist the paper is lost or stolen.

While class discussion influences some children's thinking, others remain convinced the paper was missing. The teacher does not criticize the theory for fear of discouraging the thinking that goes into making theories. Instead, she helps her class develop the courage to test their answers. She asks them to design a new experiment to determine whether the paper was lost or disintegrated. The children recreate the experiment, this time sealing the terrarium with masking tape. After three months, the tape undisturbed, the children dig for the newspaper. Most of it is gone; the remaining bits prove to the children that disintegration has occurred.

Children learn science through interactions with the physical and natural world.

Children construct their ideas about the physical and natural world based on what they know and the experiences they have. Children's interests emerge from what is right around them—things that engage their senses, that they observe, hear, feel.

As a caregiver or teacher, there are important steps you can take to encourage children's scientific exploration:

- Create an environment that offers children possibilities for exploration. As 3-year-olds sort and classify collections of leaves, 4-year-olds handle and observe guinea pigs, or 7-year-olds build simple machines, they need opportunities to describe what they see, ask questions, and find some answers.

- Offer experiences both indoors and outside. The sandbox in the yard, a walk to the park, or a trip to the zoo provide rich possibilities for scientific investigations. Materials such as tubing to crawl through, pillows of different textures, large containers, plastic tubing and colanders at the water table, microscopes, magnifiers, thermometers, and cameras stimulate new experiences. The specific materials will be different for children of different ages.

- Provide opportunities for children to work collaboratively on experiments. In this way, you facilitate social interaction and convey to children that working together is a more effective way of solving problems.

- Use the early childhood setting to convey important messages to children about scientific thinking. For example, before a cooking activity with 3-year-olds, you can hang an illustrated recipe chart to help them see there is order and method to cooking. Or you can create a height graph in the fall and again in the spring so preschoolers can see how they have grown. For young school-age children, you can display a collection of books about famous scientists, including women and minorities, so they can see many different role models.

Record keeping is part of scientific investigation.

Knowing how to record their findings will lead children to new discoveries and make it possible for them to share the results of their scientific explorations. A class of 4-year-olds, eagerly awaiting the hatching of chick eggs, mark off days on the calendar to help them discover the answer to their question, "How long will it take for the eggs to be chicks?" Five- and 6-year-olds collect tadpoles at a stream and put them in an aquarium in the classroom. The children doubt that these squirmy creatures will one day be frogs. Each day, some children draw pictures of the tadpoles, using magnifiers, and hang their pictures above the tank. After a while, children observe changes in the tank and refer to their pictures as reminders of how the tadpoles looked before.

Your role is to observe children carefully, let them become deeply engaged in their work of investigating, and, when appropriate, present them with a method of recording that organizes their observations. Chances are they will use it. Suggestions like "Draw a picture of what you see," or for older children, "Summarize your findings and share them with the class," help children develop recording skills. Record keeping includes drawings, graphs or charts, scribbles with invented spelling, and science journals.

Although very young children are not able to keep their own scientific records, you can share record-keeping systems with them. For example, collecting family photos of children from birth shows children one way that adults record change.

The children's records may not look exactly as you would like, and they may not choose to document what you think is correct or accurate. Value the work they do. Continue to present techniques for them to see. And remember that children often learn more effective recording strategies from each other when they collaborate or share their work through discussions.

Allow plenty of time for investigation.
Children need time to figure things out. If you observe children carefully, you will see when they are immersed in their work and when they are losing interest. When Mara, a caregiver, patiently holds 7-month-old Eric while he repeatedly curls a piece of her hair between his fingers, or Jan, a preschool teacher, lets Tiana have extra time to wash her hands because she gets absorbed in water play, they are letting children have time to observe and analyze their experiences. You help children develop the ability to concentrate when you watch and wait or when you intervene with an interesting suggestion.

Children need time to make repeated mistakes, to try out ideas, and to learn from one another. Their ideas remain intact until new experiences change their minds. Josh, age 4, heaps dry sand in a pile over and over, saying he is making an apartment house. It keeps falling down until Rashad, also 4, joins him and adds water to the sand; now the house stays together.

Open-ended questions help children see relationships.
Open-ended questions and statements help children observe and communicate their observations, compare, and classify. When caregivers and teachers ask questions like, "What does a bird's feather feel like?" "Tell us something about the rock's size and shape," or "Describe how the sky looks when it's going to rain," they are

helping children observe carefully as well as encouraging them to put their ideas into words.

You can help children find language to describe relationships. As children make collections and sort and classify, questions and statements like, "Tell me how these are alike," "How are these different?" or "Which is rougher?" encourage children to compare. You help them classify when you say, "Put together all those you think belong together," or "Tell me how you put your groups together."

Demonstrate strategies for solving problems.

You help children understand the process of problem solving when, instead of giving the answer or doing for children, you say, "Our door is squeaking. What do you think we could do about it?" For the toddler, you add, "Maybe we can try some oil. Would you like to come with me to get some?" Or with an older child, "Who has an idea?" Talking through a problem helps children see your thinking process. Sometimes you present strategies for problem solving when, for example, you say to the 2-year-old, "Are your string beans too hot? You can blow on them to cool them off." Use real problems from everyday situations as a chance to demonstrate to children your way of thinking—not as a chance to teach answers.

Often, real situations offer opportunities for children to think about scientific problems concerning the environment. For example, a class of third graders discuss ways people use parks. One child says, "Parks are filled with trash. People throw trash in parks." After discussing reasons why, the children are encouraged by their teacher to consider actions they might take to solve this problem. They decide to make signs, have a weekly trash pick-up, and write a letter to the local newspaper.

Putting scientific thinking into action

Infants and Toddlers

Patty, one of the teachers in an infant-toddler center, decides to take advantage of the spring weather by taking a few children on a walk. She puts Max, 14 months, in a back-pack and Doug and Katie, both 20 months, in a double stroller. As they go down a busy street, they hear a car horn. Max asks, "Da?" meaning "What is it?" Patty explains, "It's a car horn. The driver wants the bus to move." She tells the children, "Let's listen for more sounds on our walk." They hear a dog barking, a radio playing music, and a garbage can falling over. They stop to watch a cement mixer pour a new sidewalk. Each time, Patty describes what is happening and helps the children understand cause and effect—"What is making this sound?"

Preschoolers

Walking near a pond, a group of 4-year-olds are collecting leaves, twigs, stones, and other things to bring back to the classroom. Each child has a brown bag for his or her collection. Lisa stops to look at a Norway spruce, running her fingers along the pine needles. "I like how they feel," she says to no one in particular, and then moves her cheek over the tree. Lisa turns to Nina, the teacher's aide, and asks her if she wants to feel the "prickles."

Then Nina asks, "Is this pine tree like any other trees you see here?" She expects Lisa to comment on how some trees look the same as the pine but others—like the maples and oaks—look different. But Nina gets a response she does not expect. "Well, all the trees are green. That's because the pond water splashes up and colors the trees green," Lisa states with complete 4-year-old authority.

Nina encourages Lisa's thinking by asking an open-ended question. She accepts Lisa's response, noting that it is based on observation—the pond is near the trees, and the pond water looks green. Exploring patterns and relationships in the environment, Lisa makes an imaginative association with the green color of the pond surface. (In fact, the water looks green because it is reflecting the color of the trees.)

Young School-Age Children

Ms. Lordes' class of 7- and 8-year-olds are working on a gardening project; they are planting seeds in the little square plots around the trees on the school's busy city street. While digging soil, some children discover several earthworms. Their excited cries bring the other children over to look. Soon the seed planting is abandoned and they are all hunting for worms. Children remove the worms from the dirt, put them on the concrete and watch them as they stretch and squirm. Tony notices that as he was digging, his shovel chopped a worm in half, yet the creature is still moving rapidly. He calls for Ms. Lordes to come look; she asks, "Why do you think the worm is moving?" He replies, "It's getting ready to die." Sandra chimes in, "No. It won't die, 'cause worms live when they get cut." Tony does not believe this. Ms. Lordes sends the two of them back to the room for containers to transport the injured worm. She accepts the investigation of the *accidentally* cut worm. However, she does wish to instill respect for living creatures, so she discourages any children from purposefully cutting earthworms, for they will die. The other children, now totally uninterested in gardening, but enchanted with the worms, want to bring their new pets back to the classroom. Some of the more squeamish children hover by the side, nervously giggling.

Ms. Lordes suggests the children collect enough so that groups of three can each have a worm to study. Back in the room, some simply observe them with magnifiers while others make drawings. Many children measure their worms. For several days, groups of children go out and collect worms for observation. Ms. Lordes gets books from the library about worms and displays them in the classroom.

One group creates an environment for the earthworms. While studying pictures in a book, Doris observes the internal organs and shows it to several other children. Ms. Lordes encourages the children to observe the living worms carefully, to find distinct bodyparts, and to look for evidence of internal organs. She has the children draw the earthworms as they look to them through the magnifying glass.

The next day, when Ms. Lordes asks for volunteers to continue planting during outdoor time, quite a few are interested—although the majority want to collect more worms.

Ms. Lordes' plans are a framework for children's learning. When she makes her plans, she ensures that there is room for children's ideas, questions, and interests . Sometimes, as in the example above, she puts aside her plans to follow up on something new that has happened and that has caught the children's interest.

Families

David's kindergarten class is studying bakeries, and today they did experiments with yeast and vinegar. At home that night, David demonstrates his desire to continue "messing about" with science. Sitting at the table after dinner, David makes a concoction of salt, a little mustard, and what is left of the milk in his glass. Opening the refrigerator door, he asks his mother, "Where is the orange juice?"

"Why do you need it?" she asks, looking up from her newspaper. David tells her he is doing an experiment. "What are you experimenting about and why do you need orange juice?" she asks, with some irritation in her voice.

"I'm making a test," he replies with confidence. Their discussion persists for a while, and finally his mom helps him pour a little juice into his glass. But she tells him he first has to clean up the table and then he can work on the kitchen counter. To her question about what sort of test, David shrugs and says, "I want to see what will happen." In fact, what David is testing is the idea of making a test, an experiment. He is learning about the process of scientific thinking.

Exercises In this chapter, we have offered a framework for understanding the role of science in early childhood education. Here are some exercises to help you apply what you have learned in this chapter. There is a list of resources after the exercises to support you in your efforts to enhance the role science plays in your program.

1. Think of times children have come to you with a problem. What do you say? Consider some new ways to help children see your strategies for solving problems. Share your anecdotes with colleagues.

2. Look at your room arrangement and outdoor space. What are some ways your environment (materials or places) encourages children to investigate? What do you want to add?

3. Take a walk in your immediate neighborhood with one or two colleagues. Look at things from a toddler's, a preschooler's, a young school-age child's view. Record what you see. Think about how children's interests and perspectives reflect their developmental level.

4. In your conversations with children, use some of the open-ended questions and statements suggested in the chapter. Compare discussions you have had with children to those a colleague has had.

5. Use open-ended questions to have a discussion with children about some aspect of the environment. Record their responses on an experience chart. Think of some ways to extend their thinking. For example, you can ask children to think about why there are clouds in the sky. Afterwards, invite them to bring chalk, paint, paper, and water colors outside to draw the clouds. Listen to children's conversations while they work.

6. Think about how you use visual displays in your classroom to support scientific thinking. Share what you already do and what you might add with a colleague.

Resources

Chaillé, C., & Britain, L. (1991). *The young child as scientist: A constructive approach to early childhood science education.* New York: HarperCollins.

Doris, E. (1991). *Doing what scientists do: Children learn to investigate their world.* Portsmouth, NH: Heinemann.

Duckworth, E. (1987). *"The having of wonderful ideas" and other essays on teaching and learning.* New York: Teachers College Press.

Harlan, J. D. (1988). *Science experiences for the early childhood years.* Columbus, OH: Charles E. Merrill.

Hawkins, F. P. (1986). *The logic of action: Young children at work.* Denver: CO: Associated University Press.

Hill, D. M. (1977). *Mud, sand, and water.* Washington, DC: National Association for the Education of Young Children.

Mallow, J. V. (1981). *Science anxiety: Fear of science and how to overcome it.* Clearwater, FL: Van Nostrand Reinhold.

Neugebauer, B. (Ed.). (1989). *The wonder of it: Exploring how the world works.* Redmond, WA: Exchange Press.

Wilms, D. M. (Ed.). (1985). *Science books for children: Selections from Booklist 1976-1983.* Chicago: American Library Association.

About the Author:

Judy R. Jablon, M.S., is a curriculum consultant who works with teachers in Head Start and public school programs. She has been a primary grade teacher in public and private schools, including Bank Street School for Children. She has taught courses in curriculum development at Bank Street College.

14 | Art in Early Childhood

Art is a way to express our personal feelings. Using hands, eyes and mind, the artist makes an inner image external. Artists seek to express and communicate a personal vision through visual representation. Because our goal with children, especially young children, is to have them communicate just such a personal vision, we want to respond to the serious inquiries and discoveries that we see in their artwork. Art is hard, disciplined work and, at the same time, the sheer joy of "messing about."

What is art?

Art is a vital part of the curriculum for children of all ages. Art materials attract their curiosity and desire to explore. If materials are not available, children will draw with sticks in the dirt, "paint" with water on sidewalks, and build structures with mud and sand.

Why work with art?

Art stimulates children's expressiveness, which is especially important for young children who are just learning to use language to communicate. Art helps children examine some of the complexities of the real world in small manageable pieces. Through art, they can recreate and integrate curriculum experiences, including social studies, science, and math concepts. When children have many opportunities to explore and enjoy working with art materials, they discover they can make graphic or 3-dimensional symbols that others understand and respond to, just as people respond to words, numbers, musical sounds, and gestures. And working with art materials gives children a sense of pride in their own creativity.

This chapter suggests ways you can support children as they express and communicate their own feelings and ideas with art materials. It describes an approach that supports the creativity that exists in all children (and adults.) The chapter focuses on the basic materials of art—pencil, crayons, craypas, paint, clay, and collage—and how children at different stages of growth change and develop in their artwork. (Keep in mind, though, that the same principles apply to many other art and craft media, such as blocks, woodworking, stitchery, weaving, beading, and printmaking.) As a caregiver or teacher, you may want to explore and try out some of the materials for yourself in order to understand the child's experience with art—remembering, however, that your artwork will reflect your more mature way of thinking and diverse experience.

How can you make art part of the early childhood curriculum?

Developmental Phases in Art

As children grow and develop, their artwork changes too. One of the most dramatic and important milestones in cognitive development is the ability to use symbols, to make one thing stand for another. This symbolic capacity, beginning around one year, becomes refined through ages 3 and 4 and is reflected in the child's use of language and symbolic play. The clothespin becomes an airplane, the doll becomes the baby. The young child also becomes a maker of artistic symbols. She realizes that a few lines or circles on a piece of paper or a shape of clay can represent something. Now the world of artistic creation has opened up.

Throughout early childhood, new skills and understandings of visual symbols emerge, which, in turn, stimulate further growth and interest. The younger child uses broad, generalized images that become increasingly differentiated and complex, reflecting her more advanced knowledge and view of the world. Alongside these developments, the child's ability to plan and think ahead matures.

Advances in physical growth and knowledge of what their bodies can do also affect children's artistic expression. The large muscular, random movements of the toddler become increasingly refined. The whole-fist grip of crayon or brush gives way to a dextrous small-motor manipulation of thumb and index finger.

While change is not neatly predictable, general patterns in the child's artistic development do occur, although the timetable varies greatly for different children. The same child may be simultaneously doing "less mature" scribble-scrabbles alongside beginning representations of people. The age ranges for the different phases of art development should be used as general guides for children who are having consistent, open-ended experiences with the materials of art. Keep in mind that growth is uneven and that even as a new phase emerges, an earlier phase never entirely vanishes. The following stages typify the child's development as artist:

Figure 1

Figure 2

- **Exploration of the art material (ages 1 1/2-3).** Typically, the toddler delights as much in the movement of his arm, the feel of brush or crayon in his hand, even the smell of paint or clay, as in what he is producing. A child may even be looking away from the paper while drawing or painting and, once he has finished, not bother to glance at the product. He may mix all the colors together or randomly distribute marks on different areas of the paper (see Figure 1).

- **Control of the material (ages 3-4).** Older children are able to decide—and control—which lines should be long or short, wavy or straight, thick or thin, in what color and where on the paper (see Figure 2). They discover they can make patches of different colors, mixed and unmixed. Their simple, random, and amorphous lines, shapes and forms become more differentiated and controlled, reflecting their growing awareness of the nature of the material and their own activity. At this stage, 3-year-old Gabriel covers the whole paper with green of his own mixing and announces to the world at large, "I'm making a green!"

Figure 3

- **Creation of designs (ages 3-5)**. At this stage, children who have had many experiences with exploration and control combine and arrange shapes, lines, and colors into aesthetically pleasing designs. They have an intuitive and spontaneous sense of composition and of how their newly acquired knowledge about the material can be combined and elaborated into stunning, vibrant designs (see Figure 3). Three-year-old Ayasha carefully alternates the red and pink patches filling up her entire paper. Josh, at 4 1/2 , makes a roundish ball of clay and attaches long, thin, coiled shapes which radiate out like the rays of the sun or human limbs.

Figure 4

- **Early representation (ages 3-5)**. Finally, around the age of 4 with drawing, or towards 5 in paint or clay, another developmental milestone occurs. Children's visual symbols remind them of something and suddenly we hear an exclamation, "Look, it's me!" or "This is a big bulldozer!" Gradually, children begin to plan ahead what they are going to make. They discover they can make people, animals, buildings, plants and vehicles by combining simple shapes, lines and colors from their earlier experiences in art (see Figures 4, 5, and 6).

Figure 5

These early representations are not entirely realistic. It is important that you either wait for the child to identify the figure or ask if he wants to say something about his picture. The question, "What is it?" *presumes* that the child has made a representation, which at this stage may or may not be the case. Emily (figure 5), at age 4, has made many different kinds of round shapes. This could be a design, but she announces, "I made the sun, planets, and stars."

Figure 6

- **Later representation (ages 5-8)**. Children in this stage plan and organize more complete and detailed representations of their experiences and fantasies. Unlike their earlier representations of one or just a few important figures, they now often include many aspects of the environment or event. A drawing of a fire station may include details: the pole, the hoses hung up to dry, the coats and hats, the hook and ladder truck. At first, objects may be scattered on the surface in an interesting design rather than being a representation of the actual space. The colors and sizes of people and things often reflect their importance to the particular child, rather than a realistic rendering (see Figure 7).

Figure 7

201

Figure 8

Figure 9

By the time children are 7 and 8, they have a sense of themselves in relation to society. Their themes become richer, more varied, and realistic; friends, people at work and play, and settings appear as integral components of their artwork. However, they are working from their own view of the world, and, if you do not know what they have in mind, you might perceive their work as a distortion of reality. Larry, for example, is unusually skilled in depicting realistic details. He can make a profile, and he tends to includes tiny realistic details such as shoe laces. So his teacher wondered why he drew such a disproportionately long leg for the girl in his picture. Before she commented, however, she asked what the picture was about—and learned from him that the girl "is stamping her foot," and hence, the size of her leg relates to the importance of the action (see Figure 8).

Children's attempts to draw human figures provide a good illustration of this pattern of development in art. When 3- and 4-year-olds begin drawing people, most commonly a roundish shape occurs with a few marks inside and/or outside it. The inside marks may stand for the eyes, nose, and mouth, perhaps even teeth or eyebrows. What appears to be the head is the equivalent, in the child's view, of the entire figure. The short lines at the bottom of the roundish shape may possibly stand for legs and are soon followed by arms on the sides. Hair, hands, fingers, feet, and toes are likely to come next and, with increasing experience with the medium along with new discoveries, more and more details are included. Ada, at 4, knows the hand has five fingers, but as she paints she gets "carried away" and keeps on adding them until there are eleven on one hand and six on the other. Kim, at 5, carefully counts aloud to get precisely five fingers. Florence, at 7, is tired of struggling to make the five fingers small enough in proportion to the rest of the figure, so she draws a girl with her hands in her pockets. Her best friend, Betsy, states, "I'm going to have this girl wear mittens." As children's abilities develop and their knowledge deepens, body parts of people and animals or the components of physical and natural objects become increasingly differentiated and more "realistically" connected and related to each other (see Figure 9).

There is a transition phase between early and later representational work, usually between 5 and 7 years. Landscapes may become sterile and stereotyped, in adult eyes, as the child works for precision, with top and bottom lines for ground and sky, flat decorated houses with door, chimney, and window, trees and flowers in rigid lines. People, too, may be portrayed in a stereotyped fashion. For example, females may be drawn in elegant ball gowns and high heels, bedecked with jewelry. Here, the child artist is exaggerating "femaleness" in order to make her intent clear—*this* is a drawing of a female, not a male. In this case, the artwork also expresses a developmental concern with gender identity, typical of young school-age children, and reflects their tendency to define gender in rather rigid, superficial ways.

If children are given repeated open-ended experiences with art materials, and are supported in their efforts to express their ideas and feelings without undue pressure to create "realistic" or "pretty" images, the pattern of artistic growth described above develops naturally and inevitably over time.

The Role of the Caregiver or Teacher

While the approach we suggest supports children's natural and personal expressions in art, we are not suggesting that you, as caregiver or teacher, should assume a passive role. As is true of all other areas of your curriculum, you need to be actively involved in planning, supporting, assessing, and following through with appropriate art experiences over the course of the year. Your role is critical in establishing and maintaining an art program that truly reflects children's artistic expressions about their world.

In general, you:

- serve as a facilitator, making materials available in a setting where the children can work undisturbed, and motivating them to experiment and to discover;
- offer affirmation and encouragement;
- give recognition, by exhibiting some of each child's work, clearly identified with the child's name and date, in your early childhood setting;
- save at least some of each child's work in order to have a portfolio of continuous samples of his or her artwork over the school year.

Because growth is not smooth and predictable, you need to recognize where each child "is" in terms of physical, emotional, and intellectual development, and plan and set forth art materials and experiences accordingly. When to motivate a child to move into a new phase of development and when to allow him to consolidate experience with repeated and similar activities is a never-ending challenge for caregivers and teachers. In most situations, much depends on the age and personality of the child. You make your best judgment, do what feels right, and respond to what happens—not to a rigid idea of what you "ought" to do.

In Ms. Golden's first grade class, three youngsters seem "stuck." Polly is mourning a lost kitten and draws nothing else. Carlos is unhappy in a cold urban city and paints bright lush trees and beaches, like the islands from which he emigrated. While it may take months for Polly and Carlos to work through these losses, Ms. Golden respects their needs and gives them time. Another child, Bernice endlessly makes monotonous impersonal hearts and rainbows. Later you will see how Ms. Golden intervenes, encouraging Bernice to take risks and make something new.

Planning Art Experiences Over Time

As you plan art experiences, keep in mind that the basic materials for painting, clay work, collage, and drawing can be offered regularly over the entire school year for children of all ages. The materials do not change; the artwork that children create with them does. If you provide repeated age-appropriate experiences that are at the same time sequential and varied enough, you will be able to meet and provide for the changing needs and interests of all the children.

Keep in mind, too, that novelty is not the same thing as creativity. (Artists know this and they, too, use the same materials and themes again and again over the course of their lives.) A 2-year-old who has discovered that she can make jagged lines or dots all over the page is not ready to be hurried into drawing people until she has had her fill of these, which may take months. In fact, the lines and dots may reappear as elements in her renderings of people—lines as hair and mouth, and dots as eyes. Lisa, age 4, is discovering white-on-white, steadfastly ignoring her teacher's suggestions or other children's example of multicolored design paintings. For three months, she produces those subtle white paintings. Other children may paint the same design or representational figures over and over.

When children seem to be randomly going through the motions of a task with little or no personal investment or pleasure, it is probably time to vary the experience. Sometimes a new collection of patterned papers offered in collage or a large piece of colored paper for painting may be all that is necessary. Maybe you need to think about how to integrate art experiences into other areas of the curriculum to extend children's learning.

How much art you offer in your setting will depend in part on your own comfort and familiarity with the materials. As the exercises at the end of the chapter suggest, you will strengthen and enlarge your art program if you work with materials yourself.

Providing the Structure for Art Experiences

The first step is to have supplies on hand. The quantities of materials will vary depending on the number of children, available storage space, budget constraints, and children's and teacher's interests. Many materials listed below can be "scrounged" or found by asking parents, staff, friends, and local businesses for contributions. Basic materials for 20 to 30 children 3 through 8 years old may be selected from among the following:

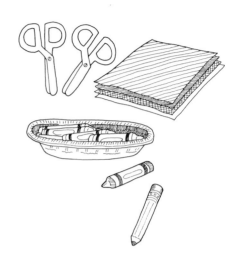

> 50 lbs. or more of clay (amount of clay needed depends on whether you recycle); one or two gallon containers of liquid white glue; at least a dozen glue brushes (inexpensive 6" brushes with metal handles found in hardware and paint stores); packages of construction paper in different sizes and colors; small glue containers (e.g., yogurt containers or other plastic cups or containers with lids); assorted visual and tactile collage materials; large and small boxes for collage materials; a variety of construction materials, such as egg cartons, oatmeal or salt containers, buttons and beads, corks, pipe cleaners, yarn, straws, tinfoil, toothpicks; white smooth papers; sheets of newsprint; gray and tan construction paper of different sizes; pencils; crayons, especially black or other dark colors for emphasis of line instead of color; craypas, or oil crayons (for older children); paint; cellulose sponges for wiping the brush; plastic (transparent, if possible) containers in pint or quart sizes for water.

If budget permits, useful tools for teachers include a paper cutter, mat knife, scissors, and wire cutter; for children, nails and screws, scissors, paper punchers, staplers, masking tape, hammer, and screwdriver.

Next, you need to provide storage and an attractive, neat work area. Shelves should be easily accessible and contain separately arranged and labeled places for clay, collage, paint and drawing materials, and different kinds of paper. One large cafeteria-sized table or two smaller tables should provide sufficient surface space for small groups of children to work on. Hooks for aprons, smocks, or cast-off shirts and blouses can be attached nearby. Adults' materials or extra supplies for the children can be put on a shelf out of reach of the children.

Young children need a structure for their open-ended explorations with materials. Adults sometimes think that children should be free from all instructions and limitations in their creative use of materials. However, too little structure can inhibit children's expression just as a too-directed experience can. Children must clearly understand your expectations for the organized routines of working with art materials. Feeling safe *and* stimulated allows them to learn and grow from new art experiences, as well as from those that are more familiar and predictable.

The art experience consists of three parts: set-up, work time, and clean-up.

By participating in all three aspects of the art activity, children feel independent as well as committed to the well-being of the classroom community. Here are set-up, work procedures, and clean-up suggestions for children working with collage (or construction), clay and paint.

Collage or Construction

For toddlers and 3-year-olds, you can provide each child with a:

- small shallow box or a box lid or paper plate to hold collage materials;
- a variety of materials: rough/smooth, opaque/translucent, patterned/plain, 3-dimensional/flat, etc.;
- a glue container and small brush with short metal handle.

If it is a first collage experience for the child, you can demonstrate how to apply paste on the background paper. Young children seem naturally to apply the paste to the main piece of paper, not on the back of the collage piece. The experience of selecting and pasting materials is manageable and sufficiently complex and motivating. Cutting paper with scissors is a separate activity, since young children are still trying to master this complex skill. Therefore, you will want to cut the materials for them.

Older children, ages 4 and up, can select collage pieces from one or more trays of attractively arranged materials in the center of the table. (They can cut additional collage materials, if necessary.) Each child should have a glue brush, with a glue pot to share with the child next to him.

In the beginning, you will need to model and help with the clean-up of sorting the various materials in appropriate storage containers and washing glue brushes in warm water.

Clay

Clay is suitable for children over the age of 3 (younger children usually do better with playdough, which they can manipulate more easily). Each child needs a large mound of clay roughly the size of a grapefruit. Children then have the choice of making large or small shapes and forms. To get the most out of working expressively with clay, the only tool necessary is the hands. Rolling pins, cookie cutters, and plastic knives are appropriate as dramatic play props for playdough, but clay is a sculptural medium and children need to be in direct contact with its heavy, soft, malleable properties. In order to emphasize clay's 3-dimensional qualities, talk about how you can build with it and demonstrate how vertical shapes can be built up (see Figures 10 and 11).

Clean-up, under adult supervision, is relatively simple for children of all ages:

- Squeeze creations into a large mound.

Figure 10

Figure 11

- Place it in the clay container.
- Add small amounts of water and a damp cloth to cover

Reconstitute dried clay by smashing with a hammer, adding water, and letting it sit for several days.

Paint

For tray painting you need:

- an aluminum cookie sheet or tray;
- 5 small containers of paint (red, blue, yellow, white, and black —they learn to mix different colors from this set of basics on paper or on the tray itself);
- 3/4" wide bristle brush with a long handle;
- a container of water and a cellulose sponge;
- a large sheet of paper, 18" x 24".

In general, children have more control of paint materials if they are painting on a table with the tray paint set-up—and there is less mess from drips. You may prefer an easel set-up, or simply not have enough table space for the children to work. However, whether working at table or easel, children of all ages should be standing in order to have ease of movement.

For a first painting experience, you should demonstrate how to:

- wet the brush in the water container;
- dab the excess water off on the sponge;
- put the brush in one of the paint containers;
- apply the brush to the paper.

After the mark or patch of color is made, demonstrate washing the brush in water and following the above procedures again. Young children will need many experiences (and matter-of-fact reminders!) before they will automatically remember to wash the brush before changing colors. In order to maintain a pleasurable painting experience, reminders about procedures should be simple, clear, and minimal.

You may want to vary the painting papers by providing:

- large pieces of construction paper instead of newsprint;
- different sizes of paper; i.e., long narrow rectangles, large squares, smaller rectangles;
- large pieces of brown wrapping paper;
- the classified section of the newspaper, especially if paper supplies are minimal.

When finished painting, the children can:

- take containers of paints that are still clear and unmixed and place them in the appropriate spot;

- take muddied containers to a pail of water or a sink for washing;

- wash their brushes, sponge, water containers, and tray and place them in the appropriate containers and spaces.

It is important to put into place routines and procedures that will prevent children from getting themselves or their clothes messy during art activities. They should wear smocks, aprons, or other coverings to protect clothing, and cleanup should include cleaning themselves.

Art in Integrated Curriculum

Art represents another opportunity for children to re-create and symbolize their experience, just as they might in block building or writing a story. As children draw pictures, paint, or sculpt with clay, they are using art to express their ideas and clarify concepts.

In a third grade study of Native Americans, some children become very involved in painting a mural of the forest. Ian is most interested in painting mountains in the distance and trying to achieve a sense of perspective; on the other hand, Carina focuses on depicting the details of a raccoon's face. A few children who prefer to work in clay shape utensils and tools as part of a diorama. For other children, designing and painting costumes for a play about Native Americans is a meaningful learning experience. In this classroom, children are offered a choice about which artistic media to use; they are given time and space to work together, problem solve ("how do you make mountains look far away?"), and express what they are learning.

The possibilities for integrating art into the curriculum are endless:

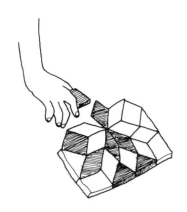

- **Art and social studies**. For a study of the neighborhood, children draw maps; a study of tropical rain forests culminates in the painting of a mural and the molding of clay animals and birds.

- **Art and science**. Children draw pictures of fruits and vegetables and of the seeds they have planted; one class draws pictures of the worms they have been observing.

- **Art and math**. After they make patterns with the pattern blocks, children recreate the designs with shapes cut out of construction paper and glue.

- **Art and reading and writing**. After a trip to a pumpkin farm, a class draws pictures and writes stories about their experience. Their work is bound together in a book, which becomes a favorite in the library corner.

In these ways artistic media can offer avenues for children to express and integrate what they are learning in all areas of the curriculum.

Working with Families and Diverse Cultures

As in any area of the curriculum, it is important to talk with parents about what their children are learning and what your goals are.

Because many parents may have had negative art experiences themselves or do not understand how art promotes their children's learning, they may need your help to better understand its value and importance. During parent or family conferences, you can show examples of the child's artwork over a period of time, explaining the changes and growth that have occurred. At a parent meeting, you can show examples of the different phases of development that are occurring in your room, carefully omitting the use of names. (If you can, use examples from children's work from a past year to give a sense of how children's art changes over time.) Showing different children's work is an invaluable way of demonstrating the great range and variety in development. You will want to stress that there is no right or wrong in judging children's art. It also helps to present an example of a child's work that you had an opportunity to observe as it was being created, and describe to the parents how the work developed.

As parents come to understand the developmental progression of children's art and appreciate the value of art in the curriculum, they will be more enthusiastic and show interest in their children's artwork. You might consider sending a letter home or talking at a parent's meeting about how to respond in a positive, nonjudgmental way to children's artwork. You can also ask families to share their own artistic work: a painter can talk with the class about how he uses line and color, a weaver can demonstrate how she uses a loom.

Putting art into action

Here are some general ideas about how to motivate and respond to children's artwork. Of course, as you put them into practice you will be making modifications for the children's ages and personalities.

In talking with a child about his work, either in getting him started or in responding to what he makes, always remember that *the way you speak* is as important as the words you use. Children are highly sensitive to tone of voice, quick to distinguish between spontaneous enthusiasm and a flat, automatic, or insincere tone. Be sure you are looking directly at the artwork you are discussing. Pointing and gesturing helps, too.

A critical feature of the caregiver's or teacher's role is being specific. Before the child starts working with the art material, you can "motivate" her to think about how she can use the material for personal expression. In simple, clear language, you give the children general suggestions or a focus in their work with the material. Two notes of caution. First, say only as much as is absolutely necessary; never overtalk a child. Second, if a child is already busy working on a project he himself has decided to do, it is wise to allow him to continue.

Some children love to talk about their work, but because artwork is a visual form of expression, other children may not wish to talk about it or may not have the language to do so. Try to bring the child's intuitive explorations and discoveries to conscious awareness by offering specifics about what is unique in what he has made.

It is usually better to talk about *how* the work is done, and leave it to the child to talk, if he cares to, about what it stands for and what it means to him. Comment on:

- lines, shapes, colors, patterns, textures;
- how they are repeated;
- how they are varied;
- how they are arranged.

Infants and Toddlers

For the toddler, as well as for older children who have had little or no art experience, the material itself is the motivation. When Eva, 18 months, sees an open box of crayons and paper on the table, she rushes over and immediately begins making marks and lines all over the paper. You exclaim, "Look at your lines. You've made a lot of them."

To Johnny, age 2 1/2, you could say, "What kinds of lines will you paint today? Long ones like you made yesterday? Or will they be short?" When Johnny indicates he is through, you might say, "Look at how your arm moved around the paper when you made this long, thick red line! Look at all the colors you mixed in your big patch here." Then you can help him lay the painting flat to dry or hang it up with clothespins.

Preschoolers

Sarah, age 4, who generally avoids working with messy materials, pokes unenthusiastically at the clay lump. You can model with another lump of clay in an exploratory manner and point out some of the things that can be done with the clay: "Look, how the clay can be rolled into long strips. It can also be flattened or pushed together to stand up high." Just talking about what you are doing is a way to help Sarah get involved and feel more comfortable with the material.

For 5-year-old Bernice, who is reluctant to start, her teacher, Ms. Golden, begins with, "What kinds of colors are you going to put on your paper today? Will you make a design? or a person? or an animal? or something else?" Bernice starts making a rainbow again. Ms. Golden says, "Yesterday you made a rainbow with lots of colors. Let's think of other ways of putting colors on the paper," while pointing to other areas of the paper. It may take several months for Bernice to have enough self-confidence to give up the stereotyped rainbow and express her own ideas. But today she does add a few squiggly lines at the bottom of the page. When she tells her teacher she is through, Ms. Golden comments, "You're holding the brush so firmly, and you've thought of other kinds of lines today."

Young School-Age Children

Christopher, at 7, has rarely used clay and seems unsure how to begin. After you suggest, "You might make yourself and a friend in clay," Christopher responds, "I don't know how." You say, "Let's think of the different parts of the body. Which part of the body will you do first?" Christopher makes a hat. You ask, "Where does it belong?" and Christopher starts making a head. As the body develops, you patiently discuss—at his request—how the head attaches to the neck and neck to shoulder, etc. You might also urge him to feel his own limbs. You ask, "What is your person doing?" He mumbles. The previous day, the class had gone on a trip to a nearby dairy farm, so you ask Christopher if he wants to include this in his sculpting (thus connecting his artwork to his other studies). Christopher says firmly, "No, this is just me and my friend Paul," so you respect his decision. Now he can work on his own. When he calls you back to see the finished figure, you might ask him to tell you about it. He probably will need no prompting now. You comment on how strongly the shoes are attached to the legs, recognizing the complex problem solving that this demanded.

Families

Noah has been enthusiastic about using art materials in the preschool classroom. During a parent conference, José, the teacher, is surprised to hear the father say that at home Noah constantly says, "What can I draw?" The other night, his father said, "Why don't you draw a bird?" Noah said, "I can't. I can't make it look good." His father made other suggestions—"a dog, a person . . ."—but finally he gave up. He feels caught in a tug of war with Noah.

José reassures Noah's father that they can find some ways to encourage Noah. He shares with him some strategies that often work in the classroom.

> When a child says he doesn't know what to do, I try to get him to talk about what he's been doing or thinking about. The other day at the park, Noah was watching a street light being repaired. When we got back to the classroom, he sat down

with a group of friends who were drawing. I asked him if he had an idea of what he wanted to do. He said no, but then I said, 'Well, you seemed very interested in what was going on at the park. What did the repair truck look like?' We talked about it and then looked at a picture of a truck. We discussed the shape of the wheels and the cab. After a while, Noah began to draw. Sometimes children need time to think about what they will draw. I'll tell them, "If you can't think of something to draw now, maybe you can in a few minutes. Let's do something else until you are ready."

Noah's father decides to try Jose's advice. Next time, when Noah feels stuck, he will ask him what kind of interesting things he saw on his way to school or remind him of the fun things they did together on the weekend. He will also try not to feel pressured to come up with an answer for Noah and will give Noah time to make his own decision about what to draw.

Exercises

1. By yourself, or even better, with a few colleagues, work with an unfamiliar material, exploring and "messing about" with it. Keep a record of how you are *feeling*:

   • before you start;

   • as you encounter the material;

   • as you form initial images in your head of what you want to make;

   • as you work, the way your images changed or modified;

   • as you view each other's work ;

   • as others' comments affect you.

2. Listen to yourself in the course of a week as you talk with children about their artwork. If possible, write down your comments. Ask yourself: "Are my comments objective and nonjudgmental? Do they focus on the process and the child's effort? Do they have the effect of motivating and encouraging the child?" Share your observations with a colleague; together, think about how you can improve your responses to children's artwork.

3. Look around your environment. Ask yourself: "Are the room and materials supportive of children's artistic endeavors?" For example, what kind of materials are available (for collage, drawing, etc.)? How does clean-up occur? How is children's artwork displayed? Identify any concerns or problems and think about how they can be resolved. Brainstorm solutions with a colleague.

4. Think about your curriculum. Are there ways to incorporate art into other curriculum areas?

5. Role-play a discussion:

   Jane Lowrey teaches 4-year-olds and her friend Reuben White teaches 7-year-olds. They have a similar problem: each has a child in class who, for the past several months, after attempting any artwork, grows frustrated with it and destroys it. What should each of them do? Keep in mind the inevitable differences in personality of the two teachers as well as the ages and personalities of the two children.

6. You and a colleague role-play a teacher-parent conference:

   • One parent accepts art in curricula but wants the child's work to be more conventional and representational.

   • Another parent wants more academics and feels that art is a "frill" and a waste of time.

   Talk these through, then reverse the roles.

7. Run a parent workshop on art. What will you present to them to "mess with"? How much direction will you give them? What ideas will you deal with in the discussion?

Resources

Biber, B. (1984). *Early education and psychological development.* Chapter 8. Children's drawings from lines to pictures (pp. 156-175). New Haven: Yale University Press.

Bland, J. C. (1968). *Art of the young child: Understanding and encouraging creative growth in children 3 to 5 years* (3rd ed. rev.). New York: Museum of Modern Art.

Dyson, A. H. (1988). Appreciate the drawing and dictating of young children. *Young Children, 43*(3), 25-32.

Dyson, A. H. (1990). Symbol makers, symbol weavers: How children link play, pictures and paint. *Young Children, 45*(2), 50-57.

Feeney, S., & Moravick, E. (1987). A thing of beauty: Aesthetic development in young children. *Young Children, 42*(6), 7-15.

Hubbard, R. (1987). Transferring images: Not just glued on the page. *Young Children, 42*(2), 60-67.

Hitz, R., & Driscoll, A. (1988). Praise or encouragement? New insights into praise: Implications for early childhood teachers. *Young Children, 43*(5), 6-13.

Kuschner, D. (1989). Put your name on your painting, but . . . the blocks go back on the shelves. *Young Children, 45*(1), 49-56.

Lord, L. (1970). *Collage and construction in school: Preschool/junior high.* Worcester, MA: Davis.

Lowenfeld, V. (1954). *Your child and his art: A guide for parents.* New York: Macmillan.

Pile, N. (1973). *Art experiences for young children.* New York: Macmillan.

Schirrmacher, R. (1986). Talking with young children about their art. *Young Children, 42*(5), 3-7.

Smith, N. R. (1983). *Experience and art: Teaching children to paint.* New York: Teachers College Press.

About the Authors:

Leah Levinger, Ph.D., is a clinical child psychologist who has studied children's drawings. She has taught at Bank Street College for a number of years, including courses in Child Development and Art as a Tool for Understanding the Development of the Normal and Special Needs Child.

Ann-Marie Mott, M.S., is the Lower School Coordinator at the Bank Street School for Children and an instructor in the Graduate School. She is also a photographer and makes educational videotapes and slide films.

214

15 | Music in Early Childhood

"If you can talk, you can sing; if you can walk, you can dance." This age-old saying expresses what modern-day educators are only now confirming through studies and child observation. Music making and dance are as natural to the human being as talking and walking.

Music can be described as the organization of sound into meaningful patterns. Even birds and animals can distinguish music from other forms of sound. No species, however, rivals humans in our ability and propensity to make music. Our neurological and cognitive systems predispose us to creating and appreciating this "meaningful organization of sound"—from earliest infancy and, perhaps, prenatally. Music play—with instruments, with songs, alone or in groups—is a primary mode of expression which, when cultivated in early childhood settings, can lead to deeply satisfying experiences of learning and communication. In this chapter, we will explore the ways in which music can be applied to curriculum, language development, and other aspects of classroom and home life.

All over the world, adults and children use their innate powers of musical expression to fulfill a variety of needs and functions.

- In a rural village in West Africa, a mother bends over her garden plot, singing and chanting to soothe and comfort the baby carried on her back.

- Driving home, a parent flips on a popular children's tape to calm and entertain a tired toddler, and finds herself humming along to "Bingo" to calm her own nerves.

- In Indonesia, a group of children sit next to elder musicians, imitating every stroke of the hand as they learn to play the traditional village instruments of the xylophone orchestra.

- In a city school playground in America, a group of third graders form a circle and start chanting, "Let's get the rhythm of the feet—ding dong!" Two first graders want to join, and soon they are incorporated in the game. Their initiation to elementary school has really begun!

Whether the society is urban or rural, highly industrialized or traditional, there is hardly an aspect of life that cannot, in some way, be associated with music. For all of us, listening to a particular song

What is music?

Why make music part of your program?

215

can evoke a whole range of feelings and memories about a personal or historical event in our lives.

The inclusion of music in early childhood education is not, then, simply a "frill" or a convenient time filler until other, more "serious" areas can be attended to. Some research suggests that musical intelligence may even be located in a special, separate area of the brain. Other studies show that in cultures where musical play is actively encouraged, children show heightened competencies in motor and communication skills at early ages. Thus, music may actually be a primary medium through which crucial aspects of learning and development are stimulated and experienced. Here are some areas where music seems to affect behavior and learning:

Language Development

The repetitive phrases of many children's songs and games help to reinforce patterns which gradually become the foundation for more complex forms of expressive language.

- *Birth to three years old*. Fingerplays, counting rhymes, and songs about daily life help very young children "tune in" to the unique tones and phrases of their linguistic environment. In a day care center, a 7-month-old coos along as her caregiver cuddles her and sings, "Hush little baby, don't say a word, mama's gonna buy you a mocking bird . . ." Sitting on his caregiver's lap, a 2-year-old cannot take his eyes off her face as she sings, "Eensy Weensy Spider." A teacher leads a group of 3-year-olds in a circle game; the children laugh with glee as they all tumble down repeatedly for "Ring Around the Rosey."

In all these interactions, children's language is being stimulated through holistic, multisensory experiences. Imitating animal or machine sounds in songs also offers opportunities to expand the sound play which is so natural to the young child. Fingerplays and circle games bring the child into close contact with an adult and into early group interaction with peers.

- *Four to eight years old*. The process of language learning through music continues into the preschool and school-age years. During free time in kindergarten, a 5-year-old shares his favorite bedtime song with three classmates in the dress-up corner. Going out the door at dismissal, all the children begin to sing "Let's Go Riding in the Car" by Woody Guthrie. Their teacher chimes in, making up new verses using the children's names ("Tanya goes riding in the car . . ." etc.). In a second grade class, a Japanese parent comes in and teaches the children a version of "London Bridge" that is sung and played in Japan. Word play and story songs with chorus and verse, such as

"Alouette" or "If I Had a Hammer," challenge the memory and growing language skills of 4- through 8-year-olds.

Socialization

Perhaps the most vital function of music is socialization. Any music ensemble, be it a rock and roll band, a group of friends jamming on a street corner, or a symphony orchestra, represents one of the highest forms of human group interaction. Listening to others, being able to pick up on subtle auditory and visual cues, holding to your own pattern while being able to hear and respond to the total group sound—all of these complex processes go into making music with others. Perhaps that is one reason why we derive so much pleasure from participating in or witnessing musical events.

For 6-month-old Rosa, listening to the voice of mother, father, sibling or caretaker crooning a lullaby while she is being rocked or held provides crucial early experiences of bonding and love. When 2-year-old Jamal is engaged in a fingerplay with his day care teacher, he is experiencing close contact, body awareness, and a trusting social interaction imbued with a sense of fun and playfulness. Sitting on the floor, a group of 7-year-olds sing and pass objects in rhythm; they are gaining skills in cooperation and concentration.

Forms of music play like these are known and practiced in every culture. These activities signify that children are participating as active members of their family and cultural groups.

Cognition and Learning Styles

In the process of singing, clapping hands rhythmically, or playing an instrument, human beings are involved with creating musical sounds. Listening to music involves not only auditory, but also physical and cognitive responses, as the mind integrates the sound waves it receives into meaningful patterns. Emotionally, too, we respond to the tones, the melodies, the movement of sound through time and space that is music. Through listening to music, the whole child becomes engaged.

Musical experiences offer children alternative modes of symbolic thinking and expression. Through listening and moving to a variety of compositions, children will soon discover that music can be used to:

- tell a story (such as Prokofiev's *Peter and the Wolf*);
- express a mood or emotion (such as Beethoven's *Ode to Joy*, or Indian ragas);
- recreate sounds from the natural or urban environment (such as Vivaldi's *Four Seasons* or Gershwin's *An American in Paris*);
- create many textures and patterns through the medium of sound (such as J. S. Bach's *Inventions*).

In these ways, memory and concept development are also being enhanced.

For many children, the opportunity to express themselves musically, to exercise their "musical intelligence," strengthens their ability to succeed in other areas, such as beginning reading and writing. Clapping along to a simple pattern of musical notation encourages directionality (left to right). Seeing and singing along with the words of a favorite song on paper can help the transition from the spoken word to literacy.

The benefits of music to learning and growth have yet to be fully exploited and recognized. Music therapists have long observed the striking effect musical activity can have on children with special needs, helping them to develop self-awareness, a sense of organization, and confidence in their ability to communicate with others. Nurturing musicality among individuals and groups of children can only serve to enhance the full realization of their learning potential.

Cultural Diversity

Music has often been termed "the universal language." It offers one of the most direct and accessible ways of experiencing the aesthetic style and feeling of a particular culture. Incorporating the music of a child's own culture into an early childhood setting creates a more homelike environment in which a child will feel more secure and validated. Knowing this, Amy, a teacher of 5-year-olds, asks children to bring in favorite records and tapes from home to play in school.

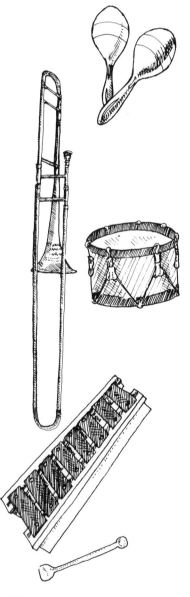

Music is also a medium through which children can extend their social awareness and sensitivity. In settings where children come from diverse cultural and linguistic backgrounds, you can broaden children's understanding of each other through the use of songs and musical games. When 6-year-old José Luis hears a recording of a Puerto Rican folk song as part of a social studies activity, he knows that his teacher is aware of and appreciates his cultural heritage. At the same time, the other children in his class are being exposed to the sounds and phrases of Spanish through a medium that is both natural and enjoyable.

Musical instruments are fascinating for young children. By playing and touching a variety of instruments, from shakers to trombones, children come into contact with the materials of culture in concrete and satisfying ways. When family members share their own musical skills and repertoire as part of a curriculum study, classroom/day care center visit, or holiday gathering, the adults, as well as the children, feel honored and appreciated for their unique heritage and family background.

In teaching and sharing in these diverse musical expressions, you are modeling the acceptance and celebration of cultural diversity that is so important in today's world.

Music can take on many forms in the early childhood setting. The extent to which music is incorporated depends greatly on your own sense of comfort and ease. Knowledge of an instrument or music theory is not necessary in order to develop successful and enjoyable experiences for your children. You can set up a wide range of experiences, from quiet listening, to singing rounds—all the way to creating an orchestra and helping children notate and conduct their own compositions. All are valid, and no special training in musicianship is required.

Music for Infants and Toddlers

For babies and very young children, there are many rich opportunities for musical interaction as part of your everyday activities with them. The soothing effect of lullabies is evident in child care practices worldwide. Infants respond to the sounds around them with great sensitivity. Rattles, shakers, bells, and chimes can be touched and played with to stimulate auditory awareness and patterning.

There are many activities you can try with infants and toddlers:

- Use familiar objects such as pots and pans, large spoons, and ladles for music play. Banging and shaking can be a source of great entertainment and independent music making.

- Sing to children during transitional tasks, such as changing a baby's diaper or dressing the toddler for outdoor play.

- Improvise your own melodies, or use a familiar melody to create your own lyrics. For example, to the tune of "Farmer in the Dell" you might sing:

   It's time to go outside, it's time to go outside
   Hi–ho the derry–o, it's time to go outside!

   Such tunes and fingerplays help to "musicalize" the child's day and can ease difficult or tiresome moments for you as well. Riding in the car, going to the market, waiting for snack, naptime, or bedtime are all optimum moments for singing and handplay.

- Build a daily song repertoire, in a language or dialect that is familiar to the very young child. This will provide a rich, stimulating, and nurturing environment. Songs for this age (in English) include:

   ∞ Fingerplays: "Where is Thumbkin"; "Open Shut Them"; "Five Little Pumpkins."

   ∞ Animal Songs: "Old MacDonald"; "Five Little Ducks."

   ∞ Action Songs: "Wheels on the Bus"; "Let's Go Riding in the Car."

   ∞ Lullabies: "Hush Little Baby"; "All the Pretty Little Horses."

Music for Preschoolers and Young School-age Children

Here are some activities you can do to create a listening environment for preschoolers and young school-age children:

- Create an atmosphere conducive to the activity at hand. Music should not be used as "Muzak"—played only for the sake of keeping a background noise going. But there are many unstructured times of the day that are suitable for productive listening; for example, restful music at naptime and lively tunes for clean-up. A joyful dance or "play along with the tape" experience at transition times can bring a group together before going on to the next activity.

- Encourage children to bring favorite records in from home. Folk music, classical music, world music, and even some "top forty" popular recordings can all be played and enjoyed. In this way, you are helping to make connections between the family and the school or child care setting.

- Record the "old favorites" in your daily routine—either with the children, or as a staff project. In this way, the children can hear favorite songs, sung "just for them," at different times of the day. A staff-made tape also helps the children develop a sense of community about their early childhood setting, as having its own identity and a special place in their lives.

- Share with the children your own enjoyment and participation. Active modeling gives children the cues they need to assure them that music making and listening are valued and important.

Creating a Music Center

Create a music center, which can be set up with tape recorders and simple instruments, and gives preschoolers and school-age children some choice in terms of the musical experiences of the classroom. The center materials should, of course, reflect the age level and interest of your group. Here are some questions to ask yourself when choosing music for children to listen to:

- Does the singer (or singers) vary tone and dynamics, or do all the songs sound the same?

- Do the lyrics of the songs relate well to the children's interests and knowledge of the world around them?

- Do the recordings include acoustic instruments as well as electronic sounds? (Children can and should be exposed to both.)

- If it is an instrumental recording, does the music vary in its sounds and textures, or does it tend to repeat mechanically?

- Does the recording, or selection of recordings, include songs and music from diverse cultural styles?
- Does the recording, or selection of recordings, reflect different moods and emotions?

Songs that appeal to 4- through 8-year-olds group include:

∞ Cumulative Songs: "The Green Grass Grows All Around"; "Alouette."

∞ Rounds: "Frère Jacques"; "Make New Friends."

∞ Folk Songs in All Languages: "This Land is Your Land"; "Hole in the Bucket"; "Jamaica Farewell"; "De Colores."

∞ Popular Songs: "We are the World"; "Reach Out and Touch Somebody's Hand"; "Here Comes the Sun."

∞ Passing Games: "I Pass My Shoe"; "Obo Esi Ni Sa"; "Al Citron."

For 6- to 8-year-olds, music task cards can be made, such as:

∞ Listen to the song, "The Grey Goose", and draw a picture of your favorite part of the song.

∞ Make up a new verse to a song and record it.

∞ Invite a friend to play along, to your own composition using any instrument in the center.

Developing a Musical Concept

For many caregivers or teachers, the idea of leading a music activity or teaching a "music lesson" can seem intimidating. However, the process of teaching music is no different from teaching any other kind of content. Important elements of music for young children revolve around paired concepts such as:

- sound and silence;
- fast and slow;
- loud and soft;
- high pitch and low pitch;
- beginning and ending.

In a classroom of 6- and 7-year-olds, the teacher, Mrs. Randolph, wants to expand her children's understanding of music. Over a period of several weeks, she shows them how to create sound patterns. She begins with a symbol system: O = loud and X = soft. She writes a pattern like this on the board:

OO XX OO XX OO XX

The children clap their hands and, once they have the idea, take turns writing out their own patterns such as:

OOOO XXXX OOOO XXXX

A few try playing a pattern on musical instruments they bring from home. Although Mrs. Randolph is not a musician and has no knowledge of conventional notation, she is helping the children to structure sounds into recognizable sequences—an important aspect of music.

Making Musical Instruments

Constructing and learning about different types of instruments offers both you and the children a way to become more comfortable with music as an art form. The attachment a young child may feel towards a homemade instrument—be it a cigar box with rubber bands stretched over it, or a can filled with gravel—paves the way for a sense of confidence in handling a guitar, violin, or drum set.

Utilizing materials from the child's home or neighborhood also highlights important concepts such as recycling and the multiple uses of familiar objects.

Here are some sample materials that may be used for making home-made instruments:

> baking pans, spoons, cookie sheets, milk containers, seeds, popcorn kernels, dried beans, flower pots, sandpaper, yogurt containers, margarine tubs, paper towel rolls, combs, wax paper, plastic bottles, bottle tops, straws.

Preschoolers and school-age children can begin to classify their musical instruments into different categories, building on their developing cognitive skills. They can think about:

- what the instruments are made of (wood, metal, cardboard, etc.);

- what kind of action makes the sound (striking, shaking, plucking, bowing, etc.);

- what quality of sounds their instruments can create (loud, soft, smooth, sharp, scratchy, echoing, etc.).

Here are some labels music scholars have developed to classify musical instruments from around the world. You may introduce them to the children, or just use them for your own frame of reference. These categories are:

- Aerophones: Sound is made by the blowing of air. Examples are flute, recorder, kazoo, bottles filled with water.

- Chordophones: Sound is made by the plucking or bowing of a string. Examples are cello, sitar, harp, cigar-box guitar.

- Membranophones: Sound is made by the hitting or tapping of animal skin (or other material) stretched across an object. Examples are bongos, snare drum, tabla, coffee can covered with a piece of heavy plastic.

- Idiophones: Sound is made by the object itself through shaking, stamping, rattling, etc. Examples are maracas, bells, chimes, rattles, soda cans filled with dried beans.

Music in the Integrated Curriculum

Music can be used to support or enrich many curriculum areas. Social studies, for instance, offers the possibility of many natural connections. Whether the study is the self, family, neighborhood, or community, singing and instrument play can be easily integrated. For example, in a study of trains, children can:

- learn folk songs with "train themes" such as "I've Been Working On the Railroad," "She'll Be Comin' Round the Mountain," "Train is A-Comin'," or "Morningtown Ride";

- dramatize the actions of a train, or role play train workers and passengers, accompanied by a home-made rhythm-band ensemble;

- accompany the telling or reading aloud of a train story with instruments, including whistles, shakers, and drums. An activity like this can be integrated into a class presentation for parents and other groups of children in your setting.

Music and science can go together:

- Place a few dried beans on the head of a large drum or tambourine. Tap gently on the edge of the skin and you will see the vibrations move the beans.

- Pour water of different amounts into bottles of the same size. Blowing into each bottle will produce a different pitch. Ask the children to line the bottles up from lowest sound to the highest sound. This will create a scale.

- Take a walk in the park and record the various sounds you hear in the environment. Later, in class, see if the children can identify the sounds.

Music and math activities are possible:

- Compare the shapes of various musical instruments. What shapes can be found inside an outline of a guitar, a kettle drum, a xylophone?

- Make patterns in groups of two, three, and four using lines, circles, or other symbols (e.g., /// // /// // or //// /// //// ////) and clap to the beats or use various instruments.

Musical expression is an inborn, innate resource that is part of our human potential. Musical interactions play an important part in the development of language, self-expression, cultural identity and community-building. Although there are children who have special musical "gifts"—which can and should be nurtured by our society—all children and adults can benefit from full and rich musical experiences in early childhood.

Putting music into action

Infants and Toddlers

Ramona, a family day-care provider, has a musical mobile over the changing table. As she changes 10-month-old Erica, she says, "Can you touch the bells with your toes? Stretch your arms—stretch your legs—stretch your fingers." Through playful interaction, Ramona encourages Erica's language development and beginning ideas of cause and effect.

Afterwards, Ramona sits on the floor with Erica and Franklin, a toddler. She has a basket full of "things that make sounds," including coffee cans filled with beans that the children roll on the floor. Erica's favorite activity is banging a spoon on the side of a pot.

Later in the day Ramona sings this rhyme with the children as they get dressed to go outside.

> Erica get your jacket on, jacket on
>
> Erica get your jacket on, just like me!
>
> Franklin get your mittens on, mittens on, mittens on
>
> Franklin get your mittens on, just like me!

Preschoolers

Leila, a day care teacher, invites a parent to play his drums with her group of 4-year-olds. They are fascinated with the different sizes and shapes. She then brings in records of drumming from around the world, and several children begin to look for "drumlike" things in the room—a teapot in the housekeeping corner turned upside down, an empty milk carton. One child calls an empty paper towel roll "his drum stick."

Leila then begins to think about making a variety of musical instruments, building on her class's interests and curiosity. She finds library books for herself to read on musical instruments and others for the children to look at. She plans a class trip to a local music store where instruments and music are sold. She invites class discussion with questions such as, "What kinds of musical instruments do you like?" "What kinds of musical instruments do you have at home?"

The children make many different kinds of instruments from materials that Leila and their parents bring in. They compare the loud and soft sounds made by dried beans, rocks, and paper clips put inside plastic containers. Some children cut wood and nail it into guitar shapes, while others lace small bells on ribbons. Leila plays tapes of the children's favorite songs, accompanied by the children's own instruments. Leila talks with the children about how they can show their families what they have been doing. They decide to invite their families to a concert, and they play their instruments, sing, and dance.

Young School-age Children

Mr. Martine's first grade class has been studying transportation. For the unit on boats and shipping, children visit the harbor. In addition to sketching and discussing the various aspects of dock work, several children record the sounds of the harbor environment on a class tape recorder. Following the visit, the children listen to the tape to identify and categorize the sounds on the recording. They then create their own symbols for the various sounds (e.g., < = fog horn). Other lessons include music and movement activities in which children re-create the many activities they observed, such as: the actions of the dock workers or the motion of various kinds of boats on water. As part of a the physical culminating activity, sea chanteys and folksongs (such as "Erie Canal" and "Blow Ye Winds") are learned and performed for the other primary grade classes.

Families

Every evening, after dinner, 4-year-old Josie and her grandfather play a favorite game. He begins to hum a popular tune and imitate the sounds of different instruments: "om–pa–pa" "ta–ta–ta–ta." As he claps his hands to the beat, Josie joins in. Her little brother, a toddler, begins to dance and clap too. Sometimes Josie's grandfather speeds up the tempo or slows it down. Josie sings along, moving her body in rhythm.

Although no one in Josie's family has had any formal musical training, they enjoy all kinds of music and share their appreciation with the children. They use music as a time to be together and have fun. After her preschool class had a parade, Josie wanted to have one at home. Her father put on a record. Adults clapped or tapped along as Josie's siblings and cousin marched around and waved scarves and handkerchiefs. This, now, has become one of the family's favorite activities, especially at holiday gatherings, when young and old participate.

Exercises

Following are a group of exercises that you and your colleagues can try out. They will help you free your own musical imagination while providing a format for developing musical concepts with young children. Body movement and visual materials are integrated into the process. This is one of the most natural ways to engage young children in musical learning. After you try out these exercises, you may want to adapt them or create new ones of your own. If you keep a written record of what you do, you will soon have a wealth of musical activities and ideas that can be implemented and enriched throughout the year.

1. Think of an experience in your childhood, adolescence or adulthood that was connected to music. Write it down, as a story, and share with your colleagues.

2. Talk with families about their musical traditions. Invite family members to bring in tapes or play for the children.

3. Develop a resource file of songs, games, and musical ideas to supplement your curriculum. You may wish to divide them into categories, such as: animal songs, holiday songs, fingerplays, lullabies, circle time songs, etc.

4. Get together with some friends or colleagues and play music together! Informal music-making can be done with the help of song books, simple percussion instruments and recordings.

5. Create a score with invented notation. Here is a way to do it:

   Materials: Recording of an orchestral piece, such as Handel's *Water Music*, or another multitextured, flowing composition. Large newsprint, crayons, school-owned or class-made instruments.

   Warm-up: Find a comfortable place to sit. Put on the recording, close your eyes and imagine what pictures the music is "painting." Stop the music and draw the scenes you have imagined.

   Development: Following the warm-up or on another day, play the music again. This time, listen for when the music is going "up" and when it is going "down." "Draw" the lines you are hearing with hand gestures, in the air.

   Then take out the newsprint and crayons to create a musical score, or "map," using any design you choose. (If you wish, you can look at an example of a modern musical score. Murray Shaefer's *Creative Music Teaching* has sample "invented scores" and further ideas.)

   These designs can show variations in pitch, beginnings, and endings for various instruments, or they can tell a story with sound. Lines, squiggles, dots, and dashes are all valid. The basic concept behind this exercise is that musical sounds can be represented visually, and that there are many ways of doing this. One of the reasons for writing down music is so that it can be played again. This is a point you may wish to discuss if you try this activity with children.

   Practice playing your score with a homemade or store-bought instrument.

   Share your work with your class or a colleague. (For classroom use, scores can be displayed or kept in a special "music composition file," just as you would keep a file folder for stories or journal-writing.)

Aronoff, F. W. (1979). *Music and young children* (exp. ed.). New York: Turning Wheel Press.

Aubin, N., Cook, E., Hayden, E., & Walker, D. S. (1981). *Silver Burdett music: Early childhood.* Englewood Cliffs, NJ: Silver Burdett Press.

Branley, F. M. (1967). *High sounds, low sounds.* New York: Thomas Y. Crowell.

East, H. (Ed.). (1989). *The singing sack: 28 song-stories from around the world.* London: A & C Black. (Available with audiocassette.)

Jarnow, J. (1991). *All ears: How to choose and use recorded music for children.* New York: Viking Penguin.

Jones, B., & Hawes, B. L. (1972). *Step it down: Games, plays, songs, and stories from the Afro-American heritage.* New York: Harper & Row.

Mandell, M., & Wood, R. E. (1973). *Make your own musical instruments.* New York: Sterling.

Schafer, M. (1976). *Creative music education: A handbook for the modern music teacher.* New York: Schirmer Books.

Wilson, F. P., & Roehman, F. C. (1990). *Music and child development: Biology of music-making.* Saint Louis, MO: MMB Music.

Winn, M., & Miller, A. (1966). *The fireside book of children's songs.* New York: Simon & Schuster.

Winslow, R. W., & Dallin, L. (1991). *Music skills for classroom teachers* (8th rev. ed.). Dubuque, IA: William C. Brown.

Recordings

Canciones para el recreo [Songs for the playground] / Suni Paz (Smithsonian Folkways).

Dance a story, sing a song / Anne Lief Barlin and Marcia Berman (B/B Recordings).

Favorite fingerplays / Tom Glazer (RTV Communications).

Peter and the wolf / Prokofiev and *Carnival of the animals* / Saint Saëns (EMI/Angel).

Rhythms of childhood / Ella Jenkins (Smithsonian Folkways).

About the Author:

Nina Jaffe, M.S., is a professional storyteller, author, and arts-in-education specialist. An advisor for the Teacher Practitioner Program at Bank Street College, she also teaches Music and Movement: Multicultural and Developmental Perspectives, and Stories, Songs and Folk Games: Multicultural Resources for Educators. She is the author of The Three Riddles: A Jewish Folktale *(Bantam, 1989) and other books of folklore for children.*

16 | Movement in Early Childhood

ovement is defined as the body in motion through space and time. It is a way to explore the world, with one's own body being the tool for discovery. Human beings start out learning about the world through physical interactions with their family members and their surroundings. Our cognitive and sensory systems are geared for making sense of the world through physical activity. Although this process continues all through life, early childhood is the prime age for learning through movement. In this chapter, we will see how teachers and caregivers can make use of various physical activities to expand and support children's learning in the classroom and at home.

Movement brings us the potential for a sense of well-being in our lives. It is through movement that we experience the power of mind and body working together in an immediate, direct way.

Children start life as physical explorers, taking in information from all their senses, as well as through motion: creeping, crawling, toddling, running, and jumping in every direction. As children's muscles, bones, and nerves grow, they need to put their new capacities to use. Whether the children are toddlers learning to negotiate stairs, 5-year-olds jumping rope for the first time, or 8-year-olds perfecting a batting swing, they put their whole mind and body to the task as they seek to satisfy the urge to move, explore, and master their world. Each new level of mastery leads to new vistas and new physical challenges.

The research of Howard Gardner (1983), a developmental psychologist, proposes that the human mind has multiple intelligences. Kinesthetic intelligence includes all the kinds of information one can learn and the concepts one can form about the world through physical activity. Its main mode is "see and do." Visual and verbal information is carried out directly through the muscles in motion as children replicate dance steps, play tag games, or negotiate obstacle courses. These activities all involve learning about spatial relationships and problem solving in a concrete, physical way.

For some children (and adults), kinesthetic intelligence is the most effective way of acquiring information and working with new ideas. It is especially vital to the needs and self-esteem of these children that they have an outlet and recognition for their physical talents. A child who excels in group games, but is hesitant to speak

What is movement?

Why make movement part of your program?

229

up in group time, can be encouraged to begin by describing the secrets of his success in dodging taggers, the plans he makes, and the strategies he uses.

Throughout life, physical developments are linked to cognitive, psychological, and social developments. For a baby, being able to crawl allows the choice of staying near or moving away from parents or caregivers and leads to the first stages of independence. A toddler who can hold a spoon can learn to feed himself; a preschooler who can ride a tricycle has mastered her first vehicle of transportation; 7-year-olds who can jump rope or play ball can learn to take turns and cooperate in group activities. Thus, it is critical for the healthy development of children's minds as well as their bodies that they have a full range of physical activities throughout the day.

Movement provides a pathway for children to learn about themselves and their world. There are many areas of classroom and home life where movement has an impact: language development, early math and science concepts, socialization, and cultural diversity.

Language Development

Body language is the child's first language. Stiffening with anger, holding out arms to be picked up, hiding the face with hands in shyness are all early expressions of feelings and wishes. Later, the child learns words for the gestures and motions he used to show anger, trust, or need. Soon, moving and verbalizing become more coordinated and children begin to follow directions. A caregiver calls a toddler in the playground, "Rosita, come around the bench over here and sit by me," and, understanding the words, the toddler approaches. Able to verbalize physical strategies, a school-age child shrieks out, "That ball is headed for left field! Back up for it!" When new words are linked to action and not memorized out of context, they are often easier to learn. For example, English-speaking children learn "brinca"—the Spanish word for "jump"—more readily when it is incorporated into a movement activity. The associations are immediate and relevant.

Movement stimulates its own large vocabulary. Words take on special significance as children try to scamper, chase, leap, or skitter as a frisky monkey would. Children learn to develop elaborate and extensive vocabularies to describe and guide movements representing falling leaves or snow.

Early Math and Science Concepts

The cognitive aspect of movement involves problem solving with one's own body. Children can be encouraged to observe the world and recreate elements of it through physical expression and interpretation. This nourishes understanding and develops their ability to symbolize experience.

Some of the basic underlying concepts in math and science include pattern, sequence, and cycles. Through movement activities, children can experience these concepts in a concrete way.

For example, colored hoops can be laid out in a line of repeating colors. Children choose one movement for each color: hop for yellow, wiggle for red, spin for blue. The pattern and sequence of hop, wiggle, spin, enhanced by lively music and anchored by the color cues of hoops, offers children another avenue for mastery of one-to-one correspondence, memorization, and patterning. (This activity calls for open space either in your classroom, a gym, or possibly outdoors.)

A group of 6-year-olds studying the butterfly cycle of egg-caterpillar-chrysalis-butterfly get a new perspective when they use movement to recreate the cycle. Children experience the slow, difficult motion of a caterpillar on the ground; then the captured and held-in stillness of the chrysalis; and finally the opening and unfolding of limbs to represent the full, free movements of the butterfly. Through physical enactment, children can internalize the sequence and repetition found in cycles.

Social Skills

Movement is especially well suited to helping a child learn how to work as an individual within a group. In many kinds of movement activities, children learn that their efforts are essential to creating and completing the work of the group. For example, working in unison with a play parachute or colorful sheet makes possible a wonderful variety of experiences in which children all lift the parachute or sheet to create a high dome overhead, or all sit inside at once and belong in a "tent" together.

In a creative movement activity with a circus theme, children learn to appreciate each other's abilities and limitations when they each take on the roles of animals and trainers. Each must learn to "read" the other person and adapt, in order to keep the activity going. Games and dances offer the children both the challenge and the opportunity of learning and using rules, strategies, or patterns of steps to be part of a physical activity that includes everyone. Whether working alone, with a partner, or in a small or large group, a child has a direct and immediate experience involving social interactions.

Cultural Diversity

In all times and places, dancing has been an expression of a people's culture, as music, ritual, and movement come together in a shared experience that is powerful for young and old alike. Games, dances, and the songs and music that go with them are part of everyone's cultural heritage. Many families have their own traditions in music and dance. These might include dancing the hora at family celebrations, the merengue at parties, or just moving all around the living room to favorite tapes. Children and their families can be invited to share these traditions. A preschool teacher asks a student and his mother to show the class a dance from his favorite tape at home. Together, they do their own version of the "Hokey Pokey." Family traditions like this can become part of the repertoire in your early childhood setting.

How can you use movement in early childhood?

Most children are ready to move any time of day. It is the adults who are hesitant. Many teachers and caregivers avoid movement activities because they are afraid a group of moving children will result in chaos. It does not have to be. Here are a few guidelines to follow:

- Plan ahead of time so you are clear about what you want to do.
- Be organized so you have all the equipment you need at hand.
- Give clear directions, telling the children, for example, to run around the circle in the same direction so no one will get bumped.
- Provide structure by saying, "When the music stops, sit down," or "You can tag someone with the ball only from the waist down."
- Begin with simple activities that can grow more complex over time.

The goal is to make movement activities safe and enjoyable for everyone.

Many movement activities can be done in your classroom. Just move the furniture aside to make space. As often as possible, you will want to take children outdoors where they will have plenty of room to move freely.

Developmental Profile
Children learn best when their developmental capacities inform the choice of activities. Knowing about physical development will help you establish a movement program in your setting. The hallmark of very young children is the "wide-base" stance. As babies push up off the floor to a standing position, they place their legs and feet a shoulder's width apart. This does not produce the familiar parallel walk of adults, but does provide a more stable position from which to venture. The weakest part of a toddler's legs are the thighs. The lifting motion of the upper leg is the last development to strengthen.

Preschoolers are upright and ready to go! They have the appearance of generalized muscle development, but still retain a pudgy look of "baby fat." The exciting challenge for children of this age is developing basic locomotor skills and hand-eye coordination. They enjoy climbing and playing with balls.

For young school-age children, hormonal changes in the form of increased androgen are causing changes in the way muscles can develop. Children begin to lose the pudgy look. Their muscles develop "definition": biceps appear, thigh and stomach muscles begin to strengthen. Their bodies crave action and an outlet to practice skills over and over, in order to develop those new muscles.

Types of Movement Activities

There is a range of activities you can include in your program. It will help to think about activities in three categories:

- **Practical Skills**. These are activities that help children develop basic movement skills, like climbing stairs, throwing, catching, crawling, running, jumping, and balancing. They include exercises, obstacle courses, and playing with equipment like balls, hoops, and play parachutes.

  Amanda wants to provide physical activity for her toddlers on a rainy day. She sets up a simple obstacle course using tables, chairs, and pillows. She invites each child to be the "Bear Who Goes Over the Mountain." She puts pairs of chairs back to back for children to climb over the mountain; tables to crawl under; and pillows to roll over. When José is hesitant, she encourages him to give his stuffed toy bear "a ride" through the course.

- **Games**. Games give children the thrill of playing together, engaging in vigorous activity, and learning to use strategies. Cooperative games work best for young children, since winning or losing is not the goal and they will not be "out" for long.

  Sarah's 4-year-olds need an afternoon outlet for their energies. Outdoors, she marks off two home bases where no one can be tagged. These are the "safe" spots for children who need a rest. She carefully chooses both girls and boys to be "It" (3 to 4 taggers at a time in a group of 15). As children are tagged with a tap from the taggers, they come to a spot near Sarah called the "Tagging House." There is only room for one person at a time. So, as soon as another child is tagged, the previous one goes back out "free." In this game, no one is out for long, and this provides a lively, vigorous group activity.

- **Creative Movement**. This kind of movement offers children a chance to express feelings and ideas through physical gestures in their own unique way. Movements are inspired by working with themes or with music, as ways to release the child's imagination.

  Miguel wants to help his kindergarten class deepen their experience of a trip to the park when leaves are falling. At meeting, he asks children to observe and call out what they see

233

as he lets a leaf fall. "Twisting, twirling, floating!" they call out. He encourages them to notice the levels of falling from high to medium to low. As children sit, Miguel asks them to use their hands as leaves: starting with them up high, then twisting, twirling, and floating them to the ground. After a few times, Miguel asks children to stand and try again using their whole bodies. As gentle music plays, they experiment with doing it alone, then with a partner, twirling around each other. To end the lesson and refocus the children's energies, Miguel asks them to sit down and do it once more, just with their hands.

Children gather important, firsthand information about themselves and the world around them as they discover what their bodies can do. The elements of creative movement provide essential experiences in three basic areas:

1. *How Bodies Move: Locomotor Skills*

These are the basic movement skills, such as spinning, jumping, leaping, galloping, hopping, crawling, running. How they are done has to do with qualities such as stiff or limp, smooth or jerky, sharp or flowing.

Carolina has just finished reading a story about rabbits to her 3-year-olds. Using the meeting area, she asks the children to try hopping (without bumping into each other) carefully and quietly like a shy rabbit. Next, they try high, strong rabbit-hops. Children offer their own versions on hopping. At last, all the "rabbits" are asked to hop to a spot where they can curl up and rest. The children have a lively experience moving to the story and also learn to control their movements in relation to each other, and to relax their bodies at the end.

2. *Where Bodies Move: Spatial Awareness*

Children learn about space by exploring how to move through it. They learn about levels by reaching arms high, then medium, then low to the ground. They learn about direction as they run, hop, or jump front and back, side to side.

Mr. Berkowitz wants to experiment with the concept of levels after observing melting icicles with his 6-year-olds. He asks his group to stand in the meeting area and make icicle shapes. The children's bodies are in stiff, angular shapes with a certain amount of muscular tension. He asks them to count slowly to 10 and start to "melt down" to a relaxed puddle shape on the floor. They take turns observing each other's icicles melting, and try new variations on their own ideas. The children learn about moving through space on high, medium, and low levels. They also experience how to make their bodies stiff, then gradually more limp and, finally, totally relaxed, as a "puddle," at the end.

3. *When Bodies Move: Timing, Tempo, Rhythm*

Children learn about the timing of movement when they go fast or slow, start or stop, move in a steady or sporadic way. They learn to time their movements to musical phrases or beats as they coordinate sound and movement.

Marika's kindergarten likes to play a game with a "Talking Drum." The drumbeats tell the children what to do. A steady 1-2 beat means that the children should walk around in a circle in the same direction; a syncopated 1-2-3 beat means to gallop; a sharp bang means to stop. The children are alert, eager not to be tricked when Marika changes the beat, or starts or stops suddenly. Later, the children invent more signals to represent other movements. This is an exciting challenge for mind and body.

Using Themes to Inspire Movement Activities

Any part of the curriculum can be the source of a movement theme. As you select an idea to explore, keep the elements of movement in mind—how bodies move, where they move, and when they move—to help focus the idea. We can use as an example Mrs. Lyons' study of bread and bakeries from the chapter "A Study of Bread and Bakeries: An Example of Integrated Curriculum."

In the discussion during bread baking, children want to know about dough changing from something sticky and soft to something hard. This idea—focusing on change from the qualities of soft to hard—suggests an appropriate movement theme. Before they start, Mrs. Lyons talks with the children about the trip to the Italian bakery and what they know about how the soft dough changes to hard breadsticks.

In movement, some children are bakers and others are the dough for breadsticks. Bakers mix and roll as the "dough" children roll about on the floor. A baker "rolls out" each breadstick for baking. When the dough is baked, the bakers stand the breadstick children upright. With Italian tarantella music playing, the children explore stiffness through stiff walking, hopping, bouncing front, back, side-to-side around the room. To conclude the activity, bakers gather "sticks" together, as though in a package.

In this activity, children recreate the cycle of bread changes and the job cycle of baking and packaging. Music, group effort, and the fun of creating a new version of a known process come together in an exciting and immediate way for children through movement. Further movement activities can be planned around making round shapes (such as bagels or doughnuts) or twisted shapes (such as pretzels). And the type of bread that the children "create" in movement can be available for snack afterwards.

Movement in Celebrations and School Gatherings
Movement, or dance, began as a powerful ritual for people to identify and express themselves in religious practice, ceremonies, and celebrations. Movement and music offer an immediate experience of cultural background, expressing the unique qualities of each person's heritage. School gatherings are an opportunity to share and celebrate those unique qualities. Further, movement lends itself especially well to gatherings of mixed ages: older and younger groups, children and parents, and grandparents.

At the end of a study on the fall season, Mrs. Simon wants to find a culminating experience that will celebrate her second-graders' work and include their parents in a festive activity. The class decides on a hoedown, a party traditionally held at the end of harvest season. Mrs. Simon reserves space in the school auditorium. Parents are invited to dance and then eat together before they go off to work. Simple circle dances like "Looby Lou," "Hokey Pokey," "Ballin' the Jack," and "Down in the Valley" are chosen. Children and parents all join in the dancing, and then enjoy a snack of apple bread baked by the children.

You as Caregiver or Teacher
You do not need to be a dancer or an athlete to provide an effective range of physical activities for children. You may already have a skill or area of comfort from which to start.

Loretta, who avoids sports and feels that she has two left feet in dance class, has become a yoga enthusiast. She can use her familiarity with yoga breathing and relaxation to devise a wonderful lesson for her children. During the day, children need a way to change pace, slow down, and relax or rest. Loretta can lead children in practice with slow breathing: in through the nose and out through the mouth a few times. Then she can teach children to relax their muscles from toe to head.

Eric brings his favorite tapes from home to share. After the children clean up the block area at the end of the day, a new space opens up where they can "dance" to the tapes. He has a collection of props for them to use: scarves, crepe paper streamers, light fabric.

Movement plays an important role in helping children learn about, explore, and exercise their physical abilities. Integrating movement into the curriculum helps children use their physical energy constructively, contributes to a more positive tone in the group, and teaches important concepts and skills. For us to grow into healthy, whole human beings, purposeful physical activity needs to be a part of our everyday lives. Whether at school or at home, movement can impart a feeling of well-being to children, teachers, caregivers, and parents.

Infants and Toddlers

Mary knows that the toddlers in her group love to practice jumping and climbing. There are not any parks or playgrounds they can use every day, nor any large space in the day care center. She thinks of the stairway. Here the children can practice climbing up and down as much as they like.

She leads them on an adventure, saying they are going to "climb the mountain and then go down and start over again." Mary tells them all to hang onto the railing. Some children climb up by the step-together method on the stairs. They improvise a song as they climb: "Here we go up the stairs, up the stairs, up the stairs. Here we go up the stairs, until we go down again." Mary realizes how useful it is to take advantage of everyday experiences as a way of adding movement to the day.

Preschoolers

The 3- and 4-year-olds in Susanna's group are engaged in a work period when several children, including Michael, a lively 4-year-old, begin drifting from activity to activity. Susanna decides the children need some physical activity, and that this would be a good time for a movement lesson.

Knowing that preschoolers are eager to master the basic movement skills of hopping, galloping, spinning, leaping, rolling, and running, Susanna chooses a theme based on re-creating the movements of various animals. She moves tables and chairs away from the meeting area to provide enough room for the children to move freely without mishap. She asks the children to keep moving in the same direction, and tells them that the only rule is not to bump into one another.

Susanna and the children talk about how animals move. Some animals have a light, free way of moving, such as birds flying or kittens jumping. Others move in a slow, heavy way, like lumbering bears or elephants. The children have many suggestions for animal movements, such as "tiptoeing" and "stamping."

For the musical accompaniment to the lesson, Susanna chooses *The Carnival of the Animals* by Camille Saint-Saëns, because it suggests the various gaits of the animals. She reminds the children that when the music is on, they may move; when it is off, they will stop. The children spend the next 20 minutes listening to the music and trying out different movements to express their ideas about how a giant sea turtle moves in slow motion, or how a flustered chicken might flap around the barnyard. Michael decides to be a scampering monkey,

Putting movement into action

an activity that allows him to work off lots of his restless energy.

When the lesson is over, Susanna wisely ends it with a calming activity: She suggests that the children be animals getting ready to sleep.

Young School-Age Children

Paul, a first grade teacher, is concerned about the amount of aggressive competition he sees among his children on the playground during recess, and how upset the children get when they are losing or excluded from play. He wants to find a way to offer them other kinds of vigorous physical activity that will be challenging, yet emphasize cooperation. He also knows that 6- to 7-year-olds are eager to practice and perfect physical skills. So Paul chooses a game called "Doctor Dodge." It involves vigorous activity, ball skills, and use of strategy, but it does not involve winning or losing.

The group is divided into two teams. A line marks the boundary between the teams. Children are given lightweight plastic balls—one ball for every four to five children. Paul chooses one or two children to be the "Doctor" for each team. He designates a spot for each team that will serve as the "Hospital."

The children begin to try to tag each other by throwing the balls to bounce off a person on the other team. If a child is tagged, he or she lies down on the ground and the "Doctor" comes to bring the child to the "Hospital." There is only room for one person in this hospital, so when the next "patient" comes in, the first one goes back out to play again.

This game provides a challenge for everyone. Those who have well-developed skills have the opportunity to aim, throw, and catch many times. Less skilled children can afford to take some risks because if they are tagged, they will not be "out" for long.

One day, it is Sam's turn to be the "Doctor." He has cerebral palsy, but has some mobility when he uses a walker. His walker becomes the "ambulance" and many children want a "ride" to the hospital "in" it. Paul notices that once Sam has brought the children to the hospital, he continues to administer "check-ups" and give advice. All the children enjoy this role play.

Families

Amy's father comes to the teacher, worried about all the energy his 4-year-old daughter has, and looking for ways to channel it. Amy's teacher, Maureen, suggests that Amy have as many opportunities as possible to play outdoors. She reassures him that even when the weather is cold, Amy can bundle up and play outside. Maureen tells him that children have high levels of metabolism and do not get as cold as adults do. She also explains that Amy's physical skills are well-developed in comparison to many other 4-year-olds, and that her competence should be encouraged. Maureen suggests indoor games, such as seeing how many different ways Amy can hop on one foot, forwards, backwards, or in a circle. She also suggests that Amy be encouraged to march, dance, and move creatively to her favorite music.

Exercises

The following exercises will help you and your colleagues develop practices and acquire resources to support a movement program in your setting.

1. Have a discussion with colleagues about your own memories or experiences with physical activity. Think about what your children's experiences are with physical activity in the classroom.

2. Brainstorm about resources that you and your colleagues have that are already comfortable for you: a favorite dance tape, a game or movement idea. Try to put them into practice.

3. Think about your daily routine. Do you already include movement activities? Are there other times you can incorporate movement skills or games? Write down your ideas and share them with a colleague.

4. Create a resource file with your colleagues. Many libraries have books, records, and tapes on movement activities that you can borrow and copy. Each person can help gather resources and share an activity they have mastered. Check local resources— library programs, local arts groups, and parents and colleagues in your school who can contribute their expertise.

5. Gather materials that can be used in movement: scarves, streamers, leaves, ribbons. Assess your available equipment and see if you can add inexpensive supplies like plastic balls, jump ropes, and plastic hoops.

6. Observe children in their physical play. Take notes on how they use their bodies, alone and in relation to others. What new information does this provide about the child?

Resources

Bryand, R. (1974). *Complete elementary physical education guide*. West Nyack, NY: Parker.

Carr, R. E. (1980). *See and be: Yoga and creative movement for children*. Englewood Cliffs, NJ: Prentice-Hall.

Curtis, S. (1982). *The joy of movement in early childhood*. New York: Teachers College Press.

Engstrom, G. (Ed.). (1971). *The significance of the young child's motor development*. Washington, DC: National Association for the Education of Young Children.

Kamiya, A. (1985). *Elementary teacher's handbook of indoor and outdoor games*. West Nyack, NY: Parker.

Recordings
African heritage dances (Educational Archives).
American playparties/Pete Seeger (Folkways).
Getting to know myself/Hap Palmer (Activity Records).
Movin'/Hap Palmer(Activity Records).
Play party dances and ice breakers for young folk/Piute Pete (Folkways).
The feel of music/Hap Palmer (Activity Records).

About the Author:
   Roberta Altman, M.S., is on the faculty at Bank Street College, where she advises leadership students and teaches graduate courses in movement and physical development. She is the Movement Specialist at the Bank Street School for Children. She is also Project Co-Director of Excellent Beginnings, a collaboration between Bank Street College and Midtown West Public School in New York City.

17 | A Study of Bread and Bakeries: An Example of Integrated Curriculum

The task of developing curriculum is a challenging one and can seem overwhelming at first. However, it helps to think of yourself as a learner embarking on a learning experience with your children. In this section, you will look at an example of a study to see how one teacher uses a social studies topic to integrate curriculum. As you read, think about other age groups, other environments, and other studies. This example is not a recipe; all effective studies reflect the individual thinking of the teachers who design them.

Mrs. Lyons, a teacher of a mixed-age group of 23 kindergarten and first grade children in an urban public school, chooses a study of breads and bakeries as a vehicle for helping her children think about how people do their jobs. She wants her children to understand that people have specific jobs and that it takes many different workers to produce our food. From a scientific perspective, she wants the children to think about physical change, and bread provides interesting content for experiments, observations, and discussions. The school's neighborhood has many ethnic bakeries and supermarkets, and bakeries are filled with interesting machines and devices that appeal to children. Mrs. Lyons likes this study topic because bread is common to virtually all cultures. At the same time, it comes in many different forms. The varieties of bread available in the neighborhood will lead naturally to discussions of different families and cultures. The children will have ample opportunities to appreciate diversity while recognizing commonalities.

Before we go on, think of your setting and age group. What are the interests of the children? What resources does the community provide? Keep your answers in mind as you read through the example.

Prior to the study, Mrs. Lyons talks with another teacher about her plans. She finds this helps her generate ideas and clarify her thinking. They discuss how the children will see wheat and grind it (activities that help children understand where bread comes from), and how they will see and taste different kinds of breads, such as donuts, pretzels, tortillas, and pita. This discussion helps her consider the range of possibilities for the study. What other ideas can you think of for a study of bread for 5- and 6-year-olds?

She begins organizing trips to stores, interviews with workers, discussions with family members about recipes—all experiences children need to gather information. She anticipates ways they can recreate their learning: block buildings of bakeries and pizza stores, songs about bakers and bread, dramatic play about bakeries, murals, cookbooks, science experiments, measurement activities during cooking, story books, wheat grinding, baking and eating.

Before beginning the study with children, Mrs. Lyons visits a pastry shop, a bagel store, a pizza shop, a Latino bakery, and a natural foods store. She explains to local merchants that her class will study breads and bakeries and asks if they can visit. The shopkeepers are receptive to her requests.

Now it is time to begin. One afternoon, she opens up discussion by asking the class, "What did you have for lunch today?" The children talk about what they have eaten and Mrs. Lyons records answers on a chart. Many of the children say they ate sandwiches for lunch. She asks them to describe the kinds of bread used in their sandwiches: white, whole wheat, pita, raisin bread. The chart remains on the wall throughout the study.

The next day she has a grain grinder and wheat berries on the table for the children to look at as they come into the room. Some children ask, "Where do wheat berries come from?" Mrs. Lyons is prepared for this question and has a book from the library with text and pictures of wheat and wheat fields. She asks the children to think about their question and lets them know they will discuss it later on. At the morning meeting, Mrs. Lyons says, "Today we will talk about flour. What is flour?" Many of the children are not sure. One child's question reveals some confusion about "flowers" and "flour." Children share stories about baking with parents and grandparents.

During the morning work period, some children use the grinder and taste the flour. They draw pictures and write (or dictate) about the grain grinder and the flour they have made. By week's end, everyone has had a chance to grind flour and to draw and write about the experience. Mrs. Lyons mounts the children's stories and drawings on pieces of construction paper. Using metal binder rings, she compiles these into a class book. The following week, Mrs. Lyons reads the book to the class during story time and then the book is added to the class library.

Knowing that the experience of making bread will stimulate the children's thinking and questions, Mrs. Lyons prepares a recipe for whole wheat bread. A parent brings in her favorite recipe for challah, a kind of egg bread, and helps the children make it. After a visit to the pizza shop, the baker gives the children the recipe for pizza dough.

Mrs. Lyons has asked a parent to bring in a small oven that the class can use during the study. She also brings her toaster oven from home. As children begin baking, they ask why bread rises. They want to know how dough changes from something sticky to something firm that can be sliced. Experiments using yeast and baking soda help them find answers to their questions.

The class takes a trip each week to different bakeries or bread shops in the neighborhood. Mrs. Lyons sometimes takes children on trips in half-groups, enlisting the support of parent volunteers.

First, they go to a bagel store. During the trip, Mrs. Lyons listens to children's questions and conversations; she records anecdotes in her notebook. Danielle asks, "Is a donut a bagel?" Mrs. Lyons acknowledges her inquiry by saying the question is interesting and Danielle should think more about it.

The next day, Mrs. Lyons presents the question to the class. She uses an open-ended statement to begin the discussion: "Yesterday, Danielle observed similarities between bagels and donuts. Let's talk about donuts and bagels." The children begin sharing stories about both foods. One child says that a bagel is bread and a donut is cake. Another child observes that both are round with holes. Mrs. Lyons's role in this discussion is facilitator; she does not give answers. Rather, she uses opportunities like these to help children learn ways to solve problems. They learn how to test their hypotheses. She wants to help Danielle think through her question. Mrs. Lyons tells the class they will bake both donuts and bagels and compare the recipe charts for similarities and differences.

The first trip to the bagel store is the basis for many experiences and many discussions. The children bring back bagels to taste and make a graph of their favorite kinds. Some children make paintings of machines and workers they saw in the bagel store.

After their paintings are completed, Mrs. Lyons talks with children about their work and listens carefully to their discussions. Through her informal conversations with children, she evaluates their learning and assesses their need for additional experiences.

The class makes a book about their trip. Each child contributes a drawing and a piece of writing. Again, some dictate stories and others write by themselves, using invented spelling. One child depicts his experience at the "bread shop" like this:

Several children build a bakery in the block corner while others construct a model of a bread factory, using boxes and milk cartons of different sizes. They use masking tape to hold them together and to tape them to a large piece of flat cardboard. Important learning is taking place here as the children discover the relationships between workers, machines, and the environment.

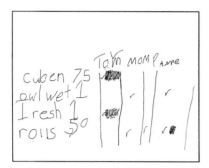

Figure 1

As the class bakes different kinds of bread, charts are hung around the room with the names of breads and recipes. Children discover their families have different names for the same bread. Around the classroom, books are displayed containing stories and poetry about breads, pies, bakers, and other related subjects, representing many cultures and customs. Some children have surveyed other classes to learn about the favorite kinds of breads of other children. Their graph, with its invented spellings, is also on display. One child prepares a shopping list. She asks her father (Tom) and her mother what kind of bread each of them would like and records their choices along with the prices (see Figure 1).

Although the study of bakeries and breads is the focal point of the classroom for several weeks, other work in the room—reading, writing process, art, music, math activities—continue as usual. The bakery study provides a rich context in which children can use their skills and knowledge from these other areas, and adds to their growing skills and knowledge in all areas.

The study that began in October will end in late November. Mrs. Lyons plans a bakery in the classroom for the culminating experience. Parents and other adults in school will be invited. She notifies parents of her plans in the monthly newsletter. Can you think of other appropriate culminating experiences?

Organizing the bakery is a big job for both Mrs. Lyons and the children. There is much planning and discussion and lots of excitement. Some items will be baked at school in small ovens in the classroom; others are baked in the large oven in the school's kitchen. Several parents take items prepared at school and bake them at home.

The bakery project sparks many new math experiences: the children keep track of ingredients used, items baked, and how many times each child has a turn as baker. They keep records of who serves, bakes, and is cashier. Real money is collected and counted. The children are ready for this because play money was used extensively in the make-believe bakery they built with blocks. Mrs. Lyons extended children's learning by designing additional math activities using play money. Now the children apply the math skills they have learned throughout the study in their real bakery.

The children are very proud of what they have learned and eager to share it with their parents. They set up a display inside the classroom including their trip books, stories, graphs and other art work for parents to see when they come to the bakery. The bakery is planned for the week before Thanksgiving. The children will sell their baked goods early in the morning when their parents bring them to school. Many parents buy breads and cakes to serve during the holiday. The bakery is a wonderful success.

Throughout the study, Mrs. Lyons reflects on how and what her children are learning. In addition to her extensive anecdotal records, she has drawings and writing from the children. She takes pictures of block buildings and constructions to help her with parent conferences and report writing.

As you read about Mrs. Lyons's study, you probably had many ideas of your own. There is no one way to create a social studies curriculum. Every group of children, every teacher, changes the quality of a study. Imagine that Mrs. Lyons teaches in a rural environment where there are no local bakeries or food shops. How might she give children firsthand experiences with other workers and their jobs?

We looked at a study for 5- and 6-year-olds. Let us consider the ways this study might change if the group of children were somewhat younger or older.

Four year-olds might well be interested in the jobs they observe people doing and will recreate trips through extensive dramatic play. While a 5- or 6-year-old makes her own baker's hat if she needs one for her play, a younger child grabs the baker's hat you place in the dramatic play area to begin her play as baker. As much as 4-year-olds enjoy mixing and kneading real bread, they are equally enthusiastic about making playdough cupcakes and pies and pizza, having serious and involved discussions as they work. An appropriate culminating experience for 4-year-olds might be a breakfast for parents and children with muffins prepared the day before. A long-range project like the one Mrs. Lyons planned would frustrate younger children because they find it hard to wait and plan far in advance.

Now that you have read about how to put a study into action, think about other topics for 4-year-olds in your community.

For older children, the study includes more writing, reading, and recording, but it continues to be rich in building, making, and dramatizing experiences. Seven- and eight-year-olds might study baking techniques used now and long ago and think about the history of baking ovens, from the fires of American Indians to the brick ovens of the early settlers, to the solar-powered ovens of today. They could build an oven using a light bulb, or make a solar-powered oven to experiment with heat and temperature. They might prepare a recipe book of breads.

A historical study of machinery and equipment used for wheat production and bread making could be a way to investigate how technology has changed through history. Older children love inventions. Through questions, speculations, and rich experiences, they begin to develop an appreciation of how people's lives have changed as a result of changes in technology.

The history of bread or baking equipment is one way to approach

Looking at integrated curriculum for other age groups

a study of long ago that begins with something from the here and now. Can you think of other topics that might be relevant to your children and your environment? A study for 7- and 8-year-olds will include visits to historical places and museums. Are there places in your community that have collections of historical material? Older children like to reenact the roles of people long ago in skits and plays. They can design costumes and write scripts for plays. These experiences provide meaningful opportunities for research and writing. Stories that they read or hear help them to imagine the lifestyles of people long ago. Films and video help to bring history to life as well.

About the Author:

Judy R. Jablon, M.S., is a curriculum consultant who works with teachers in Head Start and public school programs. She has been a primary grade teacher in public and private schools, including Bank Street School for Children. She has taught courses in curriculum development at Bank Street College.

18 | You as Teacher or Caregiver

Most of us have an image of what a teacher or caregiver *should* be. For example, many people believe that a teacher or caregiver "should" always like every child in his or her program equally. Others believe that a teacher or caregiver "should" always have the right answers. Some think that teachers "should" leave their feelings outside the classroom door, never letting children see that they are human beings who are sometimes tired, sad, or angry. How about you?

The problem with these "shoulds" is that they hide the fact that, above all, teachers and caregivers are human beings—people who are learning and growing, people who make mistakes, people with feelings, needs, strengths, and weaknesses. Though all teachers and caregivers do many of the same tasks—setting up learning environments, making decisions as they plan a program, working with parents—each one, including you, is a unique individual. Everything you do is colored by who you are—your past, your personality, your interests, likes, dislikes, and values.

You bring to the children and families in your program ideas, questions, a sense of humor, an approach to life, that no one else can duplicate. At Bank Street, we believe that you are your own richest resource. To this end, we encourage you to take a good look at who you are as a person and how that affects who you are as a teacher or caregiver.

Reflecting on who you are and what you do can be difficult, but it is well worth the effort. Put yourself in the place of Miriam, who believed that she had to like every child in her program equally.

"The first two years I worked with children," she explains, "I rushed to cover up feelings I thought were 'bad.' But in my third year, I met Henry, a little boy whose constant whining drove me crazy. I tried for months being nice to him. I smiled until my face felt as if it would crack.

"Fortunately, I had a colleague I could trust. I told him how I was feeling. He told me I wasn't alone—he had had similar experiences with other children. Talking to him helped me face the truth: I didn't like Henry very much.

"It was only when I let myself recognize my feelings that I was able to build a relationship with Henry. It began at the easel. As I listened to him talk about colors and saw how much he loved painting, I began to see a creative, interesting child hidden from me

Who are you as a teacher or caregiver?

by my feelings about whining.

"Being honest with myself was good for Henry—and for me. A weight lifted when I discovered I could be me and be a good teacher at the same time."

In this chapter, we are going to take a look at why knowing who you are is an important part of being a teacher or caregiver, and at ways you can promote your professional development. Then there will be some exercises to help you and colleagues apply what you have learned in this chapter to your daily practice.

Why is it important to think about who you are as a teacher or caregiver?

Who you are colors children's experience of your program. Your personality sets the tone, your values shape your expectations of children's behavior, how you treat co-teachers and children provides a model for how children will learn to treat one another, your curiosity affects children's explorations, and your interests find their way into the curriculum. This is not to say *you* should be the center of attention. Rather, who you are as a *person* has great impact on who you are as a teacher or caregiver.

Getting to know you can help children get to know themselves and give them insight into the grownup world which they find so fascinating. By having class pets and plants and making a terrarium, Ed Robinson shares his love of the outdoors with his second graders. He shares how it feels to be passionate about something and encourages children not only to share his interest but to develop their own. Regina Thomas, a kindergarten teacher, makes a book about herself to share with her class. By sharing photographs of when she was a child, her wedding day, her children, and the flowers she loves growing at home, she not only helps children get to know her, but invites them to make connections between their lives in school and at home. She conveys to them that who they are as people matters to her.

To take full advantage of the qualities you bring to the children you work with, you must be aware of them yourself. Because you, too, are constantly growing and changing, self-reflection must be an ongoing part of your job. You need to find ways to think about who you are. Here are some suggestions to help you begin:

Examine your ideas of what a teacher or caregiver should be.
You may be surprised to discover ideas, assumptions, or expectations you did not even know you had.

- One day Darlene, a teacher of preschoolers, hears herself saying to a visitor, "This morning they're just playing. This afternoon, we'll get to work." Her co-teacher Sandra is surprised. At their staff meetings, Darlene regularly talks about play and everyday routines as rich learning experiences. Their curriculum is based on this belief. When Sandra asks her about it, Darlene is amazed she could have said such a thing.

After thinking about it, Darlene realizes she had never been sure that "supporting" children's learning was really doing enough. As she thinks about what good teaching is, Darlene discovers in herself an old idea dating back to her own school days: a teacher's role is to stand in front of the room and teach. By holding up this old view of what a teacher "should" be next to what she has discovered over the years about how children learn through play, Darlene begins to truly believe that she is a good teacher. She can see that her classroom is a place where children learn about themselves and their world through interaction with materials, other children, and adults.

Question your daily practices.

Be open to changes. When teachers and caregivers do not look at themselves and what they do, they tend to do things out of habit. This makes it hard to respond to children's needs, which are always changing.

- It is only when she stops to question why she herself always does the serving at snack time that Maria realizes the preschoolers in her family child care program are capable of passing baskets of crackers and pitchers of juice to one another. When she encourages them to do so, everyone comes out ahead. The children gain new social skills and Maria enjoys snack-time conversations she never had time for.

Be aware of how who you are influences your teaching or caregiving.
Past experiences can shape how you respond to certain situations.

- Knowing that you had many painful separations during your childhood can help you understand why you find it hard to help the infants you work with say goodbye to their parents every morning.

- Your interests can shape curriculum decisions. For example, loving to cook may lead you to cook regularly with the toddlers you care for.

Keep a delicate balance between feeling close to children and maintaining a little distance.
Feeling connected to children can help you understand what they are experiencing. Keeping a distance—in order to be effective—helps you decide how best to respond to their needs. The challenge is being enough in tune with yourself to do both—at the same time!

How can you promote your development as a teacher or caregiver?

To be a good teacher or caregiver means you are constantly developing. Here are some suggestions of ways to keep growing:

Be a learner.
Your curiosity and enthusiasm will encourage the same in children. As a learner, whether you are studying more about children, Tai Chi, or car repair, you will take steps forward and back. Being in touch with your own feelings—of frustration when you do not seem to be getting anywhere, and excitement and pride when you master a new skill—will help you recognize and respond to these feelings in children.

Continue your professional development.
- Read.
- Take a course.
- Give a workshop.
- Participate at staff meetings.
- Join a support group of others who want to focus on a topic such as anti-bias curriculum or involving parents in meaningful ways.

Become part of a professional community.
You, like the children you teach, will be nurtured by being part of a trusting community where you can share your questions, doubts, and feelings, as Miriam and Darlene did in the examples above.
- Build relationships with other teachers or caregivers. Formal staff meetings offer you the opportunity to examine issues in depth together. Informal conversations in the hall, or getting together after work are times for much-needed "teacher talk." In one school district, teachers formed their own study group on language development.
- Consider joining a professional organization, such as the National Association for Family Day Care or the National Association for the Education of Young Children (NAEYC, the professional organization for early childhood educators who work with children from birth through age 8).

Think about why you do what you do with children.
Rather than just following a set curriculum, ask yourself, and discuss with colleagues in depth, substantial questions such as, "What can children learn from painting?" or "What is science?" Creating a program based on what you know about children is both challenging and very satisfying.

View mistakes as learning experiences.

Rather than feeling embarrassed when, for example, making pizza for snack turns into chaos, evaluate what went wrong and plan how you might handle a similar situation differently in the future.

Take care of yourself.

Teaching is very hard work. No one can continually care for others without having some of his or her own needs met.

- Take care of yourself in your setting by hanging up a favorite picture, inviting children to join you in exercising for 10 minutes each day, or bringing in flowers or a plant.

- Take care of yourself outside work by taking a long walk on the weekend or planning a picnic with family or friends.

- Think of ways you and colleagues can take care of each other by sharing a favorite muffin recipe, telling a good joke, or completing tasks you promised to do.

Become an advocate—for children, families and your profession.

- Explain to parents why children learn best through play.

- Write a letter to the editor of your local paper.

- Write to state or federal legislators about a pending issue, to share your experience and point out needs.

Infants and Toddlers

When Sharon first became an infant/toddler caregiver, she believed her role was to be the "expert." To this end, she stayed up nights reading books by noted authorities. She constantly worried that a parent might ask her a question to which she did not know the answer.

Four years later, her perspective has changed. "My experience has taught me that when it comes to children, no one has all the answers. Since I realized I could say 'I don't know. Let's try to find out together,' parents have relaxed and are more willing to share their questions and concerns. Now we can really be partners and support each other."

Preschoolers

For years, Ellen put out a small collection of about 50 wooden blocks. She felt that too many blocks would cause chaos. As it turned out, she did not have to worry about chaos, because very few children ever went into the block corner. Then, one day, a colleague, Frances, commented, "You don't have enough blocks." She followed up by inviting Ellen to visit her program. There, Ellen saw children building a farm, a highway, and a house. She felt a sense of purpose and

Teachers and caregivers in action

order, even though hundreds of blocks were being used.

Ellen added more blocks to her block corner. Children began building, but clean-up was a disaster. The chaos she had feared came to be.

Ellen decides to ask Frances to help her. Frances gets down on the floor and begins helping children stack blocks in groups of five to carry to the shelves. The children join in and so does Ellen. Over time, by talking with Frances and other colleagues, Ellen develops other block clean-up strategies.

Thanks to a trusting, supportive relationship between colleagues, a whole group of children has experiences with blocks they would have otherwise missed.

Young School-Age Children

In January, Mr. Gleason, a second grade teacher, finds himself dragging. It has been a tough first half of the year. Several children in his group need a lot of guidance. A few parents demand his attention constantly. Hoping difficult kids would be out sick and hiding behind his answering machine to avoid parents' calls is *not* what he wants to be doing.

When his neck and back began aching from tension, Mr. Gleason decids something must be done. He thinks of some ways to take care of himself, beginning with getting to school early enough to have a cup of coffee.

Stepping back, Mr. Gleason realizes he was doing too much of the work in the room himself. He makes a job chart and holds a meeting with the children about their taking on more classroom responsibilities. In an attempt to relate in a new way to the "difficult" children, he tells some jokes. Children began sharing their favorites and a joke-telling session soon becomes a daily activity.

Though, of course, children still need guidance and parents still calls, taking care of himself and stepping back helps Mr. Gleason feel more centered and gain a fresh perspective. For the first time in months, he remembers that there are many children in his class whom he really enjoys. And he begins to realize that he is not a failure, but that this is just an unusually tough year.

Families

Shelley, an 8-month-old, arrives at her family child care home each morning looking grubby. She needs a good bath. Her clothes are shabby. Patty, her care provider, begins feeling she could be a better parent than Shelley's own are. "If I were your mother," she says to Shelley, "I would take good care of you."

Feelings of possessiveness and competition are natural among adults sharing the care of the same child. They stem from a sense of attachment. But when these feelings are not recognized, they can get in the way of communication between parents and caregivers. A sense of "me" versus "you" makes cooperation unlikely and undermines the chances of building the parent-caregiver partnership that children need.

Children, parents, and caregivers benefit when caregivers have colleagues with whom to share their feelings and exchange information. If you, like Patty, are working on your own or are in a program where there is no communication, creating a professional community is a critical part of your job. If there is no professional association in your community, you might start one. It can be as easy as getting together with other caregivers once a month in each other's homes.

Exercises

Our goal in this chapter has been to help you tap into your greatest resource—you—by encouraging you to look at who you are as a teacher. Sharing experiences, insights, and feelings with colleagues can help you do this.

Here are some exercises you can do with colleagues to help you see the connection between who you are as a person and your teaching.

1. Our ideas of a what a teacher or caregiver should be are often shaped by teachers we have had. In this exercise, you will take a look at teachers you have had.

   • Think about teachers in your school years. What are their names? What did they teach? How old were you when you were in their classes? What do you remember of each?

   • Who was the best teacher you can remember? What made him or her so special to you?

   • Who was the worst teacher you can remember? What made being with him or her a negative experience for you?

   • What did you learn about teaching from the teachers you had in school? Give examples of how what you learned influences your daily work.

   Share your responses with a group of colleagues.

2. Being a learner yourself helps you inspire children to learn.

   • What is something you are learning about or want to learn about?

   • How do you feel when you try out a new skill, be it speaking a new language or paddling a canoe?

   • How do you respond when you make "mistakes," like tipping the canoe?

   • How does it feel when you begin to "catch on" and make what was a new skill your own?

- What kinds of things do people do that help you learn?
- What kinds of things do people do that interfere with your learning?
- How can your experiences as a learner shape your teaching?

Share your ideas with colleagues.

3. Every day, you are responsible for meeting the needs of many people. To do this, you must meet some of your own needs. Consider these questions:

- What can you do on the job to take care of yourself?
- How can you and co-workers care for one another?
- How can you take better care of yourself in your personal life?

4. Because every child is unique, chances are that, sooner or later (if it has not already happened), you will have children in your group whom you find difficult to work with, because you do not like certain qualities about them. No one likes everyone. But as a teacher, one of the responsibilities of your job is to resolve your feelings and build a relationship with these children. In this exercise, we encourage you to think about a child you do not like very much and about how you can get to know him or her.

- Begin by thinking of children you like. What are the qualities that make these kids likable?
- Think about a child you do not particularly like. Describe him or her in detail.
- Describe your relationship with this child and what it is you find difficult.
- Make a special effort to get to know this child. Make a series of objective observations of him or her. Observe, for example, what activities this child likes, and what makes him or her happy, sad, or angry. Talk with family members about his or her life at home. What did you learn about this child?
- Take a good look at yourself. How does who you are—experiences from your past, your likes and dislikes—influence your feelings about this child?
- Based on what you now know, describe this child again. Be sure to include his or her strengths.
- What could you do to begin building a relationship? Try your ideas and see how they work.

Doing this exercise with colleagues can be very helpful for everyone involved.

5. Becoming a good teacher or caregiver is a developmental process. Over time, as you gain experience, learn from mistakes, and work with a variety of people, you grow and change. In this exercise, we encourage you to think about some ways you have changed as a teacher. Consider these questions:

- How have you changed? For example, have you changed the way you do something, such as setting up a cooking activity, or how you feel about something, such as working with parents who speak a language you do not speak?

- What factors led to these changes?

- How does the change affect you? Co-workers? Children? Children's families?

- Is there an area in which you would like to develop further? Describe it. What will you do to help yourself grow and change?

Share your responses with a small group of colleagues.

Resources

Ayers, W. (1989). *The good preschool teacher: Six teachers reflect on their lives.* New York: Teachers College Press

Dombro, A. L. (1978). *Running, swirling, banging into walls: Autobiography of a caregiver* (ED# 180-599). Washington, DC: ERIC Clearinghouse on Early Childhood Education.

Goffin, S. G., & Lombardi, J. (1988). *Speaking out: Early childhood advocacy.* Washington, DC: National Association for the Education of Young Children.

Kreinberg, N., & Nathan, H. (1991). *Teachers' voices, teachers' wisdom: Seven adventurous teachers think aloud.* Berkeley, CA: Equals.

About the Author:

Amy Laura Dombro, M.S., headed the Bank Street Infant and Family Center from 1976 to 1983. She is now a consultant with Head Start Parent Child Center programs. She is the senior author of The Ordinary is Extraordinary: How Children under Three Learn *(1989, Fireside) and* Sharing the Caring: How to Find the Right Child Care and Make it Work for You and Your Child *(1991, Fireside).*

19 | Working with Families

First of all, what do we mean when we say "family"? Family can mean all kinds of combinations of adults and children. From the children's point of view, "family" are those people who are the foundation of their world, the people whom they feel close to and trust. Family may include one parent, two moms or two dads, step-parents, grandparents, godparents, foster parents, uncles and aunts, brothers and sisters, cousins, the upstairs neighbor who has babysat for the child since infancy. It may or may not include children's biological parents. Probably the only assumption that holds for all families is that, like the children they nurture, families are unique.

Working with families means building a relationship that allows for two-way communication between you and the other significant adults in a child's life. Through this relationship, you create a connection between the time children spend with you and their life at home. Working with families takes a wide variety of forms. It is carrying out a family's plan for the way they want their child to be toilet trained. It is telling a family about their child's day. It is sending a newsletter home. And it is much more.

Adults play different roles in a child's life. You and members of a child's family each have a place, and do not have to compete for a child's love. Family members are the most important people in a child's world. They share deep and abiding love. They are his home base—they know and care about him beyond all others. They will continue to be part of his life after he leaves your group. You, on the other hand, have knowledge about children in general and your responsibility is to support the child's growth and development in your program and at home. A child benefits by having both you and members of his family in his life—you each have something important to give.

In this chapter, we will look at why it is important to work with families and the many ways you can do it. Then there will be exercises that you and your colleagues can do together to help you develop necessary skills.

Sometimes teachers or caregivers feel that their job is only to work with children. They do not necessarily consider that they also need to work with the adults in a child's life. But who the members of a family are, where they live, how they spend their time, what their values are—all of these elements help shape each child in your group. You need their insight and information to help you build a relationship with their child.

For example, Carol, 6 months old, likes to take a break in the middle of drinking her bottle. When her mother shares this information with Carol's family day care provider, it helps her understand Carol's behavior. Having a bottle will be an enjoyable experience for both of them and get their relationship off to a good start—thanks to this simple exchange of information. In the same way, Debby's grandmother, who recognizes that transitions are difficult for her 5-year-old granddaughter, talks with the kindergarten teacher at the beginning of the school year. She describes some of the strategies that work at home, especially giving Debby advance notice a few minutes before she has to clean up. The kindergarten teacher listens carefully, so that she can learn about Debby and help her adjust to school.

The adults in children's families can keep you in touch with what is happening in the rest of their lives. It is important for you to know what is happening at home because children's behavior is affected by events, big and small, that affect their families. You can then respond to their needs and concerns. Knowing that Frank's father is away on a business trip helps his caregiver understand why he is whiney today. It leads her to offer activities that will help 4-year-old Frank feel connected to his father, such as helping Frank "write" a letter to his father, calling his father on the play phone, and reading a book with Frank about how mommies and daddies go to work and come back.

In times of family crisis, it is very important that you and families share information. You will want to tell parents how the child is experiencing the stress: what the child is saying or doing to express his concerns. Together, you and the family can find ways to help the child understand and manage what is happening.

When a child exhibits difficult behavior, working with families can also help solve discipline problems—both in the program and at home. Teachers sometimes feel that they need to show that they are in control, that they know the answer. But you do not have to offer a ready-made solution. Observing the child, raising questions, and problem solving with parents can help engage them and, together, you can find appropriate strategies. Working together also helps parents feel that they are not being blamed for their child's behavior.

Daniel's teacher, Mrs. Cohen, was concerned that he was making "put down" remarks to his first grade classmates. He would say, "That's ugly" about someone's work or, "I can do it better." Although the teacher recognized that some of this behavior was typical for this age, she was concerned that Daniel was excessive and that other children were, in turn, rejecting him. When Mrs. Cohen spoke with his parents, they told her that Daniel's older brother sometimes criticized Daniel's beginning efforts to write and read. The teacher and the parents had a conference and came up with some ideas about how to deal with Daniel's older brother (who, in fact, was feeling insecure about his *own* schoolwork) and how to modify Daniel's behavior with his classmates.

Caregivers and teachers know a lot about children. Because they know firsthand the diversity and range of children's development, they can reassure parents that "not all 2-year-olds speak in sentences" or that "some children test limits more than others do." Knowing about child development means that teachers can put children's behavior into a developmental perspective. This can be both informative and comforting to parents.

One of the most important ways that programs and families can work together is by supporting children's learning. Helping parents understand how important it is to read to their child, sharing information on what children are learning at school, and just keeping the lines of communication open between home and school can make a big difference. When families reinforce what children are doing in school and show that their learning is valued, children are more likely to be motivated and excited about learning.

Working with families includes respecting and supporting family members as *people*. Getting to know them—their individual strengths, abilities, problems, interests, and concerns—helps you find ways to involve them in your program. A parent who likes to build things may be able to build a bookcase in the classroom and show the children his tools as well as how he solves problems. Another parent may be able to send you a recipe for arroz con pollo. Family members may also need support from your program in meeting some of their needs that are necessary to the well-being of their family. These needs may include gaining access to medical, social service, or educational resources. As adults feel supported, they, in turn, will be better able to nurture the children in their family.

Establishing relationships with families takes work *and* time, just as establishing any other relationship does. Your efforts will be well rewarded and everyone will benefit.

- **Families** will gain a greater understanding of their child's development. This information can help them feel more confident and competent in their child rearing.

- **Children** will experience a trusting and mutually respectful relationship between caregivers, teachers, and families in which there is consistent and continuous support in their move from home to early childhood program.

- **You, the teacher or caregiver**, will find it easier to plan for the children in your group when you have information which helps you really know each child—information supplied by the people who know him or her best. When families have a better understanding of what you do and why, and when they feel part of what you do, they will be more likely to give you their encouragement, support, and appreciation.

To help children grow and develop to their potential, teachers and families need to work together. Your mutual goal is to provide a positive, supportive environment at home and away from home.

How can you work with families?

"Family involvement" extends far beyond baking cookies for a class picnic. Parents and other family members can take on many different roles and participate in the education of their children at many levels. The responsibility of including families in early childhood settings lies with administrators as well as with caregivers and teachers.

The involvement of families as teachers can be invited. Some programs have an established volunteer program; others hire parents directly as aides or paraprofessionals. Still others invite parents to be occasional co-teachers and to share their expertise in the classroom, perhaps to share an occupational speciality or cultural experience.

As schools change, new roles for families will continue to emerge. Families are becoming policy makers as members of a program's governance body or a school's PTA or school-based management team. Being involved in decisions that affect their children helps parents advocate for what is best for them.

Programs can facilitate the organization of parent curriculum groups or study groups around topics of interest, such as budgeting, ethnic studies, or English as a second language. Parent choice and participation in the design of courses for themselves empowers parents and other family members.

Building a Relationship

Building and supporting a relationship with children's families is part of your work throughout the year. Here are some things you can do to make your relationship strong.

- Remember that all parents want to be "good" parents. They want to do what is best for their children, even if they do not always see eye-to-eye with you about what is "best."

- Keep in mind that families' ability to participate in the program will vary. Some parents will be able to give a lot of their time; others, just as caring and concerned, will not. Some parents have more support from nearby relatives than others; some parents work alternate shifts so they cannot come to meetings. Reassure them that when they are ready to participate more in the program, they will be welcome. Also recognize that parents' involvement takes many different forms, from planning class events to sending in the family's favorite books and records.

- Shape each relationship to the particular family. Families' different needs and styles, and the personalities of everyone involved, will determine what your relationship is like. Other factors that will influence your work with families include the age of the child and how long the child has been in the program. Expect relationships to vary—each from the others, and each one itself changing and developing.

- Learn about stages of parent development. Just as children go through stages of development, so do parents. They have expectations of their infant, toddler, preschooler, or young school-age child. They must learn to deal with new behaviors and challenges at each stage of child development. For example, parents of toddlers have to come to terms with becoming authority figures. They must learn to say "no" and decide what limits to set—is it okay for their 2-year-old to jump on the bed or watch certain TV programs? Knowing that being a parent of a toddler is very different from being a parent of an infant allows caregivers and teachers to be supportive of parental growth and change.

- Use family or parent conferences as an opportunity for you to exchange information about a child. Keep in mind that working parents might not be able to get away from their jobs in the middle of the day, so conferences may have to be scheduled at different hours. At the first conference, discuss your goals for the year. Families want to know what their children are going to be learning. And you will want them to share information with you, too.

- Plan a second conference later in the year so that you can describe the progress the child has made in different areas, social as well as academic, and you can hear from the family how the child is doing at home. Share examples of the child's work, such as a painting or a piece of writing, to illustrate some of the points you are making.

- Do not rely solely on parent conferences to communicate with the family. You want to make it possible to share ideas and concerns on an ongoing basis. Some teachers designate a special time, such as 12:00 to 1:00 p.m. on Tuesdays, when they can be called at the center or school; others are willing to give parents their home number and ask to be called early in the evening. Since working parents do not always have access to a phone during the day, ask if it is all right to call them at home during the evening hours. A monthly letter to families will keep them informed about class activities.

• Communicate with families when there is something positive to say, not just when there are problems. It is wonderful to have a teacher call to report, "I just want to tell you that Valerie finally overcame her fears and climbed to the second rung of the jungle gym today" or "Jimmy really had a breakthrough this week. It all clicked into place and he read through his book with no trouble at all."

Involving Families

Many early childhood programs have found a variety of ways to reach families and involve them. No one strategy works for all; you will need to adapt your efforts to the community and the individual families.

Parent Resource Room

• Help families feel comfortable in your setting. Post your daily schedule. Label drawers and shelves so parents can find what their children need. Discuss with families ways they can participate in your room.

• Offer families resources and encourage them to create their own. If possible, your program may want to establish a special room for families. Parents can make a bulletin board displaying information about the community that families will find helpful. Above all, help parents to connect with one another. To support working parents' ability to network, make a class list with names and phone numbers. Encourage the formation of support groups. Families are often each other's best resources.

• Respect the diversity of families. See if the forms that families fill out for your program allow for many kinds of families, rather than always assuming a "mother" and a "father." The application form may be the family's first contact with the program and can set the tone for how they feel about it.

• Plan activities that acknowledge the diversity of families. Holidays such as Mother's and Father's Day may exclude children who live with one parent, a stepparent, or a foster parent. As an alternative, consider a "Family Day" celebration in which all members of children's households are honored, rather than specific members.

• Encourage family participation in learning activities at home. A family day care provider writes a newsletter with children's favorite recipes and songs. This way, she encourages families to enjoy some of the same learning experiences with their children. Another way to do this is to occasionally design homework assignments for older children that require interaction with family members, such as interviewing them about what it was like when they were in school.

- Make use of the opportunities that networking offers. Have the people who *do* come to school help you reach others. Create a Volunteer Parent Corps.

- Look at your welcoming patterns. Who is at the door to greet families? Are posted notices and newsletters understandable to parents (both in literacy level and language)? Do you need translators at school events? Think about the ways in which you invite families to participate at school. When you post "parent" meetings, do caregiving grandparents, legal guardians, foster parents, two moms or two dads, aunts and uncles feel included? Is the timing of parent or family meetings staggered so that working adults can attend too? Do you provide snacks?

- In order to reach more families, think about those places other than home and school that families go. In one rural community, sports events, especially the local high school basketball games, are major community events. They become a good place to hand out school flyers or make an announcement. Other places to post flyers about school events may include laundromats, grocery store bulletin boards, libraries, welfare offices. Involve churches in announcing school news.

- Train school support staff, like the cook or the bus driver, to reach out to families and tell them what is going on and invite their participation. As children are dropped off at the end of the day, one bus driver reminds parents that there is a PTA meeting that night.

Looking at Yourself

There are many factors that can stand in the way of open communication between early childhood staff and families. Parents who have had alienating or difficult relationships during their own schooling may not trust the school. Their reluctance to get involved has more to do with their own educational history than with you or the child in your group. Many new parents, particularly, feel threatened when their children enter school or child care because they feel they are going to be judged by people outside of the family whom they perceive to be "experts." The difference in age between teachers and parents can be a factor affecting their interaction. If the teacher is younger than the parents of the children in her program, they may talk down to her. On the other hand, if the teacher is older, parents sometimes talk to her as if she is their parent.

Some caregivers and teachers may have stereotypes or negative feelings about cultural or racial groups or different family structures, such as single parent, lesbian or gay parents. Others may find it difficult to deal with the increasing number of working Moms they have among their parents. They complain that children are being sent to school when they are sick; that children often come to school tired because parents have kept them up too late so they can spend time with them; and that parents are often late in picking up their children at the end of the day.

Working with families means taking a good look at yourself:

- Be aware of your attitudes about working with families. Sometimes your feelings—feelings you may not even realize you have—can get in the way of good communication. Here are some questions to ask yourself. Do you have an image of an ideal family? What is it? How do you feel about families that do not fit your picture? How does this affect how you work with those families? Do you have expectations of how parents should be involved in your program? What happens when your expectations do not match with how a family can or wants to participate?

- Try to put yourself in the shoes of the parents in your class who work outside of their homes. For example, a Mom may be asked at the last minute to stay late at work to finish a project. She wants to say yes to show her boss that she is a committed worker. And because many bosses do not want to hear about their workers' families, she hesitates to say, "I really have to go to pick up my son at child care." Parents, too, are often torn between their jobs and their families, just as you may be if you are juggling the demands of family and work.

- Think through your strategies of handling differences with families. Everyone has his or her own opinion about the way things should be done when it comes to young children. These opinions are often based on one's own upbringing. Chances are good that you will come up against differences. The work you have already done building a relationship will serve you well—when there is no relationship, little issues can easily become major conflicts. Sometimes you can let a difference go or resolve it on your own. At other times, you will need to work things out together. Talk. Listen. Make a plan. Put it into action. Evaluate how things are going.

- Make sure that everyone on the staff spends some time talking through their feelings and attitudes about parents. What are some ways of dealing with the staff's anger at having to handle so many children who are really too ill to be in school? Ask yourselves, why do parents bring these children when they really want to be home with them? What about the parents who seem to push their children too hard to excel at academics? Are there ways of opening up communication about some of these issues? If your program has social workers or psychologists, you may want to ask them to set up a group meeting to talk about working with parents.

Building a relationship with families takes different forms, depending, in part, on the age of the child. One of the ways in which caregivers and teachers can engage families in the process of learning about their children is by helping to make explicit key developmental tasks as they are occurring in the child's—and family's—life.

Putting skills in working with families into action

Infants and Toddlers

Separation is an important milestone for infants and toddlers. Too often, it is viewed as a problem (see the chapters "Child Development" and "Planning for Infants, Toddlers, and Threes"). But separation is not a problem; it is a normal, natural process. Some things you can do to smooth this transition for families are:

- Put up photos of the child and the parent, Grandpa, the family pets. Sometimes little children forget that their families still exist when they cannot see them, and that is scary.

- Encourage the child to bring a piece of home with him to the center: a favorite teddy bear, a special blanket, one of Mom's hankies, a tape of Dad reading a favorite story. If you are worried about its getting lost, keep it in the child's cubby until needed. Children are most vulnerable to worries and tears when it is time to eat and sleep, since these times remind them most of home. Consequently, these are the times when familiar things from home can help the most.

- As much as the family's schedule allows, stress gradual entry into the program. It takes time for young children to feel safe and secure in a new place with new people. But recognize that for many working parents, it is difficult to get time off from work. In addition to a parent, maybe another family member or friend can help transition the child.

Separation is not just an issue of children leaving their families, but of families leaving their children. Parents have a lot of concern, worries, and anxiety. Like their children, they have to learn to trust you. Many families of infants and toddlers are sharing the care of their child with you before they themselves have learned to feel comfortable and competent in raising a child. One of the goals of your work with the families of children under 3 is to strengthen their relationship with their child by helping them feel good about themselves in their new role. You can do this by figuring out ways to help them feel in control of what is happening to their child, even though they cannot be with her. To do this, you might:

- Encourage families to spend time getting to know you and the program. It is hard for parents to build up trust unless they are

265

able to spend time watching the way you interact with their child.

- Explain what kind of information you need to know each morning to plan the child's day. For example: How was their child's evening at home? Is he hungry or tired? Is anything unusual happening at home? Has their child been working on any new skills? Knowing George, 6 months, woke up five times during the night means you can offer him an earlier nap if he seems cranky in the morning. By sharing information, his parents play a part in his day even though they are across town at work.

- Share information about a child's day with her family. Include all the details of daily routines such as eating, toileting, and sleeping. Also, share a story about something a child did. A written note is one way to ensure that necessary information about the child's day is passed on to parents or other caregivers.

- Respect the family's decisions about their child's care, such as what kind of diapers to use and how many bottles a day he should have. When you cannot follow the parents' preferences, explain why, and assure them that you are still committed to providing a safe, consistent experience for their child.

- Help families feel welcome in your setting. Comfortable seating, a pot of hot water for making coffee or tea and, most of all, your attitude, will convey the message: "You are welcome here."

Preschoolers

The key developmental milestone for preschoolers is becoming part of a social group and solidifying their own sense of identity by playing together and learning from each other. Sometimes what they learn disturbs their families, whether it is learning "curse words" or desiring an expensive toy like one a playmate has. Caregivers and teachers can help parents understand how important social contact is for young children (in spite of learning "undesirable" behaviors) and help the parents find ways to reaffirm their own values.

Preschoolers, more than younger children, can use play and language to express their feelings. This enables them to help to make sense of their world and can help bridge the gap between home and school. Stan, a preschool teacher, describes how he worked with one child's family:

When his mother was hospitalized unexpectedly, Robert, 4 years old, became very quiet and withdrew from classroom activities. I knew that it would be helpful for Robert to express his feelings and concerns. During a group meeting, I led a discussion about being sick and going to the doctor; a few of the children talked about the times they were in the hospital. Robert listened but did not join in. His grandmother had told me she knew that Robert was worried about his mother and that he had really changed at home: "He cries and clings to me. He used to be so happy." I told her it was understandable for him to feel upset and, whenever possible, she could help him talk about his feelings. I encouraged the grandmother to let Robert know she would be there to take care of him.

Over the next few days, I put out a doctor's kit and other medical-type play materials in one area of the room. At first, Robert just looked at them but refused to play with them. However, when his friend, Vijay, invited him to be "sick," Robert agreed. Then they switched roles and Robert played "doctor." It was obvious to me that he was repeating some of the doctor's behaviors he had observed in the hospital. At one point, he told Vijay, "You're bad, so you have to have a shot." This was an opportunity for me to clarify for Robert that being sick wasn't punishment for misbehavior. Robert's grandmother and I talked nearly every day. I would tell her about Robert's play around the hospital theme and she would share her observations of him at home. As he played and talked more, he worked out some of his feelings and began to be more "himself," at home and at school.

Classroom curriculum can also be a way of strengthening the links between home and school. A social studies approach to curriculum, such as the one used by Bank Street, emphasizes looking at the child in relationship to others. For preschoolers, an appropriate beginning is a study of the children's families. This is an opportunity to recognize diversity in families and to forge a link between home and school. And, most important, it builds on the child's direct experience. Here are some ways that Lisa, a teacher of 4-year-olds, develops an integrated curriculum focusing on the family:

First, we talk about everyone's family: Who is in it? Where do they live? I accept whatever the children say; if they want to include their family pets, that's fine. I write down what they say on a big piece of paper. I read it back to them and we refer to it again and again. We may even graph how many people are in each family. Then we talk a lot about what families do: how they have fun, what they eat, their work. They draw pictures of their families. Each child brings in photos of his or her family. As much as possible, I have parents come in and share family traditions, like a recipe or a favorite song. We read many books on families, about new babies, grandparents, families who live on farms, in cities. Also, at Curriculum

Night, I make a point of saying, "We're going to be studying families. I hope that we have many kinds of families and households here." That gets it out in the open—I expect families to be different!

Young School-Age Children

As children grow, they become more independent and their relationships with the adults in their lives gradually change. Teachers can rely more on children for the information they need to get to know each child, and they depend less on the parent as a source of information. As a result, parents may find themselves becoming less and less involved in their child's experiences at school. You can encourage parents to stay involved by helping them understand their changing relationship with their child and with you. Just because the relationship is changing does not mean it is less important or valuable. A first grade teacher describes how a child in her class reacted to this changing relationship:

> Six-year-old Maritza had been very excited about learning to read. She began to learn to read words and short sentences. Then, suddenly, she told her family, "I don't want to read anymore." In school, she refused to participate in the reading activities. None of us understood her changed attitude until one day she told me, "If I learn how to read, then no one else will want to read me stories." She was worried that being read stories at bedtime would come to an end. Once her parents reassured her that they'd still read to her, she was ready to learn to read once again.

Knowing that school often brings about changing relationships for children and families helps teachers to be sensitive to children's needs and to find ways to ease their concerns.

It is also at this period—beginning in kindergarten and first grade, but sometimes earlier—when some parents express concern that their child isn't "learning" if he does not bring home ditto sheets and workbooks and paper-and-pencil homework assignments. Creating a dialogue—opportunities for families to express their concerns and for you to explain your classroom program—is essential.

Mrs. Harvey, a teacher of 5- and 6-year-olds, explains how she helps families understand what their children are learning:

> I think the best way is in person. Early in the year, our school sponsors a Family-Teacher Night. Every teacher talks about her goals. I emphasize that I have many goals for the children, including social-emotional ones. If they don't feel good about themselves, they can't learn. So I have the children's names all around the room and I ask parents to count how many times they see their child's name—at least five times! I

also have parents do some of the activities the children do—like use pattern blocks or make a graph of what kind of transportation their children use to get to school. So they can see their children are really learning math concepts in fun ways!

Later in the year, I invite the child and his family to a conference to discuss the child's work. I think it's important to get the child's perspective. I save examples of the child's work for the child to share and talk about. If there are issues either the family or I don't want to discuss in front of the child, we arrange another meeting or talk on the phone.

Families

The link between home and school goes two ways. Just as you want to work with families, families want to work with you to support their children, but sometimes they are not sure how. Ms. Olivia, a first grade teacher, gives families suggestions of things to do:

At first, I was hesitant to tell parents what to do. They were older than I, and I just assumed they knew best. But I've learned that I can make recommendations that parents will accept. For instance, it's been helpful to talk with parents about how they talk with their children about school.

Rather than ask, "Did you have a good day?" which is easily answered by a "yes" or a "no," I suggest parents ask about something specific such as, "Where did you decide to work today?" or "Who sat next to you at snack?" Then I invite parents to share their "good questions" at the next parent meeting. I tell them that by showing their interest, they are giving their seal of approval to the child's experience.

Another teacher describes some of the mistakes she has made with families:

I used to say, "You should do this or that." But when I told a mother, "Your daughter Josie likes to paint so much in school, you should let her paint at home," she looked at me as if I were crazy. She said, "I can't afford to buy paints. I don't have much room. Any paint on the floors and walls, and I'm in trouble with my landlord." I realized I had not been sensitive to her situation. Now I try to get rid of the "shoulds" in my conversations with parents. As it was, the mother was willing to display Josie's artwork on the refrigerator and talk about her artwork. This parent was willing to listen to me; I just had to be more sensitive to her.

Exercises

These exercises will help you sharpen your skills in working with families. They can be done with a colleague or group of colleagues.

Remember, working with families is an ongoing process.

1. Role-playing can be a useful tool in clarifying some of the issues that come up in your everyday interaction with families. Work in pairs. One of you can take the role of a teacher, the other the role of a parent. Use one of the following situations, adapting it to fit your needs, or use a situation that really happened to you or a colleague.

   • A father of a 6-year-old rushed up to the teacher one morning looking upset and asked if he could speak with the teacher in private. He began by saying that his daughter came home crying yesterday because she had been left out of a classmate's birthday party. "This is the third party that she hasn't been invited to. Last night my daughter told me that the other kids didn't want her at the parties because she's Black."

     What is the father feeling? The child? As the teacher, how would you feel? How would you respond? Share your feelings about working together to address the parent's concern. Try to be as honest and open with each other as you can. You may then want to switch roles.

   • A few days after a parent meeting, a single mother approached the teacher to complain about not knowing that the day for the group's zoo trip had been changed. The mother had made arrangements to go with her child but the change in dates made it impossible. The teacher snapped back, "Well, if you came to the meetings, you would know about these things."

     As the parent in this situation, what are some possible reasons for not attending parent meetings? How might the teacher have made it possible for you to attend or how might she notify you of what it is important to know? How might the teacher be feeling? What kinds of responses can help turn this situation into a more positive and constructive interaction? As the teacher, think about your attitude toward the parent—do you find yourself comparing her to other, more actively in-volved parents? Discuss your expectations of parents. As the parent, what are your expectations of the teacher?

     Other questions to ask include: What did the teacher and the parent have in common in this situation? How did their feelings and needs differ? What new discoveries did you make about working with families? How can you apply them to your work with the families in your program?

2. Role-playing can also be a useful tool for examining your attitudes and trying to develop strategies for dealing with differences. Make a list of several situations where you and members of a child's family have disagreed. These might include: how to handle discipline, when a parent is late at the end of the day, or an instance

in which you feel a parent is pressuring you to have a more "academic" program than you believe is appropriate.

In your role play, act out a conversation about an issue you have identified. Then have a discussion with colleagues who were listening to your role-play. What insights did you gain? How would you handle the same situation differently next time?

3. By interviewing a few families, you can also gain insight into how your program can work more effectively with families. Questions you might ask include:

   • What is it like to be a parent in this program?

   • What kinds of things make you feel welcome?

   • Have there been times when you have wanted to discuss something with a staff person but, for some reason, felt that you could not? What was the reason?

   • What would help you feel more connected to the program?

   Arrange a time—at the parents' convenience—when you can sit down and talk together without interruption. Try to listen carefully and be as open as you can to what people say. Discuss what you learned with colleagues and see if there are some changes you might consider making in your work with families.

4. Discussions with co-workers (and families) are one way to identify blocks and barriers to involvement of families in your community. Together, make a list of the obstacles, such as, families live too far from school, are insecure about language, fear the unknown, and parents of "special education" students feel isolated.

   Next, think about strategies for reaching these families that would work in your community. Think creatively.

Resources

Balaban, N. (1985). *Starting school: From separation to independence—A guide for early childhood teachers.* New York: Teachers College Press.

Berger, E. H. (1987). *Parents as partners in education: The school and home working together* (2nd ed.). Columbus, OH: Merrill.

Dombro, A. L., & Bryan, P. (1991). *Sharing the caring: How to find the right child care and make it work for you and your child.* New York: Simon & Schuster/Fireside.

Lightfoot, S. L. (1978). *Worlds apart: Relationships between families and schools.* New York: Basic Books.

Powell, D. R. (1989). *Families and early childhood programs.* Washington, DC: National Association for the Education of Young Children.

Schultz, S. B., & Casper, V. (1992). *Tentative trust: Enhancing connections between gay and lesbian parents and the schools.* New York: Bank Street College of Education.

Swap, S. M. (1987). *Enhancing parent involvement in schools.* New York: Teachers College Press.

About the Authors:

Liz Westfall, R.N., worked as Project Manager for the Early Childhood Curriculum Project from 1989 to 1991. She worked on a variety of policy-related projects in the Research Division at Bank Street College. She also worked in a clinic for homeless people. She now lives with her husband and son in South Hamilton, Massachusetts.

Amy Laura Dombro, M.S., headed the Bank Street Infant and Family Center from 1976 to 1983. She is now a consultant with Head Start Parent-Child Center programs. She is the senior author of The Ordinary is Extraordinary: How Children under Three Learn *(1989, Fireside) and* Sharing the Caring: How to Find the Right Child Care and Make it Work for You and Your Child *(1991, Fireside).*

Janice Molnar, Ph.D., is a developmental psychologist and a former member of the Research Division of Bank Street College. Her work is focused on program and policy issues related to the needs of high-risk young children and their families.

Susan Ginsberg, Ed.D., is Associate Dean and director of the continuing professional education program at Bank Street College. She has been a consultant to schools and directed staff training projects for Head Start, child care, and parent education programs throughout the country.

20 ‖ Assessment through the Curriculum

Assessment in early childhood education is a way of looking systematically at growth over time. For most educators, the word "assessment" is closely tied to the concept of "testing," which conjures up images of test booklets, answer sheets, number 2 pencils—a single event. At Bank Street, we distinguish testing from assessment. We define assessment as the complex process of observing and recording and otherwise documenting the work of children—what they do and how they do it—over time. Testing is only one aspect of assessment.

In the widespread call for school reform over the decade of the eighties, assessment has taken center stage. Alongside the renewed interest in accountability through the establishment of national standards and national testing, there has been a different kind of discourse about assessment which, though talked about as if it were new, has its roots in 19th century schools and in numerous early progressive schools. This "new" way of looking at assessment, often referred to as "authentic" or "alternative" assessment, is based on a cluster of both formal and informal assessment practices, many of which experienced teachers have always used. In this view, standardized tests, given once or twice a year, are seen as removed from what actually goes on in classrooms and, therefore, as only a limited measure of what children are learning (and of what teachers need to know in order to develop curriculum).

Meaningful assessments of children's work depend on collecting the following kinds of data over time:

- records of teacher observations of what children do (reading logs, observations of children at work, anecdotes detailing behavior or conversations, interviews with children);

- portfolios or collections of representative work of children over time (sample writings, artwork, constructions, computations);

- tests or test-like procedures (for older children, teacher-made techniques for checking up on student learning, such as informal reading inventories, tasks at the end of a unit, quizzes).

Portfolios and teacher summaries based on observations may then be used by the teacher, the child's parents, and even the young school-age child as the basis for assessing the child's work. For example, parent and teacher can sit together to look at the child's work and discuss its meaning, rather than the more usual model of

What is assessment?

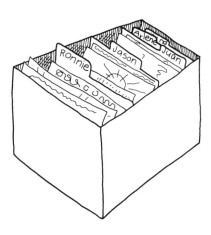

the teacher communicating to parents completed judgments on the child's progress.

Assessments made on the basis of these ongoing collections of data must:

- be centered on the substance and goals of the curriculum;
- rely upon observations and performance over time, during real, ongoing activities and work, rather than upon isolated, artificial tasks;
- recognize individual differences in style and rates of learning as well as in the knowledge, experience, and culture of the child;
- recognize not only what a child still needs to learn, but what he already knows and can do as well;
- include information about the child from parents and other family members.

Assessment is *not* used to label, exclude or track children. Rather, assessment is the systematic gathering together of a variety of data about children to use as the basis for demonstrating their learning and growth, needs, interests and strengths.

Why assess?

Thoughtful, ongoing assessment guides your work as a teacher. You assess for many reasons:

- to plan curriculum and instruction for individuals and groups;
- to identify children who may have additional needs;
- to reflect on your own teaching and evaluate how well the program is meeting your goals for children;
- to communicate with parents and other adults concerned with a child or group of children (next year's teacher or caregiver).

In this chapter, we will look at ways that assessment is integrated into early childhood programs, how you use assessments, and examples of recording systematically your observations and children's performances over time.

How can you assess?

Caregivers and teachers assess all the time as they make decisions based on what they know and observe about children; in fact, assessment is so much a part of work with children that it is easy to forget you are doing it. You assess when you allow a toddler to climb up the stairs without holding your hand. You assess when you intervene in a fight between two 3-year-olds rather than let them work it through without you. You assess when you give a piece of writing back to an 8-year-old and ask her to elaborate on one of her ideas. The challenge is to record your observations and the child's work over time so that you can use the accumulated record to evaluate and report on the child's progress.

As you assess, you have your goals for children in mind. You know that children have different learning styles, approach tasks differently, have different strengths. You may want your 5-year-olds to be able to write their names based on what you know about 5-year-olds. But your expectations of when two children will learn to write their names may be different, based on what you know about each of the children.

Observation and recording are essential parts of assessment. The chapter "Observing and Recording Children's Behavior" describes in detail how and why you make observations and record them, and suggests a variety of record-keeping techniques. Whichever techniques you use, it is important that you create a system that is the same for all children. You want to create a portrait of each child through periodic records of your observations in all areas of your program.

You also collect samples of children's work over time. Folders of written work (written stories, computations, scribbles); portfolios of drawings, paintings, and other artwork (including photos of the child's block building or other constructions)—all these gather together and preserve the record of the child's work in your program.

Anecdotes and observations, samples of children's work and products provide a solid basis for filling in checklists or writing summary reports. Consider Mrs. Smith's experience:

A seasoned caregiver of many years, Mrs. Smith was meticulous in keeping records on her preschoolers. Periodically, she reviewed each child in her program and wrote up a brief paragraph summarizing the child's progress in several areas of her program. She used these paragraphs during reporting periods when she was required to fill out a developmental checklist on each child. One summer, she takes a workshop in observing and recording and understands for the first time the difference between keeping the kinds of summary records she has always kept and observing a child and recording only what she actually *sees*, rather than what she *thinks*. She decides to try the new technique of writing down what she sees without coming to any conclusions. She creates an envelope for each child and writes on scraps of paper whenever she has a chance or sees something that she thinks is important. Periodically, she pulls out all the scraps of paper on a child and is astonished to see what a wealth of information they contain about the child's growth over time. It is comparatively easy to use the information thus collected to fill out her developmental checklist; and as she prepares written reports, she finds she has a great deal of detail to share with families about their children. Observing and recording greatly increase the information she has and aid her memory of details about each child. She is also able to document change and to modify her plans based on what she is observing.

Assessment begins with the entry of a new child into your setting or with the beginning of the year, when all or most of your children are new. Initial assessment, of a child or children, is particularly intensive and involves getting to know the child(ren) and adapting your planned curriculum based upon what you learn. In assessing the children, you also assess your curriculum and instruction and how well they are helping the children to achieve the goals you have for them. In order that your curriculum be developmentally and individually appropriate, you continually review what is happening in your program and adjust it according to your observations of change and growth in the children.

Here are some examples of initial assessments and the modifications of curriculum that resulted from them:

- Boris, a recently emigrated Russian child, enters a preschool class in mid-October. His teacher knows that he will learn English through his total immersion in it, but she also knows that he will engage more actively and confidently in learning it if he feels supported by his classroom environment. She decides to modify her instruction not only of Boris but of the other children by incorporating their diverse language backgrounds into her curriculum on families. Not only do the children learn Russian words from Boris, but they learn words in many different languages that reflect the cultures of their families. She includes stories and folktales in the library area that represent the diversity of the children's backgrounds.

- Mr. Tucci, a teacher of second graders, begins his year with a math activity that he thinks the children will be able to do. Children are given cards with multiple drawings of the same object on them—balloons, puppies, horns—and, working with a partner, divide the cards into two piles, those with an even number of pictures and those with an odd number. It takes a couple of sessions for Mr. Tucci to realize that a significant number of children in his class have no idea what "odd" or "even" means and are making the piles randomly, without a guiding rule. Mr Tucci reviews his plans for his beginning math program to include many more counting and matching activities in order to introduce his children to the concepts of "even" and "odd."

- When Danny moved with his classmates to Ms. O'Brien's kindergarten, his previous year's teacher described him as language disabled and reported to Ms. O'Brien that she had set in motion the process for him to be reassigned to a special education classroom. Ms. O'Brien thus feels that Danny will not be with her group for very long. Nevertheless, she works closely with him, as she does with all her children, focusing especially on his language development. She consults with a learning specialist and finds materials that will encourage and enhance Danny's use of language. The longer he stays, the more she sees his capabilities, and she builds upon them to strengthen his self-esteem. As he feels more accepted, his inherent sociability emerges and other children become very friendly with him. Danny learns how to share his work and is distinguished in the group for his artistic talents. His language development improves, though it still lags considerably behind that of his classmates. Ms. O'Brien reports that she herself has learned about the importance of seeing the wholeness of an individual, especially one who has been diagnosed as having special needs. Furthermore, Danny's presence in her classroom has enhanced the whole group's sense of community and acceptance of difference.

Initial assessments help you to know your children and to gauge the match between them and your program. What you find out may lead you to:

- modify your goals or some aspect of your program to meet the needs and interests of many children;

- modify your goals and instruction for one child;

- involve specialists in determining whether a child has additional needs that require special services and/or other intervention.

As you get to know your children better, you continue to gather and record data that you will use in assessment. It is helpful to have a rough idea of the times during the year when you will summarize your data on children. In all settings, the beginnings and endings of the year are natural times to make more formal assessments; beginnings and endings of curriculum units are also good times, and parent conferences are obvious occasions for assessments.

Assessment does not exist apart from your program and the goals you have for your children. What you assess is based on these goals, and your curriculum provides opportunities for children to achieve them. If you are going to assess whether your 3-year-olds are learning to use language to express their needs—a goal of your program—then your curriculum must offer them a variety of opportunities and encouragement to communicate with you and each other. If a goal for your second graders is that they become independent readers, able to select appropriate books for themselves, then your program will include a reading corner, a wide range of books, trips to the library, book sharing, and reading aloud.

In alternative or authentic assessment, like that described in this chapter, the intimate relationship between assessment and goals on the one hand, and goals and curriculum on the other, means that you assess children by observing them as they engage in the curriculum experiences and tasks you have designed for them. You assess children *through* the curriculum. In this way, you avoid the most common pitfall of standardized tests, that is, testing for skills and knowledge that were neither taught nor learned.

Putting assessment into action

Infants and Toddlers

Knowing that opportunities for physical activity are an important part of her curriculum, Susanna, a family day care provider, makes sure that the children get outside nearly every day. She also has a small slide inside. At 18 months, Nelly loves the slide, going down on her stomach, feet first. One day, Susanna notices that as Nelly reaches the top of the ladder, she stands, staring down the slide and freezes. She tries to get into position for a stomach-down slide, then turns again, squats, but freezes. Finally, she turns and goes down in her usual position, stomach-down. She does this many times, and also brings toys up the slide with her and shoves them down the slide. Susanna watches this for a day or two and realizes that Nelly is in the throes of making a transition from sliding on her stomach to sitting on her bottom. Sometimes other children are waiting to have a turn on the slide and they get impatient with Nelly.

Susanna thinks about how she can help Nelly make this transition, yet let the others use the slide. She decides that Nelly can practice with the toys in another place and sets up a "pretend" slide, putting a box under one end of a board and creating an incline. Nelly sends her toys down this "pretend" slide over and over. Susanna helps her by joining in her play; she catches the toys at the bottom and suggests that Nelly give her stuffed animal a ride down the slide too. Susanna also gives occasional words of encouragement when Nelly climbs up the slide and squats.

It is not long before Nelly makes the big change and is sliding, sitting up. By actively observing and then providing curriculum experiences, Susanna has supported Nelly's transition.

Preschoolers

Lee, a 4-year-old in Mr. Helmuth's preschool group, will not go near the balance beam during movement time. He generally stays on the periphery during movement and is minimally involved. Mr. Helmuth is concerned about Lee's lack of risk taking and would like him to use his body more. During outdoor time one day, Mr. Helmuth takes the opportunity to make some observations of several children, including Lee.

Here is what he writes:

Lee is playing tag with two other children. He is "it." He runs full tilt at first one child, then another, until he finally tags one, laughing with delight. All three children get bored with tag and move over to walk on the edge of the sandbox, using their arms for balance. Lee executes this with ease. Several other children join in this activity and Lee withdraws—he stops playing and becomes a spectator watching expressionlessly what is now a group of eight children balancing on the edge of the sandbox.

Reading over his notes at the end of the day, Mr. Helmuth speculates that Lee's problem with movement may have nothing to do with movement activities; rather, it may be that Lee is reluctant to participate because it is a whole-group activity. He decides to observe Lee more closely to test this idea that Lee is more comfortable in groups of just two or three. If, in fact, this is the case, knowing it will help Mr. Helmuth be more effective in helping Lee in large-group situations. Also, he might think about offering more small group experiences in his program to benefit Lee (and other children as well).

Young School-Age Children

Ms. Zuckermann, in her study of the Hudson River in New York City with a group of 8-year-olds, had as one goal of the study a refined understanding of the relationship of land to water and how that relationship affects human communities.

Towards the end of the study, after many trips to the Hudson and many opportunities for model making, the children make maps of New York State showing the Hudson River in relation to the larger environment. As the children make their 3-dimensional maps, Ms. Zuckermann notices that Andrea's New York State is surrounded by water—the Atlantic Ocean, says Andrea—and that the Hudson is represented as a black curvy line in the middle of the Atlantic. When she asks Andrea to tell her about her map and asks her questions about the location of the river in the Atlantic, Ms. Zuckermann comes to understand that Andrea thoughtfully built up her image through the language that was used in the study of the river: it has salty water; it is subject to tides; it empties into the sea.

These fragments of information form the base for Andrea's imperfect understanding of the geographic relationships involved and lead her to her errors which, once analyzed by her teacher, are errors that make sense. Andrea's confusion leads Ms. Zuckermann to pose the question "What is a river?" to the whole class, and she finds considerable variation in the children's understandings.

Ms. Zuckermann thus uses the curriculum, and Andrea's errors, as a means of assessment. By assessing Andrea's work and analyzing her mistaken representation of the river, Ms. Zuckermann takes a second look at the study to help not only Andrea, but other children as well, and to revise the curriculum and her goals so that they better match the children. Thus, she borrows a water table from the preschool and provides several experiences for children to build land masses with soil and water and observe what happens when it "rains" and how rivers are formed. She also revises her own expectations, to include a broader range of children's interpretations of the same curriculum. Had she merely corrected Andrea and shown her how to do the map accurately, she would have lost an opportunity to assess not only her children, but her curriculum as well. Had she given a test at the end of the unit, she would have found out what Andrea did not know, but not what Andrea was confused about or why she was mistaken in her understanding.

Families

Sarah, age 7, comes to Greta's second grade classroom barely printing. Her letters are huge, placed without regard to the lines on the paper, and are not uniform in size. The labor of handwriting inhibits her development as an expressive writer. Greta often takes Sarah's dictation during writing times to encourage her interest in writing, and is able to bring in a computer for writing periods from the fourth grade classroom. Although these measures help Sarah's writing, Greta continues to work on handwriting with her, which continues to be a struggle. Greta keeps samples of Sarah's handwriting and of her dictated and computer-written stories. Sarah's parents come to their parent conference in November very troubled about Sarah's immature handwriting. Greta agrees with them that Sarah's handwriting is developing more slowly than that of other children her age, but she is able to share with them samples of writing over three months that show improvement—smaller letters of more uniform size—from the beginning of the year. She also shows them stories Sarah has written and dictated, making a distinction for them between her handwriting, which is problematic, and her expressive ability in writing, which meets the expectations of her age group. With samples of Sarah's work, Greta is able to demonstrate her progress in one area, and her ability in another.

Exercises
1. Think about different areas of your curriculum. Develop a plan for assessing one of them over a period of time. Decide when you will collect the information. Depending upon the age of the children you teach, you might consider collecting different kinds of information:

   • observing the children as they work in this area;

- gathering samples of their work (in the case of block building or other 3-dimensional constructions, you can take photos);

- developing group measures, such as a quiz.

    Analyze your findings in terms of what individual children are learning or understanding and what is the range of children's performances. Then consider how you would change any aspects of this curriculum to be more effective.

2. With a colleague, or in a small group, exchange samples of children's writing (or, in the case of younger children, exchange observations of children's play). Discuss what information you learn about the children from their writing sample (or play episodes). Talk about what the next steps would be for the teacher to stimulate the children's learning.

3. Role play a parent-teacher conference with a colleague. If you are the teacher, discuss the general expectations for a particular age group and, at the same time, explain to the parents that their child does not fall within the age norm. If you are the parent, imagine that you are surprised to hear this news and question how the teacher comes to know this information about your child. Switch roles.

4. If you use a checklist, rating scale, standardized test, or the like with your children, try to translate some of the items back to your program and goals. Ask yourself:

   - Do the items make sense, given what I am teaching?

   - What are the different ways my children might respond to or be assessed on any one item?

   - Is there a more valid way to assess children's performance on this item (e.g., either by another means of assessment or revising the item)?

5. One of the most important ways to assess your curriculum is by becoming aware of children's errors and misunderstandings. Knowing what children do not know is critical to evaluating your program and your own teaching. Over the course of a week or longer, write down examples of children's errors. Discuss them with a colleague and focus on what you can learn from them about children's thinking and about your curriculum.

6. Select a concept that is part of your curriculum. For example, this might be a math or science concept. Develop an appropriate game that will expose your children to the concept (e.g., a counting or matching game), keeping in mind the children's developmental level. Be sure to include specific playing instructions. It could be a game played alone or with others. Try out the game with a

colleague before you give it to the children; this will help you identify ways to improve it. Use the game as an assessment tool, to assess what children are learning and understanding about this particular concept.

7. Make a plan for developing portfolios of children's work. You might want to talk to colleagues and read in professional literature for additional ideas. Begin to collect samples of children's art, writing, and other work. Periodically review each child's folder, identifying signs of progress and areas of difficulty. Refer to the child's portfolio in your conferences with his or her family.

Resources

Carini, P. F. (1975). *Observation and description: An alternative methodology for the investigation of human phenomena.* Grand Forks, ND: University of North Dakota.

Chittenden, E., & Courtney, R. (1989). Assessment of young children's reading: Documentation as an alternative to testing. In D. Strickland & L. M. Morrow (Eds.), *Emerging literacy.* Newark, DE: International Reading Association.

Kamii, C. (Ed.). (1990). *Achievement testing in the early grades: The games adults play.* Washington, DC: National Association for the Education of Young Children.

Meisels, S. J. (1987). Uses and abuses of developmental screening and school readiness testing. *Young Children, 42*(2), 4-6, 68-73.

National Association for the Education of Young Children & the National Association of Early Childhood Specialists in State Departments of Education. (1991). Position Statement: Guidelines for appropriate curriculum content and assessment in programs serving children ages 3 through 8. *Young Children, 46*(3), 21-38.

Perrone, V. (Ed.). (1991). *Expanding student assessment.* Alexandria, VA: Association for Supervision and Curriculum Development.

Pratt, C. (1948). *I learn from children: An adventure in progressive education.* New York: Simon & Schuster.

Wolf, D. P. (1989). Portfolio assessment: Sampling student work. *Educational Leadership, 46*(7), 35-39.

About the Author:

Joan Cenedella, M.S., is Vice President for Academic Affairs at Bank Street College. She has had extensive experience as a classroom teacher of school-age children, a curriculum coordinator, and school director. For many years, she was Dean of Children's Programs at Bank Street College.

Appendix A. Using The Curriculum Guide to Prepare for a CDA

Begun in 1971, The Child Development Associate (CDA) Program was designed to improve the skills of caregivers in center-based family day care and home visitor settings. It provides performance-based training, assessment, and credentialing. A candidate can receive an Infant/ Toddler Endorsement, or Preschool Endorsement. A person who works in a bilingual setting and has demonstrated bilingual competence can receive a CD with a Bilingual Specialization.

The CDA Competency Goals are the core of the CDA program. They state the skills needed to be a competent caregiver. These six goals are divided into 13 Functional Areas which define more specifically the skills caregivers need for the specific child care setting and/or age grouping. The following chart will show you key chapters in the Curriculum Guide to refer to as you work on each goal. As you use this chart, remember, it is only a starting point. Just as every area of a child's development is interconnected, so are the chapters in the Guide.

For more information about the CDA Program, contact:

The Council for Early Childhood Professional Recognition
1718 Connecticut Avenue, NW / Suite 500
Washington, DC 20009-1148
Telephone: 1-800-424-4310 (Toll Free)
(202) 265-9090
Fax: (202) 265-9161

CDA Competency Goals

Explorations with Young Children

Chapter	1. To establish and maintain a safe, healthy learning environment	2. To advance physical and intellectual competence	3. To support social and emotional development and provide positive guidance	4. To establish positive and productive relationships with families	5. To ensure a well-run, purposeful program responsive to participant needs	6. To maintain a commitment to professionalism
Chapter 1. Principles of the Bank Street Approach					X	
Chapter 2. Child Development		X	X		X	
Chapter 3. Observing and Recording Children's Behavior	X	X	X		X	
Chapter 4. The Learning Environment	X				X	
Chapter 5. The Group Process			X			
Chapter 6. Discipline and Management			X		X	
Chapter 7. Valuing Diversity	X	X	X	X	X	
Chapter 8. Creating Curriculum in Early Childhood	X	X	X		X	
Chapter 9. Planning for Infants, Toddlers, and Threes	X	X	X		X	
Chapter 10. Integrated Curriculum for Four- through Eight-Year-Olds		X	X		X	
Chapter 11. Literacy in Early Childhood		X				
Chapter 12. Mathematics in Early Childhood		X				
Chapter 13. Science in Early Childhood		X				
Chapter 14. Art in Early Childhood		X				
Chapter 15. Music in Early Childhood		X				
Chapter 16. Movement in Early Childhood		X				
Chapter 17. A Study of Bread and Bakeries: An Example of Integrated Curriculum		X				
Chapter 18. You as Teacher or Caregiver				X		X
Chapter 19. Working with Families		X	X	X	X	
Chapter 20. Assessment through the Curriculum		X	X	X	X	

N.B.: X refers to the chapters in the Guide that address specific CDA competency goals.

Appendix B. Using The Curriculum Guide for Staff Development

E ast Coast Migrant Head Start Project (ECMHSP) funded field testing of the Curriculum Guide and final work on the manuscript. Staff from Bank Street College conducted field tests in the form of staff development sessions in the fall of 1991 at two ECMHSPs: Bright Horizon's Child Enrichment Center in Bridgeton, New Jersey and Kiddie Kastle Migrant Head Start in Mt. Vernon-Glennville, Georgia.

Discussions between Bank Street College and the ECMHSP administrators, program development specialists, and the program directors pointed to the need for staff training in observation and curriculum development. At each site, the first session focused on observing and recording children's behavior; the second focused on using observations of children and knowledge of the community for curriculum planning. Written materials from the Guide were included in each session.

Head Start staff from all program areas (education, nutrition, health, social services, parent education) attended each session. Fifteen staff from the Bright Horizons program participated in the staff development sessions, and 35 staff from Kiddie Kastle. Staff had varying levels of experience and education; several were enrolled in a Child Development Associate (CDA) program. A similar training format was used at each site, with adjustments made for the size of the group and for the unique features of each program. Since ECMHSP serves infants, toddlers, and preschoolers, the training sessions focused on working with children from birth through 5 years. Two Bank Street faculty (one, a native Spanish speaker) conducted each session. Each staff session lasted a day.

Reports on the two staff development sessions conducted for Bright Horizons, ECMHSP, follow. The goals and the agenda for each day were ambitious; some areas were covered in more detail, reflecting the interests and concerns of the staff. Bank Street assumed from the outset of each session that the day's program was flexible. At the conclusion of the second report, a list of follow-up activities for a subsequent training session is presented.

Every program has unique staff needs. The sessions conducted by Bank Street College for ECMHSP may suggest how to incorporate ideas and materials from this Guide into staff development for your program. The Exercises listed at the end of each chapter in the Guide offer additional ideas for staff training.

Staff Development Session 1:
Observing and Recording Children's Behavior

Goals

1. To convey the importance of observing.

2. To develop observation and recording skills that are objective and nonjudgmental.

3. To relate categories of the LAP (Learning Accomplishment Profile used to assess children in ECMHSP) to observations of children's spontaneous behavior.

4. To develop systems for observing among classroom staff.

5. To use observation as the basis for understanding children, planning the environment, developing curriculum, and parent conferences.

6. To further understanding of child development and developmentally appropriate practice.

7. To assign observations to serve as a source for the next session's work on curriculum development.

Agenda

1. Introduction of Bridgeton staff and Bank Street staff. Purpose of our visit and history of the Curriculum Guide.

2. How Do You Use Observing in Your Work with Children?

    Staff responded to this question in a variety of ways. They use observing to understand individual children. A preschool teacher described how her observations of a boy in her class led her to suspect that he had a hearing loss. Another teacher described how she observed a toddler following an older child into the bathroom. The toddler was tugging at his diaper, indicating that he wanted it off. The teacher shared this information with the mother, who realized that her son was indicating readiness for toilet training. Other staff mentioned how they observed children to help them plan activities, noting, for example, when children were restless or had specific interests.

3. Observing Children in Photographs

    We distributed a photo of a child or a group of children, 2 to 5 years old, in a variety of settings, to small groups of staff. Each person wrote down what she saw in the photo and read it to her group; some observations were read to the whole group. This exercise pointed out that observers' biases can lead them to view the same scene differently. We discussed the amount and kind of detail appropriate in an observation.

4. Making an Observation (Handout A)

    We discussed the information that appears in the heading and in the behavioral record itself. As a group, staff listed on a chart the kind of language that should be used (descriptive, nonjudgmental) and the kind that should be avoided (words such as "nice, bad, good, because"). The child's behavior needs to stand alone, without the imposition of our biases and assumptions.

5. Examples of Observations (Handouts B, C, D)

    Staff took turns reading out loud these three observations of children, and critiqued them. The differences in language and style pointed out the value of objective descriptions of behavior. As one staff person said, "Observation A in the Handouts tells you more about the observer than about the child."

6. Group Observation of a Child from a Videotape

    We watched a videotape of a 2-year-old child at Bank Street's Family Center. After an initial viewing of the tape, small groups of staff took turns observing a one-minute segment of the tape: the child playing with nesting blocks, or painting at the easel, or building with blocks which are then kicked over by another child. Staff recorded their observations on Handout A, and several shared them with the whole group.

7. Using the Information in an Observation

    Taking the observations of the 2-year-old, we then focused on what we learned from them. First, we discussed what we learned about the child in terms of his social, emotional, cognitive, and physical functioning. Using Handout A as a guide to discussion, we also focused on how the observations of the 2-year-old might be used to plan the physical environment and curriculum, and how information could be shared with his parents.

8. Discussion of the Learning Accomplishment Profile (LAP, Chapel Hill Training-Outreach Project)

Observing yields important information for assessing children. Many of the staff were familiar with the LAP and described how they used it. For example, one teacher said that she had wanted to test the children for their balance and coordination on the balance beam. She tried to elicit their performance one day, but was unsuccessful. Another day, on a walk outdoors, she noticed many of them balancing on the top of a low wall. This anecdote pointed out how important it is to observe children's spontaneous behavior and play. We reviewed the categories of the LAP (Handout E) and, using the observations of the 2-year-old, discussed which of his behaviors could be applied to the LAP categories.

9. Systems for Observing in a Class

Staff who worked together in a classroom met in small groups. They read an excerpt, "How to Observe" from the Guide, and discussed how they could set up a system in their rooms so that they would be able to observe and record children's behavior. Each person also identified a question or concern she had that could be illuminated or clarified through the process of observing. Bus drivers, cooks, and administrators participated in a group since they, too, observe the children.

Each small group reported back to the large group. For example, the staff in a preschool classroom decided to observe the dramatic play area because they felt it was not being well used by the children. Was it a matter of providing different props, offering more adult support, etc.? Observing would give them clues. Staff who worked with infants wondered about one baby who seemed to sleep a lot—was she tired? sick? As the staff discussed her behavior, they remarked that she had periods of alert activity and that she was responsive to them. In the end, they wondered if she was sleeping too little at home, possibly because her parents valued their time with her and kept her up late in order to be with her. The staff agreed to observe her and record her behavior in the course of a typical day. Then they would use this information as the basis for a parent conference.

10. Using Observations as the Basis for Curriculum Planning

Staff viewed Part II of the video, *Social Studies: A Way to Integrate Curriculum for Four- and Five-Year-Olds*, which is a companion to the Curriculum Guide.

We asked staff to consider:

- how the teacher uses observations to develop her curriculum;
- what the children are learning.

Staff reported that the teacher's observations of the 4- and 5-year-olds' interest in their new shoes initiated the curriculum study of the shoe store, and that their declining interest four weeks later also brought the study to an end. Throughout the shoe store study, the teacher used observations to help her decide what activities would be appropriate, such as re-creating their experiences in blocks, drawings, and graphs. The children were learning about sequences, numbers, cooperation, and processes of change (e.g., repairing old shoes). Staff remarked how parents were included in the curriculum (e.g., old shoes were brought from home).

11. Review and Assignment

We asked all staff to choose a child and make three observations of the child in the next few weeks (using Handout A). The observations could be done indoors or outdoors; if possible, one should be of the child with his or her family. Staff were asked to bring their observations to our next meeting on October 26.

Staff Development Session 2
Developing Curriculum

Goals

1. To reinforce the importance of observing in the classroom.

2. To develop and refine staff's observing and recording skills.

3. To provide feedback on staff's written observations (assigned previously, September 26).

4. To relate observations of children's behavior to stages of child development.

5. To use observation as the basis for curriculum development.

6. To value diversity in children and their experiences.

7. To use the community as a source of curriculum.

8. To acquaint staff with developmentally appropriate children's literature.

9. To incorporate children's literature into integrated curriculum.

Agenda

1. Using Observation in the Classroom.

    Beginning with the infant room staff, then the toddler, and finally the preschool staff, each staff person (15 in all) read one of her assigned observations to the group and discussed what she had learned about the child. Other staff joined in, sometimes asking questions or making comments. (Some staff read in English, others in Spanish.)

    By following the developmental progression from infancy to toddlerhood to the preschool period, we were able to compare the competencies, interests, and skills at each stage. We also discussed what kinds of experiences for each age group promote the development of trust (infants), autonomy (toddlers), and initiative and competence (preschoolers). There were many vivid examples of infants' imitative behavior and early language, of toddler's motor development, and of preschooler's interest in literacy. One staff person had collected samples of a child's artwork to complement observations of his behavior.

    All staff were able to use their observations to give them insight into the individual child; however, using observations to build and modify curriculum was more difficult. Some staff were able to use their observations as the basis for positive comments to share with parents; a few staff reported that they would tell parents "he should draw at home" or "you should read to her." We discussed what kind of message "should" gives parents and how other wording is preferable.

2. Who Are Your Children, Families and Communities?

    We asked staff to think about "What's unique about your program and the families you work with?" They responded:
    - lets children be creative;
    - bilingual or will become bilingual;
    - families move or fathers move (help children prepare, adapt to change);
    - mostly married parents;
    - serves babies through 5-year-olds;
    - at home—rural, open, self-help skills are strong;
    - crowded homes—leave toys behind.

288

This exercise was an effort to help staff recognize the strength and diversity of the migrant communities. When one staff person described the children as self-reliant, she thought of it as a socioemotional characteristic. However, further discussion helped her see that in order to be self-reliant, children are problem solving and thinking; for example, "How do I get my zipper up?" "Where is there room to hang my coat?" This discussion pointed out the interrelationship of social, emotional, cognitive, and physical development. No one area of development functions in isolation.

3. What Is Curriculum?

Staff responded in these ways:

- lesson;
- plan for teaching;
- different areas (language, prewriting, thinking);
- activities in playground;
- experiences for skill development;
- food, nutrition;
- bus trip (safety, look at area, songs);
- trips;
- everything you plan for children;
- community helpers;
- science (bugs, leaves, nature, sun rays, flowers, community walks);
- social (friends, emotions);
- health (role of nurse).

We emphasized that curriculum is everything you do with children and families in your program. It is all the decisions you make—from what to serve for snack to what books to put in the library corner.

At Bank Street, we believe that curriculum should build on the strengths of children and families and affirm their diversity. Social studies is the focus as we study the child in relation to others. We start with the child and the family and broaden into the neighborhood community.

4. What is in Your Community? The Field Trip.

We paired up staff for a field trip into the neighborhood around the center. We gave each pair a trip board which asked them to record in writing or pictures what they saw, heard, or smelled on their field trip. Each pair was assigned one of these topics to investigate:

- harvest-related crops and activities;
- what people are doing to have fun;
- ten interesting things;
- ten items from nature;
- ten written signs or labels;
- ten sounds;
- ten kinds of transportation.

5. Results of the Field Trip; Developing an Integrated Curriculum

The staff came back with many varied and rich observations, which they shared with the large group. For example, the staff who observed people having fun reported people sitting on porches, talking together, playing catch, a wedding. Other staff found many signs and labels within a short distance, such as street signs, store signs, announcements in front of the church.

As staff shared their observations, we asked them to discuss also:

- three open-ended questions they could ask children before and after a field trip;
- three follow-up activities in the classroom.

Throughout our discussion, we asked them to think about how the curriculum could be adapted to children of different ages. We talked about what infants, toddlers, and preschoolers might notice on a walk, and how important it is for adults to provide rich language experiences for all age groups. We discussed how migrant children live with change and how the curriculum could reflect their experiences. For example, cooking activities would give children direct experience with change and transformation. Staff brought up the difficulties they have saying "goodbye" as the migrant children move on (which they are doing now in Bridgeton). We talked about how important it is to incorporate the children's experiences into the curriculum to help them prepare for the move and express their feelings. Together, we generated ideas with the staff:

- Take photos of the children and staff for the children to take with them, so they can remember "my friend Miguel and my teacher Carmen."
- Make books with children's pictures or photos depicting their experiences in ECMHSP to read in class and also to take with them.
- Decorate shoe boxes that the children can take with them to keep their "special things" in.
- Have the children help pack up the classroom materials.
- Bring in "moving" materials for the dramatic play area, such as empty boxes, tape to close the boxes.

One of the points made in the videotape *SOCIAL STUDIES: A Way to Integrate Curriculum for Four- and Five-Year-Olds*, was that field trips were best for small groups of children. We discussed the advantages of smaller groups: there is more opportunity for conversation and exploration, plus management is easier.

We shared with staff a variety of developmentally appropriate books on farms from the Bank Street Library. Staff were interested in these materials, and we discussed briefly how cardboard books are appropriate for infants and toddlers; how you could make your own class book of a field trip with photos or children's drawings. We distributed a bibliography on Farmbooks (Handout F).

We also distributed several excerpts from the Curriculum Guide—on Valuing Diversity and on the Integrated Curriculum.

Suggested Follow-up Activities

1. Each pair of staff re-create their trip experience in the classroom through block building, dramatic play, math, science, language arts, cooking, art, music, and movement.

2. Discuss ways to share the trip experience and its re-creation in the classroom with the children's families.

3. View Part III of the videotape *Social Studies: A Way to Integrate Curriculum for Four- and-Five-Year-Olds.*, focusing on the teacher's role in curriculum development.

4. Develop a curriculum study with staff. For example, during one of the training sessions in Mt. Vernon-Glennville, Georgia, ECMHSP staff generated ideas for the study of the local library.

We began by posing questions to staff:

1. Where does the study begin? With a trip to the library with a small group of children. Preparation of the whole group includes discussion: "What is a library? Have you ever been there? What do you think you'll see?" Throughout, we emphasized how important it is to ask open-ended questions to elicit children's understanding and knowledge. Although the library may be the focus of study, the ongoing work of the children still continues. They play, paint, use manipulatives, etc. Not every single activity has a library focus. While small groups take trips, the rest of the children are still very involved in the classroom activities. Some staff suggested that, even before visiting the library, children could make a library in the classroom; however, we emphasized that children must first have the direct experience before they can reconstruct it in a meaningful way.

2. What would children be interested in knowing about the library? What would be some of their questions? For example:
   - What are the stamps, library cards, book cards, index files?
   - What does the librarian do?
   - What happens to a torn book?
   - How do you find the books?

3. What activities back in the classroom would help children re-create their experiences and deepen their understanding of concepts. For example:
   - building a library of blocks;
   - making book cards and stamps;
   - drawing pictures;
   - sharing their favorite books.

4. What would children be learning about in a study of the library? What concepts would they be developing?
   - sequence (e.g., checking out a book);
   - jobs people do;
   - various functions of a library (including tape and video collections, xeroxing);
   - language (e.g., words such as "author," "illustration," "due date");
   - responsibility for and care of books;
   - emerging literacy (e.g., learning about reading and writing).

5. What else could be included in a study of the library?
   - learning about other places to get books: bookmobile, bookstores;
   - learning about book making as children make their own books or invite authors into class.

6. Curriculum planning for children under 3 years focuses on everyday routines and play. They, too, can learn about the library. In small groups, infants can visit the library; toddlers can take out library books and certainly will be fascinated by the rubber stamps.

Handout A

Observation Sheet

Name of Child:

Age:
Setting:
Date:
Observer:

Behavior Observation:

Discussion of Behavior Observation

1. What did you learn about the child from the observation? (Think about physical, social, emotional, cognitive, language development and the child's strengths.)

2. What did you learn that will help you in planning the physical environment? (Think about the room arrangement, materials, etc.)

3. What did you learn that will help you in planning the curriculum? (Think about the child's interests, style of learning, etc.)

4. What did you learn about the child that you can share with his or her parents? (Think about what is unique and special about the child.)

Handout B

Sample Observation

Name of Child: Jane

Age: 1 year
Setting: On changing table sitting up.
Date: June 7, 1991
Observer: Ruby

Examine these two observations and discuss their differences.

Observation A

Jane is a cute little girl. She likes to play and laugh. She is beginning to talk.

Observation B

I just changed Jane. She reaches for the bottle of baby lotion. She puts it on top of her head. It falls off. Jane laughs. I laugh too. Jane picks up the bottle and taps it in her right hand several times. (This is how I usually get the lotion out.) She says "Ba-ba" while she does it.

Handout C

Sample Observation

Name of Child: Daniel

Age: 4 1/2 years old
Setting: Art area: Daniel and Carlos and Susan are drawing.
Date: March 15, 1991
Observer: Kevin

Examine these two observations and discuss their differences.

Observation A

Daniel bothers Carlos at the art table. Daniel is mean and not a nice boy to Carlos. Carlos should learn not to cry and not to take things so seriously.

Observation B

Daniel leans over Carlos' paper: "I want to make a monster." He picks up a pencil and starts to make a mark. "Noooooo" shouts Carlos. Daniel does it again. Carlos begins to cry softly. Daniel says, "OK. I won't do it."

Handout D

Sample Observation

Name of Child: Maria

Age: 3 years old
Setting: Outside on walk to park
Date: 10/12/91
Observer: Susana

Examine these two observations and discuss their differences.

Observation A

Maria likes to go to the park. She knows some colors but she should know more colors at her age.

Español
A María le gusta ir al parque. Ella sabe algunos colores, pero a su edad debería saber más colores.

Observation B

Maria and I are walking together. I ask her in English, "What color is your shirt?" She answers correctly, "Azul." She points to a lady's blue skirt as we pass by. I ask her if she sees something orange. She looks around and points to a white truck.

Español
María y yo estamos caminando juntas. Yo le pregunto en inglés. "De qué color es su falda?" Ella responde correctamente, "Azul" y me señala la falda azul de una señora que pasa cerca de nosotras. Le pregunto si ella ve algo "anaranjado" o de color "naranja." Ella mira a su alrededor y señala un camión blanco.

Handout E

Learning Accomplishment Profile (LAP)

Gross motor development (large muscle coordination, strength, stamina)

Fine motor development (eye-hand coordination)

Pre-writing (stages of grasping writing instruments, the role of finger and easel painting, and pre-writing skills)

Cognitive development (intellectual functions such as reasoning, problem solving, and knowledge)

Language development (expressive and receptive language)

Self help (ability to cope independently and responsibly with skills of daily living)

Personal/social/emotional (self-esteem, perception and knowledge of personal life, interpersonal behaviors such as cooperation, ability to relate to a group, sensitivity to others, and helpfulness)

Adapted from the *Learning Accomplishment Profile* (Chapel Hill Training-Outreach Project)

Handout F

Farm Bibliography

A resource for parents, caregivers, and teachers that contains books (for toddlers and preschoolers) related to farms and farming.

Aliki. (1974). *Go Tell Aunt Rhody*. New York: Macmillan.

Baxter, K. M. (1978). *Come and get it: A natural foods cookbook for children*. Ann Arbor, MI: Children's First Press.

Ehlert, L. (1990). *Color farm*. New York: J.B. Lippincott.

Florian, D. (1989). *A year in the country*. New York: Greenwillow Books.

Florian, D. (1991). *Vegetable garden*. New York: Harcourt Brace Javonovich.

Garland, M. (1989). *My cousin Katie*. New York: Thomas Y. Crowell.

Gibbons, G. (1988). *Farming*. New York: Holiday House.

Ginsburg, M. (1980). *Good morning, chick*. New York: Greenwillow Books.

Kightley, R. (1987). *The farmer*. New York: Macmillan.

Kunhardt, E.. (1989). *I want to be a farmer*. New York: Grosset & Dunlap.

Lenski, L. (1942). *Little farm*. New York: Oxford.

Lenski, L. (1968). *La granja pequeña*. New York: Henry Z. Walck.

Marston, H. I. (1982). *Machines on the farm*. New York: Dodd, Mead.

Miller, J. (1989). *Farm noises*. New York: Simon & Schuster.

Rogow, Z. (1988). *Oranges*. New York: Orchard Books.

Turner, D. (1988). *Eggs*. Minneapolis, MN: Carolhoda Books.

Turner, D. (1988). *Potatoes*. Minneapolis, MN: Carolhoda Books.

Usborne, P., & Swallow, S. U. (Eds.). (1972). *Leche*. Barcelona: Editorial Molino.

Windsor, M. (1984). *Baby farm animals*. Washington, DC: National Geographic Society.

Wykeham, N. (1979). *Farm machines*. Milwaukee, WI: Raintree Children's Books.

Index

Family conference, 261
    diversity, 112
Family crisis, 258
Farm bibliography, 298
Freud, Sigmund, 26

G

Goodbye ritual, 133, 134
Group process, 77-88. See also Community
    characterized, 77
    conflict resolution, 82-83
    creating, 80-83
    diversity, 83
    exercises, 85-88
    family, 84-85
    humor, 81
    infant, 83
    language, 81
    learning environment, 81
    preschooler, 84
    problem solving, 82
    resources, 88
    scheduling, 82
    toddler, 83
    trust, 77
    usefulness, 78-80
    young school-age child, 84
Group time
    characterized, 97
    discipline, 97
    management, 97

H

Health, learning environment, 62
Hello ritual, 134
Heredity, development, 26
Holiday, diversity, 110-111
Home. See Family
Humor
    discipline, 94

    group process, 81
    management, 94

I

Identity, diversity, 104
Individual appropriateness, 11
Individuality, 18
Infant
    art, 210
    assessment, 278
    caregiver, 251
    child development, 38, 127
    cognitive development, 28-29
    curriculum development, 129
    developmental profile, 27-30
    discipline, 98
    diversity, 113-114
    emotional development, 27-28
    family, 265-266
    group process, 83
    learning environment, 66-69
    literacy, 169
    management, 98
    mathematics, 184
    movement, 237
    music, 216, 219, 224
    observing and recording, 53-54
    physical development, 27
    science, 194
    separation, 133-137, 265
    snack time, 141-142
    social development, 29-30
    teacher, 251
Integrated curriculum
    art, 208-209
    bread and bakeries study, 241-246
    case study, 241-246
    characterized, 145
    concept learning, 148
    evaluation, 154-158
    exercises, 158

The Busy Classroom

Patty Claycomb
Illustrated by Linda Greigg

From dinosaurs to ocean mysteries, this easy-to-use book gives teachers a monthly calendar with a fun-filled learning experience for each day.

ISBN 0-87659-159-4   Gryphon House

10028   Paperback $14.95

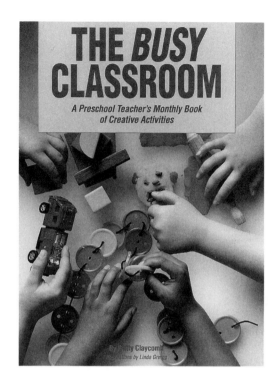

Changing Places: A Kid's View of Shelter Living

Margie Chalofsky, Glen Finland and Judy Wallace

Illustrated by Ingrid Klass

Changing Places captures the voices of eight homeless children, ages 6-13.

"... a wonderful little book, gentle and moving, and I hope it will be read by children."

> – Jonathon Kozol, author,
> **Savage Inequalities in America's Schools**

ISBN 0-87659-161-6   Gryphon House

10029   Paperback $4.95

Story S-t-r-e-t-c-h-e-r-s® for the Primary Grades

Shirley C. Raines and Robert J. Canady

The teacher's favorite whole language curriculum — now with 450 fresh new teaching ideas for grades 1-3. Each of the 90 well-loved children's books is the basis for five cross-curricular activities including writing centers.

" Raines & Canady have lost nothing of the creative insight and imagination that makes their work the best of its kind."

  — Jim Trelease, author,
  The New Read-Aloud Handbook

ISBN 0-87659-157-8   Gryphon House

10026   Paperback $14.95

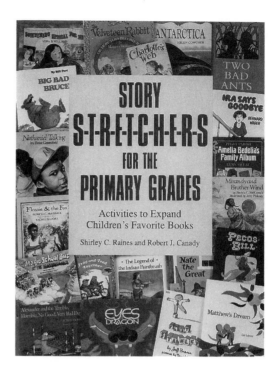

Earthways: Simple Environmental Activities for Young Children

by Carol Petrash
Illustrated by Donald Cook

Even very young children can learn environmental concepts – and earth-friendly ways of living – through the imaginative activities in **Earthways**. The extensive teacher unit shows how to set up an earth-friendly classroom. Contains stunning illustrations.

ISBN 0-87659-156-X   Gryphon House

10024   Paperback $14.95

Simple Environmental Activities for Young Children

Earthways

by Carol Petrash

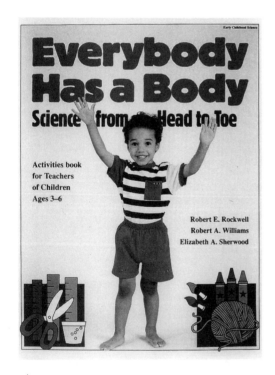

Everybody Has a Body: Science From Head to Toe

Robert E. Rockwell, Robert A. Williams, Elizabeth A. Sherwood

Illustrations by Laurel J. Sweetman

Children will gain mastery of the basic science process skills – observation, inference and prediction – while exploring the first environment they encounter – their very own bodies.

ISBN 0-87659-158-6   Gryphon House

10027   Paperback $14.95